P9-DYB-531

RIGHTS and GOODS

Other Books by Virginia Held

RIGHTS and GOODS
JUSTIFYING SOCIAL ACTION

Virginia Held

THE FREE PRESS
A Division of Macmillan, Inc.
NEW YORK

Collier Macmillan Publishers
LONDON

The Free Press
A Division of Macmillan, Inc.
866 Third Avenue, New York, N.Y. 10022

Collier Macmillan Canada, Inc.

Printed in the United States of America

printing number

1 2 3 4 5 6 7 8 9 10

Library of Congress Cataloging in Publication Data

Held, Virginia.
  Rights and goods.

  Includes bibliographical references and index.
  1. Political ethics.   2. Social justice.   I. Title.
JA79.H44   1984   172   83-48758
ISBN 0-02-914710-7

Contents

About the Author

VIRGINIA HELD is professor of philosophy at the City University of New York, Graduate School, and Hunter College. She has also taught at Barnard, Dartmouth, and Yale University and has directed a National Endowment for the Humanities seminar at Stanford University Law School. She has studied in France, and received a Ph.D. from Columbia University in 1968. She is on the editorial boards of *Ethics, Hypatia, Political Theory,* and *Social Theory and Practice.* She was for a time on the staff of *The Reporter* magazine, and has written on social and political affairs for a wide variety of publications.

Acknowledgments

So MANY persons have offered their thoughts on parts of this book that I cannot sort out the labor of each or acknowledge adequately the contributions even of those who have been most helpful. But among those who have commented on various segments of it, I wish especially to thank the following: Kathryn Pyne Addelson, Sidney Axinn, Kurt Baier, Hugo Adam Bedau, Stanley Benn, Max Black, Jeffrey Blustein, Sissela Bok, Harry Bredemeier, Peter Caws, Norman Daniels, Joel Feinberg, Alan Gewirth, Mary Gibson, Carol Gould, Mark Halfon, Sandra Harding, Gilbert Harman, Robert Heilbroner, Diana Meyers, Sidney Morgenbesser, Onora O'Neill, Susan Rae Peterson, Christine Pierce, John Rawls, Joseph Raz, David A. J. Richards, Amélie Oksenberg Rorty, Steven L. Ross, William Ruddick, M. B. E. Smith, Robert L. Thompson, Judith Jarvis Thomson, Richard Wasserstrom, Carl Wellman, and Kenneth Winston. For suggestions on the manuscript as a whole, I am especially grateful to David Braybrooke, Larry May, James Nickel, and Laura Wolff.

The writing of the book began while I held a Rockefeller Foundation Humanities Fellowship in 1975–76, and I am grateful for the time that grant provided. A sabbatical during 1981–82 from the City University of New York and Hunter College permitted another sustained period of work on the manuscript. The support and understanding of the university, the college, and my colleagues at both have been important to me.

For some chapters of this book, I have drawn on various of my previously published papers. I thank their publishers for permission to use selected passages.

I wish the final version more nearly approached what my various friends and critics thought it should be. I am grateful to all who have tried to strengthen whatever contribution the book may make to the progress of moral inquiry.

VIRGINIA HELD

New York City
September 1983

Chapter 1

Introduction

A SURGE OF interest in ethics is fully apparent. Books and articles in "applied ethics" stream onto the cultural scene; new journals spring up to deal with the actual problems of policymakers, doctors, jurists, and environmental activists. Words pour forth at frequent conferences on "professional ethics." "Codes of ethics" are written and debated and revised for legislators, engineers, business employees, police officers, and nurses. Social scientists increasingly recognize the normative aspects of their work, and try to decide how they ought to shape the disciplines of economics, political science, and sociology.

In many ways these developments are encouraging. Many more sincere persons than a decade or so ago are concerned with moral issues and are trying to make their society a morally better one. Morality is no longer thought of as prudery. Ethical concerns now often elicit respect rather than ridicule. The discussion that takes place often increases the sensitivity of participants to the moral issues involved even when it cannot produce "answers" to the moral dilemmas with which people are surrounded.

And yet there are dangers. The most serious danger is that applied ethics will become worthy of the bad name that casuistry acquired. Moral arguments were constructed by clever casuists to support what-

1

ever positions people wanted to take; by the nineteenth century every serious moral philosopher lamented the resulting devaluation of ethical discourse.

Especially when the money to pay the "applied ethicist" in the period ahead is likely to come from a corporate interest or self-serving professional group, the dangers are extreme that ethics will become a form of ideological public relations or institutional advertising. But this is a possibility to guard against, not a reason to brake the forward movement of moral investigation.

The growth of applied ethics that has taken place has demonstrated our need for moral theories. Without appealing to moral theories, we cannot make headway with such concrete problems as whether the use of nuclear weapons to defend Europe against attack would or would not be morally justifiable, or whether we ought or ought not to fund abortions for women who cannot pay for them, or whether we ought to increase or decrease taxes to pay for public transportation or health services or education. We need theories about justifiable means of defense, about what rights are and which ones we have, and about the legitimacy of taxation for various purposes. We need theories that we can apply to the particular problems at issue. And we need a way of connecting the theories with the contexts to which we are applying them, together with knowledge of the characteristics of these contexts and of the likely consequences of alternative actions within them.

Most moral theories that we might be inclined to look to are "ideal theories," theories that attempt to construct a view of what justice or moral rights or the public good could mean in an ideal society. The foremost example in recent years is presented by John Rawls in his book *A Theory of Justice*; it is designed for what he explicitly calls a "perfectly just society."[1] The difficulty with ideal theory is that it suggests only what we ought to do in an ideal society, not what we ought to do here and now, given the very unideal societies in which we live, and given that we do not yet have a "global society," however imperfect. Actual societies are the results of war, imperialism, exploitation, racism, patriarchy—the imposition of the will of the strong on those who have been overcome. Nowhere do we have a society that remotely resembles the "community of free persons" evoked by various ideal theories.

How we ought to connect an ideal theory with our actual situations is not at all clear, yet it is in relation to our actual situations that we must find solutions to moral problems. In my view, we ought to appeal to moral theories that do connect with specific contexts, especially with some areas of applied ethics in which we have a grip on what some problems are and what some solutions to them might be like. It is this sort of theory that I shall try to suggest in this book.

I shall argue that we ought to begin with the point of view of a sincere moral agent with experience of the problems in question, not the point of view of an ideal observer removed from our actual reality. We should then develop a method for understanding and dealing with actual moral problems. The method I shall advocate will be a version of the method of reflective equilibrium offered by Rawls, revised into what I call the method of experimental morality.

Different Moralities for Different Contexts

We should then proceed to devise moral theories and to experiment with them. If the theories turn out to be suitable for one area but not for others, that may be an acceptable outcome, rather than a source of discredit to the theory. Moral theorists in the past have made the mistake, I think, of looking only for a moral theory that would answer questions about what we ought or ought not to do, and what sorts of things are good or bad, in any domain. Thus a Kantian moral theory tells us that no matter what kind of action we are considering, we ought to act in accordance with the categorical imperative[2] without regard to the consequences of the action. And utilitarian moral theories recommend that for every context we ought to seek to bring about as much happiness as possible.

This approach may be compared to what it would be like to search for the one true unified scientific theory that could explain everything that happens in any domain. Although this may be appropriate as a distant goal, it is not the best way to proceed at present, and it was certainly not the approach that allowed the initial development of the various sciences. We have developed more limited domains of inquiry, such as physics, chemistry, biology, economics, sociology, and psychology. And we do better to work with different theories in different domains than to worry very much about a general theory to cover them all.

In ethics, our search for a single theory to cover all moral problems has led to an unwillingness to pursue the separate inquiries that might be most fruitful. I shall argue that in conducting moral inquiries we ought to develop different theories for different domains. We should not let the lack of a unified theory impede our progress. A moral theory appropriate for a political context may not be appropriate for a family context. A moral theory that can recommend what a judge ought to de-

cide may be unsuitable for advising an industrial manager on what
ought to be done.

We need, I think, a division of moral labor. Different persons in
different roles in different domains of society *ought* to develop and to experiment with different moral approaches. These approaches will include some very general and abstract moral principles together with intermediate-level principles appropriate to the domains in questions,
such as principles about the justifiability of enforcing respect for rights
to speak freely, or principles about the responsibilities of one generation for the environment of a future generation. The danger of fragmentation with a division of moral labor is, I think, much less than the danger of stagnation in moral inquiry if we refuse to accept a measure of
differentiation.

Frequently in the past various descriptive or normative models have
been put forward as appropriate for describing or judging the whole of a
society composed of legal and political and economic and personal and
other components. But these models have been derived from consideration or study of some part of a society and then extended purportedly to
take in the whole. For instance, a model of an egoistic society may be
constructed by assuming that the self-interested pursuits of much of
economic life characterize all social activity. How faulty such a view is
can be seen by considering the behavior of a parent sacrificing much for
the sake of a child; such behavior simply makes no sense on the egoistic
economic model. Or a model of society in which everyone can be guided
all the time by rules resembling laws may be constructed by supposing
that a society is merely a legal system writ large. But such a view is
highly inappropriate for contexts in which rules and laws have little to
offer, the context, for instance, of artistic creation. To say that a moral
rule "permits" various styles of art, or of life, is often to say very little.
We may be interested in choosing between the various styles permitted
by the rules to which we are committed.

I shall argue in this book that we should accept the suitability of
partial views for partial contexts. We should try to improve the normative thinking we do, and the practice of morality we engage in, in the
special domains in which we concentrate our efforts. The efforts of some
people should be devoted to seeing these parts in relation to one another, but we should not think that morality demands us all to do so all the
time. Too often the attempt to devise moral theories and systems that
can encompass all problems leads to so much vagueness, unclarity,
grandiosity, and indeterminacy in applying them that these theories
and systems are actually applied to almost nothing.

To accept a division of moral labor, admitting that our models are only partial, and to do our best within them offer much more promising prospects.

The Prospect of Progress

To consider the disparity in the development of scientific theory and of moral theory since about the seventeenth century is to be both stunned and saddened. On the side of science, we have a substantial measure of agreement that we know how to proceed. The birth and growth and achievements of one science after another have fed our confidence that physics is able to acquire knowledge, that chemistry supplies answers to important questions, that biology is a science in which knowledge accumulates. All these sciences allow human beings progressively to gain knowledge, understanding, insight into the ways of the natural world. Of course, many theoretical problems remain. Philosophers still debate what is the nature of matter, whether space is absolute or relative, and whether our perceptions are of an external world or of phenomena as they appear to us. And many questions of method are in doubt. But the sciences proceed. Scientists do their work. They produce theories, they test them, they accept some and reject others. The results affect us beneficially in many ways and threateningly in many others. But there is little doubt that the results *do* affect us, that the theories of science are not idle speculations but, often enough, powerful achievements.

Compare now the situation of moral theory. We are very unsure what it is, what we want it for, and what to do with it. Are there moralities the way there are sciences? Are moralities merely beliefs that given groups of people happen to have? If so, what besides "morality" shall we call general proposals about the moral beliefs people *ought* to have? How shall we proceed to conduct moral inquiry? Are moral theories ideologies, like communism or capitalism, say, or are they general theories about how human beings ought to judge moral issues, or to behave, like utilitarianism, for instance, or egoism? Or can't we begin to answer such questions until we decide about such metaethical issues as whether moral judgments can have any cognitive content at all, or whether they can do no more than express subjective preferences or emotional attitudes? Can moral judgments be true or valid the way scientific statements can? Can human beings have knowledge in the area of morality? Can they have grounds in experience for accepting or rejecting moral theories?

In the territory that moral theory would occupy if we could decide what it is, we still look to writers of many centuries ago, not out of historical interest as we look at early scientific hypotheses, but because we are not at all sure that what we now think on many aspects of moral theory is very much better. To say this reflects our acknowledgment that moral theory and moral inquiry are in a quite pathetic state.

Perhaps part of the problem is a mistaken notion of what moral theory is or should be. I shall try in chapters 4 and 15 to give an account of what an adequate method of moral inquiry would have to include. I shall argue for a view of moral theory that will see it as far more tied to practice and experiment, and far more analogous to scientific theory, than is usually thought. With such a conception of moral theory, we would be able to see, I think, more progress taking place than we are sometimes aware of. Normative inquiries in the particular domains I shall discuss *are* taking place, and they are sometimes fruitful. If we understand how such inquiries can best proceed, with an accepted division of moral labor between such domains as the legal, the political, the economic, and the personal, we shall perhaps be able to see the directions in which more significant progress could take place in the future.

I shall examine the arguments for a measure of social cooperation. While egoism, appropriately limited, may be an acceptable basis for a given range of activity, it cannot yield the grounds on which human beings can construct or maintain society. The existence of society requires a measure of trust between its members. For such trust to be possible, relations that transcend both egoism and altruism are needed. For trust to develop, the members of a society must tacitly agree on the general basis according to which they will constitute a social entity. Social contract theories have attempted to suggest the terms of agreements that could provide a foundation for society. I shall suggest some essential elements that would have to be included in such understandings if we think of them as offering a basis we could agree to here and now, rather than from some nonexistent ideal position. These understandings will constitute the basis on which we can agree to live at peace with one another, to settle our conflicts through legal, political, economic, and other institutions, each with its own appropriate normative assumptions. These understandings will establish the framework within which we can, individually and collectively, pursue our visions of the good or beautiful.

The framework agreed to will establish various realms "within" a society, such as the economic, the political, and the legal, and will recognize various domains "outside" it. In delimiting such realms, we can make moral judgments at a more general level to treat a given range of problems, at a less general level, in a given way. We can do this by creating "roles" that persons are to fill. These "roles" will have specifications about how those who occupy them ought to behave and about the objectives they ought to seek. Each individual is then morally responsible for accepting the more particular normative recommendations appropriate for the roles he or she chooses to occupy—roles such as that of voter, legislator, doctor, manager, friend, and co-worker.

I shall try to suggest the kinds of moral theories that those in various roles ought to appeal to. The moral theories will be different for different sorts of roles in different areas of society. I shall explore the kinds of moral theories and moral positions appropriate for the acceptance of membership in a state, for decisions within a legal system, for activity within a political system, for economic exchanges, for close relations between persons, for determining the place of culture in society, for shaping the environment, and for existing in a world of nation-states.

I shall conclude with some reflections on how morality ought to be pursued in practice, with inquiry that is free of the domination of the powerful. Such inquiry will bring about, I think, the development of such fields as normative sociology, normative economics, normative law, normative politics, and normative psychology. All will be branches of applied ethics, pursued by philosophers and others from other areas of inquiry and activity. They will supplement, not replace, the existing, descriptive social sciences.

Such fields will be moved forward by the "experiments" of certain citizens and workers and professionals who are sincere about moral inquiry. They will be moved forward also by philosophers willing to develop moral theories that address themselves to the moral problems that confront us in the world in which we actually live.

Chapter 2

The Revival of Ethics

ETHICAL problems always have been and always will be with us. The problems do not disappear even when they are least discussed and even when the culture and the academic discipline of philosophy, of which philosophical ethics or moral philosophy is a part, are least helpful in offering advice for dealing with them.

At times the focus of attention has been on problems that should have been but were not recognized as moral problems. Those paying attention to such problems have often turned to the social sciences to find suggestions for addressing them. They have treated "morality" as the beliefs of the society being studied, or as the personal preferences of whoever might invoke it. But a recognition of the prevalence of moral problems that *are* distinctively moral, and of the need human beings have for answers to ethical questions, has unmistakably grown in recent years. This has led to a groping for foundations for morality itself, not just to studies of existing moral opinions. And it has led to an attempt to apply existing moral theories to actual problems, even when the theories did not lend themselves well to such an approach.

The search for good advice on ethical issues has been conducted outside the field of philosophy and within it. Only gradually has there been a growth of interest in what philosophers might have to offer in the way of ethical advice.

Tradition and Religion

Many people look to tradition or to religion for guidance in moral matters. Both are of limited value for this purpose. Consider tradition first. Virtually every tradition one can point to, identify oneself with, or build on will be questionable in some ways. Virtually all existing traditions are, for instance, deeply sexist. Hence, if one appeals to tradition as a source of one's values, one may have to accept the charge of denigrating women. If one denies that one is sexist, one admits that one approaches tradition selectively, accepting some aspects of it and rejecting other aspects. In doing so, one admits that principled commitments take priority over tradition, since one has already accepted independent criteria with which to evaluate tradition, criteria that provide grounds for accepting some aspects of it and rejecting others.

The same arguments apply if we include religion among the traditions we might look to as a source of values. Plato's argument in the *Euthyphro* remains conclusive: we can claim that we ought to do what religion recommends only if we have independent grounds for deciding that what religion recommends has the additional feature of being what we ought to do. [1] Then we will be claiming that we ought to do something *because* it is right, rather than *because* religion recommends it.

We can continue the argument as follows: *if* something is right or good, religion and tradition ought to recommend it. But those of us who have no psychological reasons to continue the argument in this way, since we can be moved directly by our understanding of what is right or good without the assistance of religious formulations or traditional emotional ties, have no *moral* reasons to continue it this way. Many people have good reasons to be interested in tradition or religion, but morality need depend on neither. We can approach morality directly, deciding on our commitments and projects on the basis of our methodology of moral inquiry. This will encompass the suggestions of tradition and religion, but only as some suggestions among others. And it will put all such suggestions to the test of our developing and accumulating moral experience.

Applied Ethics

In recent years more and more philosophers have become interested in applied ethics, which deals with actual moral problems rather than with merely abstract moral theory. Some philosophers have imagined themselves to be—and some others have caricatured them as supposing they are—persons of superior wisdom and understanding, deciding whether to grace the world with their truths. The image is unfortunate, whether the philosopher's motives are generosity or some sort of *sagesse oblige*. Nearly always, philosophers have more to gain than to lose in venturing beyond the academic enclave and exploring the real world in all its moral ambiguities and traps.

Some of us have argued in recent years for a politically active role for philosophers, holding that we should take stands on matters of public policy and perhaps even take actions, *as philosophers* and through our professional organizations, not just as private citizens. This approach has not, to put it mildly, swept through the profession, and the recent proportion of action to talk has been as low in the Society for Philosophy and Public Affairs, created in the early 1970s for philosophers to deal with actual rather than merely abstract moral problems, as in the American Philosophical Association (APA). But the character of the talk, in the APA and throughout the profession, really has changed, as issues of public policy and of actual problems are rather routinely included among the concerns of philosophers in a way that would have been unthinkable, and considered highly unprofessional, fifteen or so years ago.

The relation between philosophy and its attention to actual problems seems in important ways rather like the relation between scientific theory and work in the laboratory, in the field, or in practice. The issues for philosophy, then, are somewhat parallel to those being debated at present within the social sciences; on the one hand are scholars developing subtle and elegant but probably scholastic theories, and on the other hand those favoring more work at the grubby level of observation, practice, and real problems. A good example is economics, where the most socially concerned members of the profession find it harder and harder to remain unmoved by real problems, even though such problems often lack the fascination of the increasingly intricate mathematical theories on which the profession has concentrated for many years.[2]

For many philosophers, the turning point was the war in Vietnam. The hopeless inadequacy of philosophy in the face of the enormity of this horror brought many philosophers to rethink what seemed to them the appropriate way to "do" philosophy. For others, the need to pay attention to concrete problems may have been apparent sooner, or later, but the changed focus is certainly no longer confined to a small group of like-minded persons.

For the most part, philosophers are approaching these issues from a point of view distinctly different from that of *any* of the sciences or other formal disciplines as now usually understood. In most cases they are starting deliberately from a *moral* point of view and dealing normatively with these issues, and the illusion that the issues in question can be adequately handled by the social sciences or by the legal profession, with no more than a little cleaning up of conceptual confusion by philosophers, has finally been given up almost entirely. This is an important and helpful and, I believe, irreversible development. In other cases the philosophic interest has been more descriptive than prescriptive, but again, it has recognized the gross deficiencies in the supposedly descriptive accounts of much recent work in the social sciences, where ideologically laden terms and frameworks have been passed off as value-neutral.

Within the normative philosophical approach, we can distinguish levels of theory and practice, and we can see what some of us have been doing in recent years as directing attention to the level of practice instead of exclusively or primarily to the level of abstract theory, whether metaethical theory about ethics or theories about the *most general* moral principles.

It is not at all surprising that we are encountering difficulties. The distance between theory and practice is probably wider in moral philosophy than anywhere else, since philosophy is the most theoretical of all the disciplines in question, and yet the practice in question here is the most individual and particular: the practice of personal, autonomous moral decision and action.

And, in contrast to the sciences, the vast intervening layers of theory are usually just plain missing. We simply do not yet have, although we greatly need, recognizably distinct and developed fields such as moral sociology, moral economics, moral psychology, and moral legal theory. What we need are university departments or their equivalents providing jobs and institutional support for responsible, independent, continuous research, publications, discussion, teaching, and the like in these areas comparable to what is now provided for inquiry into strictly empirical questions and purely empirical aspects of these fields. The lines between them should not be fixed or firm, but some division of moral labor should be facilitated. In such new areas, inquiries are needed that combine moral considerations with the relevant empirical material and that come up with specialized moral theories that can, with further inquiry, be progressively improved.

Of course, there will be disagreements about the moral principles and values that ought to be accepted or assumed and applied in these areas. But so is there disagreement about the scientific hypotheses we ought to accept. The social sciences to a very high degree pursue their work in terms of competing theories, not well-entrenched truths to which all agree. Moral inquiries can proceed with comparable internal differences and still achieve progress.

Psychology, for instance, does not give up or fail to get lavish government and university support because it cannot settle the disputes between behaviorists and cognitivists. There is no good reason why moral inquiries should not proceed in special areas such as politics, economics, and international affairs without waiting for a resolution of the arguments between Kantians and utilitarians.

Scholarly competence is certainly as much needed in dealing with specialized moral problems as in dealing with specialized empirical problems. Yet often, all we have in these large areas between pure moral theory and real problems are the underdeveloped theories and seldom impartial observations of politicians, religious office-holders, journalists, and self-proclaimed social critics—and now, finally, of a few philosophers venturing beyond their own areas of competence, where they sometimes encounter a few radical social scientists, apt to be unemployed. It is not surprising at all that the efforts of philosophers in these areas are sometimes unimpressive. Philosophers are not necessarily the best persons to explore this territory. But as long as it is being so inadequately explored by others, we might do well to encourage the efforts of philosophers to point the way.

Practice and Theory

Attention to actual problems has had some good effects, and few bad effects, on ethical theory. Not long ago even the silliest versions of simple subjectivism and emotivism, according to which moral judgments could do no more than reflect our own personal "druthers," had to be accorded considerable dutiful respect at a theoretical level, because so many very intelligent philosophers took them very seriously. We now waste far less time than we used to in getting started. We no longer need to justify the very idea of moral inquiry. We can now give roughly the same attention to skepticism in ethics as to skepticism in epistemology, an amount that should not be negligible in either case, but should not be excessive either, as it certainly used to be in ethics.

A recognition of the pressing reality of such actual moral problems as poverty at home, starvation abroad, the disappearance of political critics in some countries, and the ever-present threat of nuclear war have led almost all moral philosophers to see that moral theories which deny the meaningfulness of moral arguments and assertions need no longer be taken seriously. And questions of value are no longer reduced to the shared values, however irrational, of existing societies or groups. The task of morality is to evaluate the beliefs and values people have, not merely to describe them the way an anthropologist or sociologist would; moral inquiry is prescriptive.

This is not to say that most philosophers today consider ethics "objective." Those who have argued for objectivity or nonrelativism or both have hoped to establish the possibility of enough intersubjective agreement for moral argument to advance; they have argued for the justifiabiility of asking for reasons to sustain positions that purport to be moral, and for the defensibility of continuing to search for solutions to moral problems, rather than giving up with a shrug as soon as the debate leaves the empirical or logical planes and enters the moral one. If those philosophers who now defend subjectivity[3] and relativism[4] in ethics are willing to concede the meaningfulness of moral argument and not just of its empirical and logical components, as they seem to want to, the rest of the argument is of somewhat minor importance for ethics itself—comparable, one might say, to the somewhat minor importance for science itself of the disputes between Kantians and Humeans over how we can or cannot know that certain causes have certain effects. The latter disputes continue to be important for metaphysics and philosophy of science, and the argument about objectivity and subjectivity will continue to be important for metaethics or philosophical thinking about ethics; but the important moral theories with which to guide action can be developed and criticized, as can scientific theories, without waiting for answers. And this has been happening. Led by their admission of the meaningfulness of political argument to an admission of the meaningfulness of the moral components in such arguments, many philosophers have applied themselves to actual moral problems.

Observing the way judges seem to be engaged in weighing the strengths of various reasons for and against their possible decisions has also deeply influenced contemporary ethics. And if judges themselves fall short of providing full-scale moral arguments for the decisions that they, unlike philosophers, cannot avoid making, philosophers have begun to reconstruct their judgments and advise on future stands.

The effects on moral theory have been salutary. Looking carefully at the issues surrounding the actual bombing of population centers for political objectives, or the actual overriding of persons' rights for the sake of the smoother functioning of an existing organization, may give us far more relevant insight into the grounds on which we should, for instance, accept or reject consequentialism in ethics[5] than we can get from a consideration of the merely theoretical and hypothetical issues involved. The same can be said for various philosophical areas within the domain affected by moral theory, such as political philosophy and philosophy of law. One of the best issues with which to test the adequacy of our commitments to various theories about political obligation and the relation of law and morality has been the issue of civil disobedience. Attention to its actual occurrence, and to the arguments appropriate for actual instances of it in various forms and for various purposes in recent decades, has certainly sharpened and improved theoretical debates.

In considering the practice in the light of which to judge theories, direct experience may be crucial, as I shall argue in chapter 4: one goes there and sees the families torn apart by war, or one experiences, oneself, discrimination and humiliation, or one goes to jail in protest, or one exercises, oneself, the power of government. But next in importance would seem to be consideration of the direct experience of others, as one has it through reportage and testimony and reflections on these. Attention to real experience can be very important from the point of view of reliable moral inquiry, at least in addition to the more usual hypothetical cases of philosophical discussion. And we need not be disturbed that the problems to which philosophers have addressed themselves in looking at issues of applied ethics are those forced upon them by the historical reality in which they live, rather than more nearly problems chosen by themselves. The moral theories we should be looking for are those needed by human beings in a historical context, with given kinds of experiences, and not just those in which philosophers are most interested. Nor should we be disturbed that the problems are taken up as if they could be dealt with piecemeal. For their very independence from one another can sometimes help give them reliability as tests for moral theories.

Recent developments illustrate what some of us have long thought, that ethical theory can develop adequately only in combination with attention to its application, through a continual revision of theory in the light of practice, and through continual adjustments at various points in the network of moral commitments in the light of decisions elsewhere.[6] Decisions at the level of moral and metaethical theory can best, if not exclusively, be made with an awareness of their implications at the level of practice, and in the light of decisions made, to some extent independently, at the level of particular problems.

Moral Rights

The focus of much recent moral philosophy has been on rights.[7] Given the powerful influence of political and legal thought on philosophers working in ethics, this is quite understandable. Rights are real. Legislators really write them into black-letter law, judges really decide who has which, and groups of shouting people really demand them.

But moral rights are more than this. Moral rights are stringent entitlements yielded by valid moral principles, and we can claim our moral rights even if a given society fails to recognize them or is unable or unwilling to assure them in practice.[8]

John Rawls has been only one of many moral philosophers who have recognized that a respect for rights is of primary importance and that we need a moral theory that will show us why. Rawls has presented for this purpose a theory of rights, not of the tainted kind that legislators bargain over, that judges make, or that interest groups assert, but of the ideal kind that would follow from the principles that ought to be fundamental in a perfectly just society, principles that would give us conclusive moral reasons.

As I have said, a theory of what our rights would be in an ideal society may not be satisfactory in answering questions about what our moral rights are here and now and about what we ought to do to bring about their assurance in actual societies. Can other moral theories provide more help?

There has been much agreement that what has been called *act-utilitarianism* cannot provide an adequate basis for serious rights. Act-utilitarianism recommends that among the actions open to us, we perform those which will produce the most happiness for all who will be affected. This would seem not only to allow but even to require that if many people will be made very happy by disregarding the interests of a few burdensome and pathetic ones among them, and the latter are too demoralized to care very much, this should be done. But what about the *rights* of these few? we may ask. Does not a person have a right to live, even if the sum total of happiness would be slightly increased if that person were disposed of? Does not a slave have a right to be free even if this will decrease the overall happiness? Does not the right to speak freely, or not to be punished if innocent, have to be upheld even when it inconveniences and even substantially burdens the majority? Anyone who takes rights the least bit seriously will agree that it does. The act-utilitarian may protest that these problems will never arise in an actual situation; at the level of moral theory, what to hold if they were to arise is problem enough.

And so those with inclinations toward utilitarianism—and who wishes to discount human happiness?—have looked to what has been called *rule-utilitarianism*. On this theory we should decide what to do in particular cases by referring to a rule—such as a rule assuring rights to live, not to be enslaved, to speak freely, not to be punished if innocent, and so on. *Rules* should be judged on the basis of whether adherence to them (alternative versions consider conformity or acceptance) will maximize happiness or not, but we should not try to judge individual acts themselves on utilitarian grounds. Thus, even though, in a particular case, preventing the free speech of an irritating journalist might greatly please the vast majority of people affected, a rule guaranteeing free speech can be thought to contribute to the maximization of happiness over the long run, and this person's free speech should be assured because of such a rule.

Several serious objections make rule-utilitarianism a questionable foundation for rights. Given any particular contemplated action, we can never know whether we ought to do it because a rule we think contributes to overall happiness tells us always to do so, or not to do it because a different rule claiming that *it* contributes to overall happiness (the rule might be one specifying exceptions) tells us not to. We could only know which rule to adopt by judging particular cases such as the case over which we are pondering. If in *this* case happiness would be increased by doing it, that supports the first rule. If in *this* case happiness would be increased by not doing it, that supports the different rule. To decide which rule to adopt, we have to judge particular cases, so we are back with act-utilitarianism. Just because doing it has increased happiness in most cases so far considered is no conclusive reason to think that most possible cases are like those cases considered rather than like the one in front of us, especially in human affairs. To go back to our example of the unpopular and irritating journalist, if we find in enough particular cases that curbing free speech will contribute to an overall increase of happiness, we will have to abandon our rule guaranteeing free speech. We will have to abandon such a rule if we are utilitarians, which will be a reason for many to abandon utilitarianism in the context of rights.

J. J. C. Smart's argument against rule-utilitarianism has never been adequately countered. Smart recognizes that there may be useful rules of thumb to guide us when we do not have the time or ability to calculate accurately the utilities that will be produced by a given action. But, he asks, "is it not monstrous to suppose that if we *have* worked out the consequences and if we have perfect faith in the impartiality of our calculations, and if we *know* that in this instance to break [rule] R will have better results than to keep it, we should nevertheless obey the rule?"[9] Instead of accepting the act-utilitarianism Smart then defends, however, most philosophers have recognized that a right that would evaporate when respecting it in a given case would cause a decrease of utility is no real right. Rights that are real will thus need stronger foundations than any form of utilitarianism can offer.

Another large difficulty with utilitarianism of any kind as a theory of rights is that it seems unconcerned with how the aggregate of goods it aims to maximize is distributed. Justice, fairness, and equality seem to require that we pay attention to how the goods are divided up and not just to increasing their sum total. William Frankena, writing helpfully about ethics even during some years when few others were doing so, summed up this argument thus: "The point is that an action, practice, or rule may maximize the sum of good in the world, and yet be unjust in the way in which it distributes this sum," so that an action, practice, or rule that may bring about less happiness but divides it more fairly may be morally superior.[10] If this is so, a utilitarian ethics will inevitably be defective, for we surely have rights to be treated fairly.

An aspect of rights that no version of utilitarianism can account for is that we seem to recognize that rights ought to be respected for their own sake, rather than merely for some further benefit they may bring about. Thus persons' rights to decide freely for themselves about a wide range of matters are deemed worthy of respect even if such persons use their freedom to make themselves and others less happy than a benevolently authoritarian government might make them. The case for rights just does not rest on any such calculation of happiness. The "right to make a mistake" is one of our most treasured rights, irony and all. Respect for a right to freedom or autonomy for its own sake is deeply embedded in our political and legal and moral thought; it crowds utilitarianism from the stage of moral rights.

If rights cannot be based on utilitarian foundations, the most promising source for them has seemed to a number of philosophers to be a hypothetical social contract. But what we would agree to from such a hypothetical position does not really answer the question of what we ought to agree to here and now, and so this ideal foundation for ideal rights may remain disturbingly remote from the actual rights we may seek to assure. If moral principles yielding rights are appealed to directly, the questions we may raise about which rights there are may be no harder to handle and may be more persuasively answered. I shall discuss these issues further in chapters 7 and 8.

Goods and Goals

Rights and the obligations they entail are not all that morality is concerned with. Rights provide restraints within which various goals may be pursued, but the goals themselves need to beckon and be sought responsibly. Rights are not the same as what it is "right to do"; sometimes we ought to *have* a right but, on a given occasion, we ought *not* to exercise it. But the same grounds may well provide a foundation for the rights or entitlements that ought to be assured to persons and for a decision about what it would be right to do.

At the level of moral theory, for the sake of increasing the theoretical resolvability of problems, there have been efforts to define the right in terms of the good, and thus rights and the obligations they imply in terms of the good consequences they may bring about and the bad consequences they may avoid. To hold that acts are right or wrong because they bring about good or bad consequences, rather than because the acts are inherently right or wrong apart from their consequences, is called *consequentialism*.

The reasons to resist consequentialism as a foundation for rights and obligations are compelling. The arguments considered already against utilitarianism apply to all forms of consequentialism, a major form of which is evaluating consequences in terms of utility. The alternative mistake, to suppose that if we take rights and obligations seriously we will have done all that morality advises, has been less well recognized, but the point is as important. We can respect persons' rights and fulfill our obligations to them and still have a world without joy, beauty, playfulness, or love. Such goods should be sought even after we have respected rights and fulfilled obligations.

Not all goods to be pursued are mere interests or wants that we happen to have and should strive for efficiently rather than as bunglers. Some are ideals we can choose. Though we may be stuck to some extent with wanting what we want, deciding what to strive for is up to us.

Of course, not all "goods" have moral value. Many of the economic products often labeled "goods" may be matters of indifference to morality, and some may be more bad than good. But in deciding which outcomes to try to bring about and which means to use to produce them, we need to evaluate alternative states of affairs and ways of achieving them. To do this we will try to ascertain which ends and means are better or best, and these decisions will often involve the moral evaluation of nonmoral goods. We may decide that very different alternatives are equally valuable or that some should have priority over others.

This does not mean that if we recognize the moral worth of a multitude of goals, we need to accept the "pluralism of values" view of Isaiah Berlin and others. Berlin has argued that we seek various ends that are incompatible, yet make absolute claims upon us; we will thus inevitably be faced with tragic choices between conflicting absolute claims. In Berlin's view, some persons may choose equality as an ultimate value, others freedom, others beautiful art; a coherent scheme of values to which all could agree is not in principle possible.[11]

To hold this, however, may be to confuse principles concerning rights with choices concerning goods. We can agree that persons' conceptions of the good will diverge and that, although not all such conceptions will be equally admirable, persons can legitimately pursue a pluralism of admirable goals. But their recognition of principles of freedom, justice, and equality yielding a system of rights for human beings is not a matter of preference or of choice between goods. Such principles do not depend on preponderant preferences or good consequences any more than on the sorts of utilitarian calculations we have discussed. Nor is the ordering and meshing of such principles at the level of their application in actual schemes of basic rights, however dramatic, a matter of preference or of consequences. There is tragedy enough in the suffering of actual persons deprived of their rights without mourning the tragic figures who chose the wrong side of the great debates of history concerning human rights. Yes, those who fought for slavery suffered, but let us not confuse this with the suffering of the slaves.

Respect for an adequate scheme of human rights represents a sort of rock-bottom requirement of morality, and how to reconcile what seem to be such conflicting claims as those between freedom and equality does not, again, depend on preferences or consequences.

Tolerance of a pluralism of goals is compatible with a shared respect for human rights. That all persons ought as moral beings to adhere to principles assuring respect for rights can be asserted and defended. We can then combine a respect for rights based on principles that are not themselves preferences or goods, with room for a variety of preferences and goods to be sought within the bounds of rights.

In pursuing our goals we often assert our interests. Interests are not the same as rights, since we may have rights to do what it is not in our interest to do. (See chapters 9 and 10 for further discussion.) Consequentialist arguments are suitable for decisions about interests, though not for decisions about rights.

In addition to theories concerning moral rights, we will need moral theories that evaluate the worth of various goals and preferences and interests. That something satisfies the interests of persons, or increases what can be called their utilities, may often be an indication of its moral goodness, but an additional judgment that the kind of utility in question has moral worth will be necessary. Often, the moral judgment should be to let diverse preferences flourish, and that they do flourish in varied ways will itself be a morally good consequence of various decisions, especially political and social ones.

Political decisions based on a preponderance of interests will often be necessary, and utilitarian calculations will often be a suitable basis on which to make decisions concerning the public interest. But the public interest is not everything of moral importance any more than rights are everything. Our political policies can seek to promote a flourishing of diverse preferences rather than the imposition of majoritarian interests on all. And moral discussion can promote the nonimposed choice of lives and cultural expressions that seek human fulfillment rather than mere increased consumption.

Just as we have learned to live with a broad range of religious toleration (stopping short of tolerating violations of human rights), so could we learn to live with a broad range of social toleration. The old disputes about sexual morality, proper living arrangements, personal and cultural styles of life are appropriately interpreted as discussions largely concerning tastes and preferences, and, at their more serious, about ideals of the good life. Debates about rights are not. We cannot tolerate violations of basic rights the way we can tolerate the diversity of preferences and of views of the good life.

Our understanding of moral rights has made substantial progress in recent years. We can hope that this will be followed by comparable progress in understanding what sorts of goals and consequences are morally good. We need to decide which objectives are appropriate for political choice, which for shared cultural pursuit, and which for private passions. It can be hoped that moral inquiry will enhance our abilities to imagine, to appreciate, and to choose between the diverse goods that a serious regard for rights allows. [12]

Chapter 3

The Division of Moral Labor: Roles

EACH OF US is more than the occupant of a role and more than the occupant of all the roles we are in, and each of us should always decide as a moral person, from as morally comprehensive a position as possible, whether we are justified or not in occupying any role or set of roles. We should never forget Plato's admonition that if good people refuse to govern, they will be governed by those who are less good than they are.[1] But once a conscientious moral agent finds it permissible or better to occupy a role, that person can often achieve more in that role by concentrating on that manageable segment of moral concern reflected in the role than by trying to do the entire job of morality all at once and single-handedly.

Perhaps we can see the justifiability of what is called *role morality* when we think about what we want and expect doctors to do. We do not want doctors to decide when an operation may be justified on an entire range of moral grounds, but primarily on *medical* grounds. This is not to say that a doctor should be empowered to impose that decision, but that he or she should *judge* in terms of a person's health whether the risk is worth it or not. We do not want doctors judging on political grounds, or on grounds of a patient's life-style, whom to treat and whom to leave untreated. And we do not want the advice of persons who are not doctors to be accorded as much standing as that of doctors on the purely medical question of whether an operation would be medically advisable. We want the doctor to act in behalf of the patient with respect to the patient's *health*. The value to be served—the patient's health—is relatively clear and unambiguous, and this has great advantages. We do not want doctors to step too far outside this role. Of course, doctors now do so: they often decide that they will treat those who can pay their fees and not treat those who cannot. But we might conclude that this decision should not be up to the doctor, rather than suggest that an even wider range of nonmedical considerations should enter into the doctor's decision.

We can certainly say that the medical profession as a whole ought to concern itself far more than it now does with the health of the population as a whole.[2] This entails obligations on the individuals within the profession to do so as individuals. But especially in the situation where adequate medical care would be provided for all equally, we would want a given doctor to be concerned primarily with the health of a given patient, rather than with all other considerations. Until health care in the United States is more equitably distributed than it is now, it is understandable if a doctor chooses to be a political activist rather than a doctor. But if we build an obligation to try to assure adequate health care for all into the role morality of doctors, as we ought to, we would still not want doctors to concern themselves as doctors with all the other aspects of morality *besides* the health of people as much as they concern themselves with health.

We have become accustomed to distinguishing between *having* a right and *exercising* a right. There may be good reasons for us to have a right, but at the same time better reasons for us not to exercise that right on given occasions. For instance, it is important that a right to speak freely be assured by the legal system. But on a given occasion we may do more harm than good in exercising this right by insulting those whose support we need for a given reform. We need a similar distinction with respect to roles. To justify the existence of a role is not the same as to justify a person's occupying that role. And the question of whether there ought to be persons in a given role is different from the question of the behavior the role ought to prescribe. In the world as it exists, there may be good reasons for the roles of soldier and general. But in the case of an outright war of aggression based on national greed, generals ought to resign and soldiers ought to refuse to fight. No one ought to occupy the role of general or soldier except when the fighting is to be done for justifiable reasons.

As a distant goal, the "withering away of roles" may be an attractive vision. The nonrole of "being human" might, if fully worked out and acted on by fully moral persons, preclude the need for roles and for all the institutions that define and structure them. But we should not be so blinded by the vision that we fail to pay attention to how existing roles and institutions could be made less oppressive and less conducive to moral waste.

Roles and Norms

ROLES ARE ESSENTIAL

What is a role? Social scientists interested only in accurate description see roles as patterns of expected behavior within societies. They may describe the norms or rules to which those in given roles subscribe, and the norms or rules they act upon, and find a social structure in a pattern of roles. But from the point of view of morality, we must be able to *judge and evaluate* the roles that exist and to *prescribe* the norms that ought to guide persons in them. It is not enough merely to describe roles.

From the moral standpoint, a role is often thought to be a set of rights and obligations.[3] This definition is appropriate for many roles, such as that of judge or letter carrier. But it overinstitutionalizes the concept of role. Consider the role of social critic or political activist. It would be hard to specify the rights and obligations of such roles, and yet we can certainly evaluate how well persons perform these roles. Does the social critic, as gadfly, irritate insensitive bureaucrats and provoke authority that is excessively entrenched? Does the activist succeed in organizing the discontented and in focusing resentment on some realistic target before discontent erupts into blind explosion? Some roles should be judged almost entirely in terms of the good or bad consequences brought about by them and by those in them. Yet consequences are not the terms on which rights and obligations should be based. So a role may be a set of rights and obligations, or of goals and competences, or some appropriate combination. In any case, it ought to be guided by moral considerations.

The affinities between the term "role" and its dramatic associations are appropriate. In Dorothy Emmet's words, "A role is a part someone plays in a pattern of social activities."[4] The role can be occupied by a succession of persons. We can judge both the roles themselves and the ways different persons in different roles act their parts. And we can especially ask, from a moral point of view, how the drama we all are engaged in should be improved.

Clearly, different roles are in fact guided by different norms of behavior. I shall argue that they *ought* to be guided as well by different moral norms and different segments of moral concern. Many moral philosophers suggest that when a person in a role is acting as a moral agent rather than "merely" as an occupant of a given social role, the person should be guided by the norms of morality, which, they claim, are the same for everyone.[5] I shall argue, in contrast, that persons in roles should be guided by appropriate segments of morality rather than by the whole of morality, and that the moral norms for various roles are not all the same.

Sorting out which moral principles and concerns should have priority for which social roles will be a major task of this book. The roles and structures of roles that characterize societies ought to be evaluated on moral grounds and ought to be transformed, by those occupying such roles and structures and by those able to affect them, into morally justifiable patterns of activity.

"Public" versus "Private" Morality

If we try to understand how moral guidelines might appropriately differ for different professions or different areas of activity, we may be led to consider a distinction with a lengthy history, that between the morality fit for the "public" realm and that fit for the "private" realm. Many moral theorists have thought that the moralities suitable for these different domains ought to be different. They have often written of the existence of a "private" world in which people can behave decently, honorably, and considerately, and of a "public" world in which people are called upon to engage in deceit, manipulation, and violence.

Machiavelli has provided a classic statement of this view: "You must realize this: that a prince, and especially a new prince, cannot observe all those things which give men a reputation for virtue, because in order to maintain his state he is often forced to act in defiance of good faith, of charity, of kindness, of religion."[6] The role of "prince" or political leader has thus been thought to require a set of prescriptions in conflict with morality. Max Weber has developed the idea for the modern politician. In his view, morality has to do with ultimate ends only and can indicate little about the legitimate means a politician may or may not be justified in using. The politician must be concerned with direct consequences, and morality cannot help him in evaluating them. The viewpoint of morality and the viewpoint of a political leader are in Weber's view "fundamentally differing and irreconcilably opposed."[7]

Many others see professional roles in a parallel way as requiring the persons in them to behave in ways that would be immoral for others. While I agree that persons in different roles ought to behave differently, this will not be because morality is suitable only for ideal or for private contexts. It will be because morality, which ought to guide us in all contexts, ought to guide us differently in different contexts.

Stuart Hampshire has developed a recent version of the contrast between public and private morality. He would have us rely on the "respectful rituals" we have been brought up with, rather than on the abstract formulas of major public moralities. He invokes the "gentleness" and "virtues" of families and traditions.[8] Along with many others, he emphasizes the importance of practice in achieving virtue, advising us to recognize the prohibitions in a particular "way of life," and urging us to be suspicious of an overly rational and theoretical approach to morality. But the practice he evokes turns out to be such that it may be suitable for a protected enclave only, not for the world beyond.

A moral theory that focuses on the virtues, advocating such dispositions as temperance, loyalty, and charity but treating these as abstract virtues, or dispositions that only very privileged persons can cultivate, may be as remote from actual realities as a morality that constructs abstract principles of justice, equality, and liberty suitable only for an ideal world. Some moralities that appear to emphasize practice rather than theory actually deal with no more than ideal practice, or theoretical practice. When I speak of practice as distinct from theory, and argue for its importance in developing adequate theory, I shall be referring to a notion of practice quite different from that of privileged enclaves and idealized societies.

Hampshire relies on what "feels natural" in moral contexts: "One may on reflection," he writes, "find a particular set of prohibitions and injunctions, and a particular way of life protected by them, acceptable and respectworthy partly because this specifically conceived way of life, with its accompanying prohibitions, has in history appeared natural, and on the whole still feels natural, both to oneself and to others . . . its felt and proven naturalness is one reason among others for accepting it."[9]

What "feels natural," however, in the sense of usual, customary, or expected for most people throughout history has been oppression, domination, and fear. We shall return to this point later; let us here return to the question of roles.

In Hampshire's view, the "public" realm is one where power is exercised over others. The "assumption of a political role, and of powers to change men's lives on a large scale, carry with them . . . a new kind of responsibility,"[10] he writes. He attempts to defend a morality that contrasts with utilitarian calculations. In the morality he defends there are absolute prohibitions, things that simply are "not done" because a morality prohibiting them feels natural to us. They would include "serious moral constraints—serious in the sense that they regulate killing and sexuality and family relationships."[11] His examples are notably unspecific, but he thinks there is a large overlapping "between the claims of good manners and moral claims"[12] and that a man simply does not betray a friend. He does not provide an example of what, in his morality of habits, would count as betraying a friend, but private morality is thought to set the standard from which public morality must be a departure.

In my view, the contrast between the levels of morality and immorality that can reasonably be expected of persons in "public" and in "private" roles is often artificial. There are both awful choices and routine choices everywhere.

Consider the following account. Whether it is precisely true or not is unimportant:

> Larger ships passed them by, the seas were heavy and their food, water and fuel ran out. They drifted; sometimes they used their clothing to fashion a sail, and at other times they turned the makeshift sail into a fishing net. . . .
>
> Dao Van Cu said the captain and his group told another teen-age youth who had joined the group at sea to commit suicide so that the others could eat him. He pleaded for mercy, and the matter was put aside while the captain and his companions went to sleep.
>
> The terrified youth fell upon the captain as he slept, Dao Van Cu said, and in the ensuing fight the boy jumped overboard and drowned. . . .
>
> Dao Van Cu said that at this point the others held a discussion among themselves and gathered around him. . . . Later that day, his ailing young companion died and was eaten by the others, and he said this gave him a respite. . . . His life was spared, he said, only because on July 26 their boat reached the shore of a hilly island that is part of this colony.[13]

First, we can wonder whether this should be classified as a "public" or a "private" horror. In many ways it is both. The same can be said about much family violence.[14] This violence occurs within the "privacy" of the family but involves the "public" event of assault.

Of course, that it is difficult to classify many events as either "public" or "private" would not negate the fact that many events are more or less clearly one or the other. But we should not forget that many aspects of life, whether "public" or "private," have *no* rules, and this is true not only in the extremes of lifeboat situations where life itself in its starkest form is at stake, but in all the psychological and occupational lifeboat situations where one ambition assaults its rival and one ego's rise requires the fall of another. And as soon as we consider that the social rules which allow some events to be "private," and to "feel natural" are themselves "public" rules, we must wonder about the division.

At the level of ordinary morality, nearly all of us are participants in Machiavellian constructs of one kind or another. Consider the economic disparities that allow some of us to enjoy the "private" lives we lead while others barely survive. If we continue to live at a level unjustified by moral principles of equality, we are implicated in the use of the power that our institutions give us against the defenseless. These institutions give us power that is greater than the handgun of a mugger or the rifle of a revolutionary, but what supports our positions is power rather than morality. There are almost no regions of society in which we can not use the possibilities that our positions of power yield; we ought to use them more for good than for evil. But the power of the prince is not unique. It is one form of power among all the others. A morality that does not connect with the context of power, or with the power surrounding isolated "private" enclaves of "gentlemen" or "executives" or "professionals" or "friends," is not a morality fit for the real world.

As should be clear by now, the traditionally "private" realm is shot through with relations of power. Those acting within this realm seldom escape the "dirty hands" they associate with the traditionally "public" realm. [15] This is clearly true of the economic activity imagined to be taking place in a "private" sphere outside the "public" sphere of government. But it is also true of all that is left even after we recognize that the modern corporation is anything but "private."

The women's movement, for instance, has made it obvious enough that "the personal is political." Patriarchal and "public" social rules give men far more power than women in the supposedly "private" domain of the family, while denying women the chance to enter the "public" domain on equal terms. [16] Persons who worry about how the role of public official might affect their moral purity might do well to consider how the roles they are already in have affected it.

At present, the circle of the family is not at all "private" in a reasonable sense. Still, we can imagine the public and the private being distinct. We can imagine the family being in a distinctively private domain, and we can imagine other areas of private relations between human beings—relations of friendship and affection or of rivalry and conflict—which the public order might in some morally justifiable way allow but not further affect. Shared consumption and cultural production might also be in such a private domain. I shall explore some of these possibilities in chapters 11 and 12.

If the two domains could be thought of as separate in this way, then would the contrast between private morality and public immorality or amorality be valid? I do not think so. Betrayal, callousness, and the exploitation of the goodwill of others will still be possible and will probably not be infrequent in the genuinely private domain allowed by any public rules. In contrast, vast numbers of clearly public decisions could involve, and probably can be expected to involve, the routine carrying out of morally benign rules and activities, such as those to prevent fires from occurring and to collect the garbage.

Role Morality

If we acknowledge, then, that "private" morality in the traditional sense of "private" is a mystification, what are the implications? One is that nearly all morality is role morality. We can specify the set of circumstances within which we are making a moral recommendation, not by ignoring the background, but by identifying it and clearly assuming it.

Our first moral judgments will then have to concern whether it is justifiable to be in that set of circumstances. We could always stop being in that set of circumstances by ending our own lives, as the existentialists have taught us. To be human is to be responsible for accepting or resisting the claims of the roles in which we find ourselves, and to choose which further roles to occupy or to try to achieve and which to refuse to accept. If we are citizens of the United States, our judgment from the point of view of morality would have to address the question whether we can justifiably continue to be a citizen of a state such as the United States. The role of citizen is one we must take responsibility for being in. Similarly, if we are parents, or employees of a corporation, or social workers, or voters, we occupy roles for which we must accept responsibility.

We may believe that the way to deal with this is to try to do the best we can: to work for the least morally objectionable corporation we can, to try to change public policies into more responsible ones, to choose clients or teach students who deserve our efforts rather than those who will pay the most or bring us the most prestige in terms of what a corrupt society admires, and so forth. Since the psychic cost of moral alienation is often quite high, the sacrifices may be much less than the person making them at first imagines. But self-deception about the extent to which we sell ourselves is often deep.

The danger of claiming that all morality is role morality is that we dissolve the useful distinctions we should wish to preserve between persons in such particular roles as those of the physician, the lawyer, or the governmental official and those not in these roles. In the view of some writers, to make morality into role morality weakens the claims of morality on the persons in such roles, as they hide behind their roles and disclaim responsibility for their actions.[17] I disagree. For reasons that I hope will become clear in this book, I think the claims of morality will be strengthened, not weakened, by becoming an intrinsic part of the roles that persons occupy. But for this to happen, morality must be applied differently to different roles, and the various roles must give priority to various moral principles and moral objectives.

We should not imagine that we can take any "ordinary" context of citizens or family members and see it apart from the social organization that structures it. Gender roles are among the most rigid. It makes conceptual sense to talk of persons apart from the gender roles they occupy, and reducing the extent to which many roles determine behavior makes sense, especially as an objective to be sought. But the extent to which persons have so far been able to exist outside gender roles has been very limited. Similarly, the extent to which we can divest ourselves of the role of citizen of a rich country or member of the middle class or beneficiary of a good education is very limited. There is more danger in failing to see the roles that pervade so-called ordinary morality than in failing to see persons in the roles of legislator, doctor, or teacher as also persons.

Roles and Conditions

We might consider construing role morality as specifying conditions. Instead of suggesting that role morality "conflicts" with "ordinary morality," we might understand it as specifying a set of conditions—being a lawyer, doctor, public official, or parent, for example—that are not present for persons not in that role. The conditions will be different for different roles. We can specify what they are for different roles and then try to specify what moral implications these conditions have. Then, since the conditions *are* different, morality will frequently recommend different actions for persons in these conditions than for persons not in them. It will, for instance, recommend different actions, with respect to a drowning child, for persons who can swim and for persons who cannot swim. And morality will recommend different actions for a person who is a surgeon than for one who is not a surgeon. But then morality will just be doing with respect to roles what it does everywhere, ordinarily.

"Conditions" may be a misleading term here, however, since a role is not only or even primarily an empirically given condition such as having a certain kind of knowledge or behaving in accordance with a socially determined set of expectations. A role is also a set of norms or rules concerning behavior. In accepting a role, we accept these norms. In being a lawyer, we put ourselves in a condition of "being a lawyer," but this should not be understood merely in terms of making the empirical description "That person is a lawyer" true. In being a lawyer we are also acting in accordance with such judgments as "It is morally permissible to be a lawyer." And we are accepting the norms constituting the role of the lawyer in that society as valid norms. Similarly for all the other roles we choose to be in.

Many roles are such that we voluntarily put ourselves into them and can voluntarily take ourselves out of them in a strong sense of "voluntary." Thus we are responsible for being in them in a much deeper sense than we are responsible for being alive or for being citizens of a given country or the parents of a particular child, though we are responsible for being in the roles of citizen and parent also.

A role is different from the knowledge that a person in the role has, although a person usually has the knowledge as part of being in that role. The person with the knowledge a physician has might have a moral obligation to help in a medical emergency even if she has given up the role "doctor." Or a person may fill the role "legislator" by being elected, but he may lack the knowledge of government which anyone in that role ought to have.

Some roles cannot easily be separated from the conditions that persons may involuntarily be in. Once one is a parent, one cannot cease to be a parent as long as one is alive, and then one is a dead parent, though one can step out of the role of parent in various ways. No one else can become the genetic mother or father of a given person, but the *role* of mother or father is not the same as being this. In choosing to stop being the parent of a given child in the sense of accepting the role, a person may do grave damage to the child. But in choosing not to use the medical knowledge one has in the role of physician, or in choosing not to exercise the political skill one has in the role of official or citizen, one may also do serious harm. All this only shows that we are morally responsible for not being in roles as well as for being in them.

Roles must be structured in ways that take account of empirical realities as well as of appropriate norms. In a society in which there are no means to train doctors, there may be persons concerned with helping the sick to recover, but none who can fill the role of what could be called, without distortion, "doctor." In a different way, roles have certain built-in limitations. For instance, although parents might split their monetary resources equally among all the children in their neighborhood, or even all the children in the world, it would be logically impossible for them to split the moments of their sustained attention equally among all the children in their neighborhood, let alone the world. If they tried to do so, the attention would no longer be of the sustained and continuing kind that children seem to need to develop in psychologically healthy ways.

Some roles give persons more power, authority, expertise, and the like than others, and each role adds to the characteristics of persons in different ways. But it is better to recognize the differences between various roles than to imagine differences between persons-in-roles and persons-not-in-roles. And we should seek the moral guidelines appropriate for the roles we choose to stay in or to take on.

We look to morality to guide us in acting in the roles we occupy, and to recommend to us how we ought to give up, take on, revise, and restructure the roles into which society is organized. Morality as it now exists is highly inadequate for the task, but it has been improving in recent years as philosophers and others have turned their attention to the actual moral problems of actual persons enmeshed in actual social roles.

A Division of Moral Labor

I argue in this book that different sorts of moral arguments are appropriate for different contexts, and I try to indicate the sorts of moral theories and practices that can be expected to be fruitful for the conduct of moral inquiry in various domains.

In a paper published in 1975, I distinguished what seemed to me to be the different moral considerations appropriate for justification in legal contexts, on the one hand, and political contexts, on the other.[18] I shall expand and develop the arguments for such a position in chapters 7, 8, and 9.

Justification may, in general, take different forms. The most fundamental distinction between forms of justification is that between deontological and teleological arguments. Within either form, justification may be of particular acts or decisions, or of prescriptive generalizations or rules of which these acts or decisions are instances.

Deontological arguments judge an action, or kind of action, on grounds of its intrinsic nature. Is it a lie? Is it a promise? Or is it an instance of a rule such as, for example, "Keep your promises"? The rightness or wrongness of the action or kind of action depends on its intrinsic nature, apart from the consequences it happens to have. Teleological or consequentialist arguments judge an act, or kind of act, on grounds of consequences alone. Are the consequences of this act productive of happiness, or would the performance of acts of this kind cause unnecessary pain? The rightness or wrongness of the act or kind of act depends on the consequences it brings about, regardless of its supposed "nature."

With both deontological and teleological arguments, either we can judge acts in isolation or we can judge the rules or normative generalizations of which these actions are instances. Different theories have different positions on this matter. But with both act-deontological and rule-deontological arguments, justification depends on the intrinsic nature of actions. With both act-teleological and rule-teleological arguments, justification depends on the consequences of acts.

Some philosophers maintain that the distinction is not important or interesting. Andrew Oldenquist, for instance, writes that "the traditional teleological-deontological distinction does not mark two fundamentally different theories about what is relevant to the rightness of an action but instead only distinguishes two alternative ways of saying the same thing. . . ."[19] I do not find such arguments convincing. They seem rather like asserting that induction and deduction are not really different because we can use either to talk about the same subject matter and, often, we can come to the same conclusion using either one. Of course. But inductive and deductive forms of argument remain importantly different. At least one major difference between deontological and teleological arguments is that judgments about the intrinsic nature of an action may be judgments of which we can be *certain* (for instance, "It's a lie"), whereas judgments about its consequences are judgments of which we can never do more than estimate the probabilities.

In chapters 7 and 8 I shall show why deontological justification ought to be employed in arriving at judicial decisions, and in chapter 9 why teleological justification ought to be used in arriving at political decisions. This does not mean that within either system, departures are never or even seldom made; it means that these forms of justification are especially appropriate for these domains and should be the primary forms of moral argument used in them. The moral deficiencies of legal and political systems are in part the result of their inherent tendency to employ one form of justification to the neglect of the other; their moral strengths are in part that they try out the particular form of justification appropriate to them, and this trial run, so to speak, can then be subject to criticism and correction on the basis of the other form and of moral justification employing a combination of both deontological and teleo-logical considerations.

One can further indicate, I think, that questions of rights and inter-ests are best approached through different kinds of moral arguments. It is the primary responsibility of the legal system and the courts to assure respect for rights and the fulfillment of corresponding obligations, and it should be the primary objective of the political process to satisfy col-lective and individual interests. I shall discuss these claims in chapters 7 and 9.

In addition, it seems to me that the room a society might be justified in allowing for egoistic pursuits should be different in differ-ent domains. I shall argue in chapter 10 that *if* the economic and social rights of everyone in a society to the means for a decent life and ade-quate self-development are respected, then, to the extent that the socie-ty could be considered apart from the rest of the world, the society might be justified in allowing economic activity over and above what was needed for this, to be conducted as an egoistic contest. If persons could voluntarily enter or not enter such economic contests and if the culture and the rest of the political and social system could be insulated from the outcomes of them, then the society might allow such contests if a maximization of interests would be served thereby. If Adam Smith is right and a trading instinct is not only a British but also a human characteristic, it may be worse to suppress the instinct than to provide an outlet for it. If, after they have fulfilled their obligations to one an-other, humans choose to organize parts of their lives to make room for trading games, and to award those who make special efforts in them special prizes, morality might have few grounds for objection.[20] Mar-kets are not necessarily immoral.

Egoism, however, cannot provide a basis for the fundamental moral rights that ought to be reflected in law and society, nor for many of the goals the political system ought to pursue. From the positions we are actually in, positions that bear little relation to the hypothetical ones of social contract theories, egoism does not yield sufficient trust to hold society together. Society requires trust and cooperation. Cooperation and our decisions to accept the societies we are in depend on more than egoism, though not on altruism, as will be explained in chapters 5 and 6. So arguments based on self-interest are not appropriate for many issues.

If many human beings do not have a natural inclination to trade and compete economically,[21] they can choose, without being hampered by moral judgments that competition is best for everyone, to organize economic and certainly cultural life in noncompetitive ways. Even if competition is conducive to efficiency, once the claims of rights have been satisfied, persons may justifiably seek goals other than efficiency.

Culture and imagination will be especially important in suggesting how persons might contribute to what would be collectively good in itself rather than merely conducive to individual self-interest. The creation of a shared sense of joy, of arrangements to allow groups of people to work at what would be fun and amusing and spontaneously intriguing, might, for instance, come to be seen as far more suitable goals for the organization of much activity than mere increased production or greater efficiency.

In some other contexts, egoism is decidedly out of place. In the more intimate relations between lovers, friends, family members, sometimes neighbors, and fellow members of groups in hostile surroundings, a high degree of mutual concern is appropriate. I shall explore some of these issues in chapter 11.

Throughout this book I shall try to show how our inquiries can proceed with the most plausible moral approaches available, and how these approaches should appropriately be different for different contexts. And within given domains, we can experiment with and improve our moral inquiries and practices.

The Conduct of Moral Inquiry

My argument concerning the division of moral labor is not the same as the "functionalist" one that different institutional structures have different "functions" which can be judged in terms of their causal contributions to making the social system "stable." We can always ask, at a moral level, whether a given social system ought to work and remain stable, and we will sometimes conclude that it ought to cease to exist. My argument, in contrast to the functionalist one, claims that different segments of the society ought to concern themselves primarily with, and be judged in terms of, different segments of morality.

The case I make can be plausible only if one's conception of morality includes both deontological and teleological components and allows for different resolutions of the tension between egoistic and communal claims in different domains. A pure Kantian, a pure utilitarian, a pure egoist, or a pure communitarian would find the analysis I present hard to reconcile with his or her morality. In my own view, an adequate morality could be developed by none of the above. In chapters 4 and 15 I explain how I think the elements of morality ought to be combined in a cohesive theory and pursued through the use of a method quite different from, and yet in important ways analogous to, the method by which scientific truth is pursued. The method relies on moral experience.[22]

The divisions between the legal, the political, the economic, the personal, and the cultural contexts of a society are of course not clearcut. But I believe there are examples of what may clearly be thought to belong to one domain or another, and it seems helpful to try to delineate the different types of moral arguments most appropriate for each. For everyone to try to be equally concerned about the whole of morality all the time may lead to the dismissal of morality as hopelessly complicated, irrelevant, or vague. The search for moral validity in such separate domains as the psychological and the sociological may be more fruitful than trying to find one moral theory into which to force all the problems. A division of moral labor both at the level of practice and at the level of theories about what the practice ought to be and what moral recommendations concerning it are valid, will have a better chance of leading to the improvement of the ways we seek to develop morality than will any search for the one true unified moral field theory of everything anyone might do.

A Comprehensive Morality

If it is correct, as I shall argue, that different sorts of moral arguments are appropriate for different contexts, will we ever approach comprehensive moral positions? If, for instance, legal justification is best approached deontologically, and political justification best sought teleologically, what claims to moral justifiability can legal or political justifications make?

In a sense *all* decisions are moral decisions. But we seem to be able to make moral decisions to treat given ranges of decisions some other way, to adopt more limited decision procedures for such ranges, and to create roles guided by more limited moral considerations. Take the procedure of flipping a coin. We decide that this is not an appropriate way to decide the question "Shall one tell the truth?" We decide that it is an appropriate way to decide which of two movies to see if one is equally interested in both. Once we make a prior moral decision that a given procedure is appropriate for a given kind of issue, then we can make decisions on the basis of that procedure without calling the procedure, and the morality of its outcome, into question every time, although the prior decision that the procedure *is* appropriate should be reviewed every once in a while along with all our other beliefs and commitments. And once we create various roles with specific responsibilities—that of the judge, for instance, to uphold justice or of the physician to safeguard health—we can be guided by the normative recommendations suitable for that role without calling the morality of the activities within the role into question at every moment, although the moral justifiability of the entire role ought to be periodically reviewed.

We seem to make fundamental moral decisions that certain kinds of problems are appropriately decidable politically, on the basis of good consequences, and largely in terms of aggregationist considerations of maximizing interest satisfaction. In such contexts, majority votes, a welfare census,[23] bargaining between competing interests, and so on, become limited procedures appropriate for deciding certain issues. These procedures can be subjected to teleological moral judgments about the values of the interests satisfied and the appropriateness of the methods employed to achieve various goals.

We seem to make a moral decision that different procedures are appropriate for the range of legal rights as opposed to political interests. (See chapters 7 and 9.) Here we expect legal decisions to be made largely in terms of distributive rather than aggregationist considerations, to reflect considerations of fairness, justice, and impartiality through judicial procedures. These procedures can be subjected to deontological moral judgments about the moral rightness of the legal rights and obligations recognized and the validity of the rules that express them. And so on for the other domains where we decide to use a partial rather than totally comprehensive view of morality to guide us.

If one adopts a method of moral inquiry that includes deontological and teleological arguments, one might say that legal and political justifications each provide judgments that have the standing of moral claims to be subjected to the more balanced as well as rigorous requirements of moral justification. A purely political ethics could ride roughshod over basic moral rights and obligations; a purely legal ethics could freeze a given set of rules into rigid moral insensitivity. At different points in history, it may be appropriate to give the *advantage* to one form of justification over the other. When little change is necessary, most decisions may understandably be legal or quasi-legal; when rapid change is called for, most decisions may well be political expedients that look to the future. Normally, in a relatively stable yet satisfactorily open social system, the legal and political systems should perhaps be kept in balance, along with the other systems of society. The claims to moral justifiability made in their judgments should perhaps be given approximately equal weight, and an awareness should be maintained that these judgments are almost always morally inconclusive, not only because of the human fallibilities of their makers but also because of the limited forms of justification they inherently employ.

And if our method of moral inquiry rules out neither egoism nor altruism, we may discover the ways in which some activities and relations are best guided by self-interest and others by concern for and attachment to other persons. At a time when the claims of community become oppressive, to encourage the expression of individual preference may be in order. But when a society is in danger of dissolving into a collection of dubious contracts between economic egoists, the values of cooperation and social harmony should be encouraged or rescued. (See chapters 5 and 11.)

There is a normative component to all action and decision, whether it be in a legal, political, economic, social, international, or personal context. But the component differs in these different spheres, and I shall try to suggest the ways in which the relations between ethics and these various spheres can best be construed. I shall also try to suggest what a close examination of judgments about actions and decisions in these various spheres may tell us about ethical theory at an abstract and more comprehensive level.

In trying to fit the separate inquiries together, we can often find that given actions or rules are equivalent when judged from one point of view, but that one is superior to the other when judged from another point of view. This will give us a reason to favor the one judged superior from some other point of view even though we continue to hold that it ought primarily to be judged on the basis of the first point of view. For instance, we can recognize that moral rights ought to be respected, and that the legal system ought to assure that those rights appropriately made the object of legal enforcement ought to be assured. An issue of

rights such as our rights to free speech ought to be treated as primarily
an issue to be handled within the legal system. From the point of view
of the legal system it may be justifiable to enforce rights to free speech
through the coercion of those who fail to respect the rights of other persons to speak freely. However, coercion is in itself a wrong. It is only
justifiable for reasons that override a prima facie ("at first sight") principle forbidding persons from coercing other persons. Persons have rights
not to be coerced any more than is compatible with a like respect for all
others. If respecting rights to free speech requires coercing those who
fail to respect such rights, that is not a violation of a person's rights not
to be coerced. We can judge this on deontological grounds. But, as between two methods of enforcement, if a given level of compliance can
be achieved with the use of a lower degree of force or with a less unpleasant kind of force, we can respect rights equally with either method.
Then, on teleological grounds, we can judge that the method using less
force, or a less unpleasant form of force, is the morally better method,
because it has better consequences. We can reach this conclusion even
though we should maintain that the question of rights to free speech,
which rights justify enforcement, should not itself be judged on teleological grounds. We should not, for instance, allow an infringement of
such rights merely because it will bring about a general decrease of un-
pleasantness or a lowering of the average of force used in a community.
When rights are at issue, only if the alternative methods are judged
equal on deontological grounds would we be justified in considering
them on teleological grounds.

Similar approaches may be helpful for other issues as well. If
alternative economic policies, in a domain appropriately to be guided
by self-interest, serve the interests of persons equally well, but one policy contributes more than the other to the feelings of shared concern for
one another among members of a community, that would be a reason to
favor it. Or if, in a family context, the level of mutual attachment is already sufficiently high, but a given action can substantially serve the
self-interest of one of its members without threatening the feelings of
closeness within the family, that is a reason in favor of such an action.
We can reach these conclusions, again, without giving up the recognition that the primary grounds for choice of certain economic activities
should be their contribution to interest satisfaction, and without giving
up the decision that for family contexts, fostering the sentiments of
mutuality to an adequate degree should be our primary concern.

We should try to connect our decisions to treat given ranges of issues separately. And we should try to do so in some other way than by

subjecting each decision to the full but impossible scrutiny of a comprehensive moral analysis and judgment. What makes this possible will be our method of moral inquiry. As it indicates to us that we are indeed making moral progress in normatively guiding social roles, we can consider our decision to treat that range of issues in that way morally justifiable.

We may often make more progress in a limited domain of moral concern than we can at the level of a comprehensive view of how these domains should be related to one another. Instead of being a source of dismay and despair, this should encourage us to continue with our inquiries in whatever areas we can best explore.

Chapter 4

Moral Theory and Moral Experience

MANY CONTEMPORARY moral theorists warn us about the distorting aspects of our actual experience. They suggest that in the situations we are actually enmeshed in, our moral judgments may be unduly colored by self-interest, emotional attachments, a lack of impartiality. Moral theories that may be quite different in some respects often share the view that judgments which are specifically moral can best be arrived at by thinking about hypothetical situations or by an exclusively rational process. They advise us to judge moral problems from the point of view of an ideal observer or a purely rational being. I shall argue that this advice is mistaken. In trying to arrive at valid moral theories, as in trying to arrive at true empirical theories, there is no substitute for experience. I shall try to show that actual experience is a more reliable locus in which to "test" moral theory than is hypothetical experience. And I shall try to show that the theories resulting from employing what I call a method of experimental morality will be better and more nearly valid than theories that result from purely rational or hypothetical approaches.

Actual versus Hypothetical Experience

What is the appropriate place of actual experience and what is the appropriate place of hypothetical experience in the development of moral theories and judgments? R. M. Hare, in *Freedom and Reason*, warns us repeatedly of the dangers of anything less than pure impartiality. We must, he says, disregard the selfish feelings we may have in our actual situations, and take the point of view of the universal prescriber, Hare's version of the more traditional "ideal observer," giving equal weight to the interests of all.[1] Although Hare thinks we should not be the "completely dispassionate and apathetic" observer Roderick Firth might favor,[2] Hare claims that "hypothetical cases will do as well as actual ones" when we undertake "to test the moral principles that suggest themselves to us by following out their consequences and seeing whether we can accept *them*."[3] Elsewhere he positively recommends the use of hypothetical cases for the kind of moral thinking we should do "in a cool hour" to select the principles to employ in the heat of actual experience. He says that his theory "secures impartiality by a combination of the requirement that moral judgments be universalizable and the requirement to prescribe for hypothetical reversed-role situations as if they were actual."[4] And he argues that when we are prescribing universally, we ought to do it "as rationally as possible."[5]

Hare does believe we need actual experience rather than just stories, and that it is "important not to take all the examples in one's moral thinking out of fiction, as the young and those who have led sheltered lives are apt to do."[6] But this advice is offered by Hare for the sake of descriptive accuracy, since "story-books" do not help us much "to separate what is really likely to happen from what is not. . . ."[7] Hare does not recommend, as I shall, actual experience for the distinctively *moral* assessments we require in developing moral theories.

It may be that the very idea of appealing to an ideal observer is a mistake, as has been argued against Firth. It may be that in choosing criteria for what an observer would have to be to be ideal, we would have to appeal to the very moral judgments we would be looking to the ideal observer to make for us.[8] I shall not pursue this line of argument. Rather, I shall try to consider what reliance we should place on something like an ideal observer *if* we could recognize what judgments we might come to from such a point of view.

Let's consider the method of reflective equilibrium suggested by Rawls by which we might hope to arrive at a satisfactory moral theory.[9] What sorts of judgments should we, in employing this method, bring into the set of judgments between which we seek equilibrium? Rawls holds that they must be "considered" judgments.

Though his moral theory is distinctively different from Hare's, Rawls tells us in a way that is quite similar to count among our "considered" moral judgments only those we could arrive at when we are not influenced by the emotional coloration or distorting bias of our actual situations. We should, he thinks, discount those judgments we may make "when we are upset or frightened, or when we stand to gain one way or the other."[10]

As envisaged by Rawls, the method of reflective equilibrium would have us bring into line our most general moral principles and our most particular moral judgments. With respect to justice, Rawls holds, "we acquire a skill in judging things to be just and unjust, and in supporting these judgments by reasons. . . . What is required is a formulation of a set of principles which, when conjoined to our beliefs and knowledge of the circumstances, would lead us to make these judgments with their supporting reasons were we to apply these principles conscientiously and intelligently. A conception of justice characterizes our moral sensibility when the everyday judgments we do make are in accordance with its principles. These principles can serve as part of the premises of an argument which arrives at the matching judgments."[11]

In his paper "The Independence of Moral Theory," Rawls explains that in his view, "People have considered judgments at all levels of generality." Such judgments, he writes, can range "from those about particular situations and institutions up through broad standards and first principles to formal and abstract conditions on moral conceptions. One tries to see how people would fit their various convictions into one coherent scheme, each considered conviction whatever its level having a certain initial credibility."[12] But no judgments that can count as considered should be affected by the self-interest with which we may view the world from the point of view we are immediately in.

Peter Singer and some others have expressed skepticism that we can ever arrive at "considered judgments" that can differ from whatever judgments we just happen in fact to have.[13] The judgments we happen to have may have been picked up from prejudiced childhood influences, from foolish traditional ways of responding, and the like, and are morally suspect. I do not doubt that we *can* have considered judgments of the kind Rawls recommends, but I question whether the judgments between which we *ought* to seek an equilibrium ought all to be of the kind Rawls recommends.

Hare recommends a procedure of lining up general principles and particular judgments that is somewhat similar to what Rawls recommends, but for Hare, the particular judgments are to be the result of imagining how we would feel if we were in the other person's shoes. Through this process we should arrive at judgments that we can consistently universalize: We cannot accord ourselves special privileges, but must recognize that if it is right for us to do something, it is right for anyone similar to us in similar circumstances. At varying points, both Rawls and Hare suggest comparisons between this method for ethical inquiry and the method of scientific inquiry. [14] But at other points, they compare their method for ethical inquiry with the construction of mathematical theories, and this analogy is much more revealing of their developed views on ethical inquiry. In *A Theory of Justice*, Rawls explicitly characterizes his objective as the development of a "moral geometry," [15] and this characterization is repeated in "The Independence of Moral Theory." [16] Hare considers ethics, like mathematics, to be neutral as between the theories developed within the conceptual framework that is all ethics or mathematics in his view can provide. [17]

For both Rawls and Hare we ought to come up with both general principles and particular judgments from a point of view in effect outside ourselves, a point of view of pure thinker or pure sympathizer. The difficulty, however, is that if we are to discount judgments whenever we are upset or stand to gain, as Rawls recommends, we cannot include judgments from our own real situations and dilemmas. It is almost always the case that to discount experience in which we stand to gain or lose is to discount experience. Although not all of us are upset all the time, anyone with a grievance or a conscience will be rightly suspicious of the contentment that would allow us not to be in the least upset by the situations about which we are trying to formulate considered judgments. And if we are to put ourselves wholly in the positions of others, as Hare recommends, we remove ourselves from the positions we are actually in. To take the point of view of the ideal observer is to abandon the point of view in which our experience is real.

If we follow the advice of either Hare or Rawls, our particular moral judgments will not address the questions "What ought I to do in this situation here and now?" or "Is this actual outcome good or bad?" They will only be impersonal judgments about others or judgments about imagined situations, and whether they apply or not to our own actual situations will remain in doubt.

The Reliability of Experience

I question the grounds for supposing that if we imagine ourselves in a situation and judge that in it we ought to perform a certain act, but then find ourselves actually in that situation and judge that we ought *not* to perform it, the latter judgment is faulty and the first judgment reliable. We might, in contrast, take our chances with the second judgment and conclude that *this* is the judgment that should be universalized or should be given greater weight as suitable for entry into the set of judgments between which we should seek reflective equilibrium. I shall try to show why we ought to do so.

Peter Singer goes even further than Rawls and Hare in the direction of making ethical inquiry, like mathematics, a purely rational exercise. He is so suspicious of particular judgments, supposing that they will always be corrupted by our upbringings, that he thinks we should not rely on them at all.[18] He even discounts particular moral judgments based on experiments of the imagination. But one might, in contrast, be equally suspicious of what we take to be self-evident moral axioms. They, too, may be the product of corrupted or excessively sheltered upbringings. So when we ask which judgments we are to seek reflective equilibrium between, or which universalizable judgments we are to accept, we should not, I think, agree to discount the actual experience we actually encounter. We should, on the contrary, insist that we go out of our way to encounter more of it.

There is nothing wrong with considering hypothetical situations to make meanings explicit and to clarify an issue—I shall use many hypothetical cases myself. The point is rather that when we must choose what moral position or action to take on a matter about which we can now clearly see the issues, it is not at all obvious that we ought to rely more heavily on the judgments we think we would come to in hypothetical situations laundered of our actual feelings and interests than we should rely on the judgments we come to in actual situations. This is not to say that actual situations are always to be favored either, only that the actions we take and the judgments we come to in actual situations may sometimes constitute a sort of *test* of our theories in a way in which hypothetical situations cannot.[19]

The issue is not the same as the problem of weakness of will, though the two are often confused. When a person imagines that in a given situation her considered judgment would be that a certain action would be right, and then, when finding herself actually in that situation, her considered judgment is that it is wrong, her change of heart is sometimes dismissed as simply a rationalization arising from weakness of will or disinclination to do what she otherwise "knows" to be right. But this may well be a mistake. Quite possibly, her earlier judgment was the rationalization of a learned prejudice or myth, and the judgment of actual experience is the more valid in terms of genuine moral insight and inquiry.

Neither Rawls nor Hare places any requirements on us to acquire the kind of morally relevant actual experience that might affect our judgments. But do we not have to recognize that, often at least, the poor and powerless have a more adequate understanding of the wrongs they suffer than the well-off and powerful who imagine what it might be like to be deprived? There was a time when Rawls showed concern for this problem. In his 1951 article "Outline of a Decision Procedure for Ethics" he wrote, "The more interests which a person can appreciate in terms of his own *direct experience*, the greater the extent to which he satisfies [the] first test" for a competent moral judge. The test required that a moral judge have a "sympathetic knowledge" of human interests.[20] And in discussing a procedure for "defining" the class of considered moral judgments,[21] Rawls then said, "it is required that the case, on which the judgment is given, be one in which there is an *actual* conflict of interests. Thus all judgments on *hypothetical* cases are excluded.[22] But such concern seems lost in *A Theory of Justice* and subsequent works.

And while Rawls thinks the competent moral judge should judge cases involving others rather than himself, we must point out that in the case of morality, where the rules we choose will be rules we must apply to ourselves as well as to others, the moral judge will have to realize that the difference between judging for others and judging for oneself characteristically disappears. So this condition of Rawls's may be impossible to meet, *unless* the cases are *only* about others and thus relevant only to our hypothetical rather than our actual selves.

Interestingly, Hare also, in *The Language of Morals* (1952), never lost sight of our "ordinary ways of using words."[23] From that perspective, the judgment "That would be the right action for you to take" was seen as referring to actions we face or may face here and now. With *Freedom and Reason* (1965), however, Hare draws us into the realm of ideal beings in an ideal world, losing touch with the actual problems that confront us as actual persons.[24]

Let us consider some cases. One person, Aphra, is unemployed and without savings. Another person, Benno, is an employed taxpayer. Both ask themselves whether taxes should be increased so that the government can become the employer of last resort to provide jobs for those who cannot find them. Aphra, let us say, thinks they should. She thinks that any adequate theory of justice will have to be compatible with her considered judgment that everyone who seeks employment in a society capable of providing it should be able to find a job. She is willing to universalize this judgment and imagines that if she were in Benno's shoes, she would still hold the same view. Benno, on the other hand, thinks taxes should not be raised for this purpose. He thinks that any theory of justice to which he could subscribe will have to allow for this considered judgment. He is willing to universalize it and believes that even if he were out of work and poor, he would not want a government program to create jobs. Both Aphra and Benno, in a way they believe to be conscientious, come to certain considered judgments they believe to be well founded. Both imagine what they would hold if they were in each other's actual situations, and continue to believe that they would have the same considered judgments.

But suppose that now, ten years later, Benno is also unemployed. And suppose that now his considered judgment undergoes a change, and he comes to think that higher taxes to create jobs for all would be a good idea. And suppose that Aphra has in the meantime acquired job security and is assured of future employment. Remembering how it felt to be unemployed, she continues to be willing to pay higher taxes so that others need not be unemployed. Should we really suppose that the judgments these persons have arrived at on the basis of their actual situations are more suspect than the allegedly impartial judgments they thought they would arrive at on the basis of what they imagined they would hold if they were in the other person's situation?

Or consider another case. A young man, Carl, is in the armed forces of an oligarchical Latin American state. He is given, let us suppose, orders to destroy a village held by rebels. Given his previous moral beliefs and his understanding of the situation, the complex network of his considered moral commitments suggests to him, let us say, that he ought to obey orders and destroy the village. Carl imagines actually doing so and continues to think that he ought to obey orders. But in the midst of the actual, live experience, he changes his mind, not because the situation is different from what he anticipated, but because his judgment of what to do in it is different. If this is weakness of will, perhaps he will recognize it and continue to think that he ought to have destroyed the village but lacked the nerve to participate. In this case the equilibrium in the moral judgments to which he considers himself committed is not upset. But it may sometimes be the case that the change is *not* due to weakness of will and that the best and the brightest in the field disagree with those at home for the best of moral reasons.

It is not hard to imagine in the case considered that this might be so. Then, if, at the level of actually deciding what particular action he ought to perform, he decides the contrary of what his previous network of moral beliefs recommended, and if he continues to think that he did the right thing in not participating in destroying the village, he will have to revise his scheme of moral beliefs to make room for this new considered moral judgment. Such revisions often have to be very substantial, causing personal crises and major redirections of people's lives. Of such revisions, among numbers of persons, are moral revolutions made.

Experience versus Theory

An objection may be raised that the validity of any judgments made in the heat of personal experience will be distorted by a human tendency to suppose that whatever actions we have performed can be justified, or a tendency to bend our principles arbitrarily to suit our interests of the moment. But insincerity and self-deception are possible at every level. What I am trying to suggest is a method of moral inquiry for those committed to it, not one for those prone to evade the moral requirements that will result from employing it.

In wondering whether an action conflicting with our theory resulted from weakness of will or from a genuine change in our considered judgment concerning what we ought to do, we should notice that the very upheaval in our moral beliefs that may result from a genuine change will give us reason *not* to rationalize that whatever we in fact did was the right thing to do. From the point of view of having a set of moral judgments in equilibrium with which we can live our lives, it will be *easier* to dismiss deviations from it as the result of weakness of will than to have to face the task of theoretical revision that will be required if we acknowledge the apparently deviant judgment as the one we now consider valid.

Certainly it would be a mistake to suppose that every time a person's considered judgment changes in actual circumstances as opposed to the same circumstances imagined, the change is caused by weakness of will or personal bias. A conviction that the new judgment is not caused by weakness or bias will not always be mere delusion or rationalization. And in the case in which the change is a genuine shift in con-

sidered judgment, if an equilibrium existed prior to this, it will be upset. It is this situation with which I am concerned, and it is my claim
that the considered judgment arrived at through real experience instead
of through disembodied reflection may be *more* important, serious, and
reliable for moral theory than its ideal counterpart. And if we cannot
obtain actual experience of our own relevant to our moral conclusions,
at least we should rely more on actual experience that we learn about
secondhand, on reports or literary accounts of the actual experience of
others, than on our own mere imagined experience.

Is there not commonly a disparity between what we imagine or even
predict that an experience may be like for us and the reality of that experience itself? Are not the formal constructs of expectation often overwhelmed by real experience? But why, then, should moral theory be ex-
empt from the implications of this?

Of course, the distinction is not without difficulties, since
imagining is itself a part of experience in the broad sense, but I think
we all know well enough what is meant here in distinguishing an experience or action that we imagine from an experience or action in which
we are actually engaged. And the distinction in deciding between the
moral judgments arrived at in the two cases seems clear enough.

The metaphors of hot and cold may be misleading, as in "heat of experience" and reflection "in a cool hour." Some persons are passionate
about abstract principles and cool toward their immediate surroundings. Imagined experience can often be more vivid and affecting than
actual experience. I wish to deal, not with the moral significance of the
warmth or vividness of the experience, but with the moral significance
of its reality of unreality.

Hare claims that "if we enter imaginatively into a hypothetical situation, and think about it *as if* it were going really to happen to us, we
logically cannot have desires about it which are different from those
which we would have if it *were* going to be real. . . ."[25] Being actual or
being hypothetical are not "things about" objects or events; they are
not characteristics that could affect our desires. This seems to me a de-
batable claim, but even if it is granted for the *logic* of desire, it surely
cannot be claimed that the moral judgments we conscientiously arrive
at in actual situations cannot differ from those we conscientiously arrive
at in hypothetical situations. Of course, we cannot hold that in an actual and a hypothetical situation that are exactly similar in all morally relevant respects, the judgments "X is right" for one and "X is wrong" for
the other can both be valid. But the issue is, *which* is valid when they
disagree? I fail to see why hypothetical experience should be taken to be
morally superior to actual experience.

It might be argued that the difference here is less significant than I am suggesting.[26] A person in the midst of experience may reach a decision on whether he or she will take "X is wrong" to be valid or invalid, but if the requirement to be willing to universalize is applied, and the judgment given up if it fails this requirement, what would the difference be between the approach I am suggesting and that of Rawls and Hare? The difference, I think, might be very great, for the judgment to be universalized might be the reverse of what it otherwise would be. In the second example I discussed, it was supposed that prior to the experience, Carl's considered judgment, which he was willing to claim was also valid for any similar person in similar circumstances, was "I ought to destroy the village." After the experience, if he changed his position from within it, the judgment he would now claim to be also valid for anyone like him in similar circumstances would be "I ought not to destroy the village." How much more difference could we ask for?

One result of including the judgments arrived at in actual experience among those that are taken to be morally relevant is that claims for a moral point of view in direct conflict with self-interest may have to be more modest than most moral philosophers acknowledge.[27] But in developing demands for respect and concern for others, we may have to make demands that are not excessive and yet are persistent. Doing so may be a necessary feature of any moral theory adequate for the dilemmas of actual persons in existing contexts.

The Limitations of Ideal Moral Theory

We seek moral theories to guide us in deciding which actions to perform and which to refrain from. We seek a method of moral inquiry to provide us with progressively better moral theories, theories that can be applied in action, and maintained or improved upon or replaced, for reasons that ought to be persuasive to those who conscientiously undertake to employ the method.

Deeds themselves—committed or omitted—are concrete and particular. Their descriptions must be particular enough for us to locate them at least roughly in history. And the imperatives and judgments that can guide and evaluate our actions will require descriptions that locate actions in some context of human activity, such as the political, the economic, or the personal.

The actual circumstances in which action takes place can only be addressed in theories concerning persons and circumstances that are less than ideal. For a society in which everyone always does what is ideally right is no real society, and institutions that are altogether just and conducive to good are not actual institutions. Hence, any ideal theory developed for such ideal societies leaves us with problems of how to connect it with our actual circumstances and with problems of what it requires of actual, imperfect persons.

A method that I take to be a version of the method of reflective equilibrium can, I think, be developed and employed in various actual contexts of human activity and can become adequate for the moral inquiries we ought to undertake. It will be better understood as a method of experimental morality.

The method is not suited to yield the ideal theories of which Rawls's theory of justice is an example; it is more suitable for developing what he calls "partial compliance" theories—theories about how we ought to act in societies that are not perfectly or even almost perfectly just or moral. Since, in my view, partial compliance theories *are* what we need for the pursuit of morality, this characteristic of the version of reflective equilibrium that I am proposing constitutes an argument in its favor rather than one against.

There are two separate questions concerning partial compliance: do we have partial compliance with moral requirements suitable only for ideal beings, or do we have partial compliance with moral requirements reflecting only a basic minimum of what might be required of any ordinary human being? It seems that in any actual situation we have no more than very partial compliance with even very minimal moral requirements. The dilemma, then, is that if we set moral requirements too high, as including what would normally be thought of as beyond the call of duty, supererogatory, and extraordinarily benevolent, we risk bringing the whole enterprise of morality into disrepute, as it asks the impossible.[28] On the other hand, if we are going to judge any actual situation of partial compliance to minimal requirements as being in need of improvement, from a moral point of view, we need a conception of something closer to ideal by reference to which the actual situation can be judged to be deficient.

Rawls recognizes that for some aspects of our actual situations, we need partial compliance theories; his list of these includes "the theory of punishment, the doctrine of just war, and the justification of the various ways of opposing unjust regimes, ranging from civil disobedience and militant resistance to revolution and rebellion. Also included here are questions of compensatory justice and of weighing one form of institutional injustice against another."[29] But Rawls thinks we must begin with ideal theory because "it provides . . . the only basis for the systematic grasp of these more pressing problems. . . . The nature and aims of a perfectly just society is the fundamental part of the theory of justice."[30] And in *A Theory of Justice* he claims to offer an ideal theory for a well-ordered society, a "strict compliance" theory, where "everyone is presumed to act justly."[31] From his list of the sorts of partial compliance theories we also need, Rawls offers some discussion of only two: civil disobedience and conscientious refusal, but his recommendations concerning these are for "nearly just" societies with only minor lapses from perfect justice. Hence the applicability of even these theories may be in doubt. *No* existing society, for instance, can be imagined to be "nearly just" with regard to the half of its population that is female, and of course it is not only women for whom all existing societies are distressingly unjust.

The difficulties with ideal theory can most easily be seen, perhaps, in a political context. Moral problems often arise in political contexts and need solutions within such contexts, solutions that are justifiable in a normative and not merely instrumental sense. But political contexts are not even describable without reference to the actual interests of actual individuals and groups. Yet such interests find little place in ideal theory. In actual political contexts, moral issues arise in questions of maintaining or furthering or harming actual interests, and in deciding between actual interests in the almost ever-present situations of conflict between them. We cannot hope to deal with such questions in a real political context without considering the actual interests being felt, asserted, claimed, or at least thought about in them. For persons to adopt the point of view of an original position would require of them, from their actual positions in any actual society, large losses or gains.[32] Those privileged by actual arrangements would have to be willing to sacrifice actual self-interest to a very high degree, while those deprived would gain very substantially.

Various other theories such as utilitarian ones begin with what they call "interests." But they ask us to appraise these from the point of view of an ideal observer so far removed from our actual points of view that the ideal observer must consider each individual with total impartiality. And those to whom this impartiality is to extend may be not only ourselves and our friends, but all existing individuals. It may even be not only all existing individuals but all individuals of all generations, no matter how far into the distant future.

The context of actual political reality, however, requires us to ask how much sacrifice of actual self-interest on the part of the actual persons we address it is reasonable to expect, from a moral point of view.

Starting with where people are now, immersed in their existing situations, what is reasonable to ask of them? What are the actual obligations of actual people enmeshed in privilege and deprivation? These actual obligations will undoubtedly be quite different from what would
be the obligations of hypothetical persons in an ideal world, and also
different from what would be the *most* morally admirable actions that
actual persons could take in excess of duty in their actual world.

The sacrifice of self-interest involved in any change and in any
maintenance of an existing arrangement is a problem both for the privileged when they are asked to yield and for the deprived when they are
asked to wait. All those with grievances that are not rectified immediately sacrifice their interests. If the aggrieved have unrecognized rights
to justice, morality may still demand of them restraint in bringing
about the realization of such rights, but how much restraint is it reasonable to expect of those wronged by an actual institution? And morality
will require those unduly advantaged by actual institutions to surrender
some of their interests, but what limitations on the immediate
dismantling of the social structures from which they profit can reasonably be insisted on? (See chapter 5.)

Definitions and Tests

In the paragraph just concluded I have used words such as "rights,"
"justice," "privilege," and "grievance." The defenders of ideal theory
would suggest that we need first of all to understand the meanings of
these terms before we can proceed to discuss and evaluate actual societies in which persons have, for instance, rights that are not being respected by actual laws and practices. I certainly agree that we must develop conceptions of what we mean by such terms. What I deny is that
the resulting definitions or schemes are adequate as moral theories.
They are, rather, rational constructions or stipulated assumptions, and
until they go beyond mere rational coherence and are tested in experience, they do not provide the theories we need for our actual situations.

The issue is separate from the question of whether "wide reflective
equilibrium," as developed by Norman Daniels, can give us more than
the mere coherence possible in narrow reflective equilibrium. Daniels
suggests that we seek arguments concerning alternative "fits" between
general moral principles and particular moral judgments by appealing
to other *theories* beyond moral ones.[33] He offers as examples of other
theories a theory of the person and a theory of procedural justice; I

should think another example would be a theory of rationality. But we could ask of all of these other theories, too: are they to be ideal theories or not? And it is this latter question that I am asking about moral theory.

Of course, it may be questioned whether Rawls's theory *is* as ideal as he suggests. One is often surprised, in reading Rawls, at the way he supposes that from an original position of equality, persons contracting together would develop institutions with such an astonishing similarity to many of those with which we are familiar. His theory of justice has sometimes been criticized as being a sophisticated apologia for a liberal capitalism that is somewhat more egalitarian than usual, rather than a delineation of a timeless notion. I think such an evaluation is unjust, but any reader must recognize Rawls's conception as sharing various assumptions and perceptions of a certain historical period and thus as being a somewhat questionable candidate for an "ideal" theory of "justice" or "social justice." But his theory is offered to us *as* an ideal theory.

Suppose we were to concede that it is as ideal a theory as Rawls intends. Insofar as it is, it seems to rest not on a reflective equilibrium between our considered judgments, but on a quite different ground. Along with his efforts to argue for his theory as reflecting a consensus of our considered judgments, Rawls attempts a quite different task. He tries to derive his principles of justice from indisputable rational premises. This is the route of the original position, with its rational presuppositions. (See chapter 10 for further discussion.)

Even at the level of purely rational principles, there are great difficulties in deciding what reason suggests, especially, for instance, in agreeing or not with the maximin rule of rationality assumed in the difference principle. (See chapter 10.) But even if such difficulties could be met, when the principles are based on such rational premises, it is not at all clear that the results, insofar as they constitute a *theory* of how societies ought to be organized rather than constituting merely formal definitions of such terms as "justice" and "liberty," *would* mesh with our particular considered judgments. In effect, we are left with the task of subjecting the rational construction to the method of reflective equilibrium. If the rational construction fails this test, we will have to decide whether to revise the rational construction or abandon the results of the "test." My point is that we *will* be faced with such decisions in the pursuit of morality. And moral theories adequate for our purposes must, I think, pass the "tests" of according with our particular judgments in actual cases if they are to be valid for actual persons and actual actions. Derivation from rational premises will not suffice. (See chapter 15.)

The decision problems we face in actual circumstances are problems that cannot be dealt with in terms of ideal theory. Discussion of them will have to deal with acceptable rates of progress, and with justifiable procedures and policies and actions for realizing rights and satisfying interests, *given* the complex arrangements existing at any given time, which the theory will have to be able to take account of and offer recommendations for.

Nations, governments, corporations, and the relations between actual human beings have come about as a result of the triumph, through war and exploitation, of those with greater power over everyone else. Moral theories guiding us on what we ought to do must connect with this reality. Ideal theory cannot do so without a large amount of interpretation and purported application. But the "considered judgments" with which we will confront our rational constructions must be developed from within such reality. Otherwise, if they merely follow from the theory, any argument appealing to them will be circular.

The Context of History

To engage in moral inquiry we must assume definitions of our moral terms. Concepts and assumptions will be needed concerning what constitutes unjust privilege and what progress should be progress toward. However, in pursuing morality, we must have theories that go beyond our definitions and assumptions. We need to answer questions about how partial a given level of compliance can justifiably be at a given time, about what morality demands in the way of progress, and about how progress ought to be made.

Even the actions we perform, and thus our judgments about them, will differ depending on the actual contexts in which they take place and the actual intentions with which we perform them. For instance, the act of paying one's taxes when most others pay theirs is a different act from paying one's taxes when most others don't pay theirs.[34] And applying the category of race in, say, a professional school admissions policy is a different action when its purpose is to increase equality in the society than it is when its purpose is to perpetuate inequality in the society.[35] Handing someone money as a gift is a different action from handing someone money as a bribe,[36] yet reducing deprivation may require, in an actual context, payments that are closer to the latter than to the former.

In a perfectly just society there will be no such actions as paying one's taxes when most others don't or performing what would otherwise appear to be a questionable action to *increase* justice. But to exclude such actions from what our moral theories can apply to is to exclude the moral reality with which we are surrounded and to leave us bereft of theory at just those points where our need for it is most desperate.

Furthermore, the way we become aware of even the most basic requirements of ideal theory seems tied up with the process of experiencing a given set of arrangements in a historical context. Consider the formal requirements of equality of opportunity, and then consider the question of the morally legitimate grounds on which an employer may choose to hire or not hire an employee. That sex is not a legitimate ground on which to exclude persons was often not realized, even by many observers who thought themselves impartial, until the issue became a matter of public debate. Whether the environment was deserving of moral consideration was hardly discussed as a philosophical issue until the 1970s, when the environmental movement brought philosophers to recognize the problems and to begin to think about how they might best be dealt with.

A historical context thus seems necessary for recognizing the judgments to bring into equilibrium, if we use them in developing the content of the formulations of ideal moral theory. To merely begin to understand what could be agreed to in, for instance, a hypothetical original position or from the point of view of an ideal observer may require judgments deeply affected by historical circumstances, even if some aspects of our more purely formal assumptions could transcend such actual contexts. The judgments we arrive at from the contexts we are in do not merely reflect existing rules and practices. They may clearly reject them, but their terms can refer to existing realities in ways in which the terms devised for ideal contexts may be unable to.

Some philosophers have argued that our "considered judgments" are not independent of our moral principles, but follow from them. In this case such judgments can in no way be used to "test" the principles, and the method of reflective equilibrium is dismissed as circular. I do not share this view. We do indeed, it seems clear, arrive at considered particular moral judgments apart from and sometimes in conflict with what we take to be our moral principles, and the search for an equilibrium is a continuous task.

Other philosophers deny that we can ever arrive at ideal moral principles; they see even what appear to be pure rational constructions as generalizations from historically conditioned relative judgments and hence as principles that cannot be independent of particular cultural outlooks. I do not share this view either. It does seem possible to construct some historically neutral ideal moral principles. The difficulty is not that such principles are impossible to imagine, but that they do not constitute moral theories. Either they are so formal as to have no substantive content, or they have a status comparable to mere definitions of terms rather than to moral theories that can be, or have been, put to the "test" of actual experience.

In seeking moral theories that can have validity for actual human situations, we must, I think, subject the abstract formulations suggested by reason or imagination or generalization to the "testing" that can be provided by considered *particular* moral judgments which we arrive at from the point of view of actual experience, independently of such abstract formulations. (See chapter 15 for further discussion.) If an equilibrium can thus be achieved, we can consider that the moral theory has stood up to the "tests" of experience and has withstood the realities of the moral lives of actual human beings grappling with the dilemmas of interest, of sacrifice, of power, and of responsibility.

What we seem to need most, then, are moral theories that allow us to prescribe for and evaluate actual social and legal and political and economic and personal arrangements and relations, and the actions of actual persons within them, within actual historical contexts.

The Discovery of Applicable Moral Theory

An alternative approach to the one of developing abstract moral principles directly, and then, with interpretation, trying to submit the resulting theory to "testing," might be to take any existing or concretely proposed set of social, legal, political, economic, or personal arrangements, structures, institutions, or sets of actions, and to consider them as embodying a hypothesis about how society ought to be organized or acted in.[37] The hypothesis would include a number of very general principles, such as, perhaps, that government ought to be based on consent; a number of institutional interpretations, such as, for instance, that a legislature elected every few years on the basis of majority vote, with one person having one vote, ought to be empowered to enact enforceable laws; and a number of intermediate judgments concerning outcomes that the arrangements ought to yield, such as that rich and powerful individuals ought not to be able to buy decisions favorable to them by controlling legislators.

The principles assumed to lie at the foundation of the given arrangements will seldom be as explicit or discoverable within the arrangement as they might be, for instance, when stated in a constitution. Determining which moral principles to take to be included in the hypothesis would require much debate and deliberation, but nothing would prevent the consideration of alternative hypotheses or alternative formulations of what was taken to be the hypothesis reflected in the given arrangement. And of course varying particular judgments concerning what the arrangement should yield, what actions it would encourage or rule out, would have to be considered. A principle such as Rawls's first principle of justice, or his claim about the priority of liberty, could easily be among those assumed to underlie some set of actual or explicitly proposed institutions, fitting together with a set of particular judgments about equality and liberty. The method of reflective equilibrium might then be quite suitable for developing partial compliance theories with which to judge whether and how actual arrangements ought to be maintained, and when and how they ought to be changed. And the method of reflective equilibrium would be more suitable for this than for the development of ideal theory.

Suppose, for instance, that we take that provision of the U.S. Constitution calling for "equal protection of the laws" as embodying, in the law, a fundamental moral principle concerning equality that we could try to formulate in still more general terms. And suppose we then consider particular moral judgments that may or may not be in equilibrium with the equal protection provision. A court in California, for instance, decided that the financing of public school education through local taxation was in conflict with the constitutional provision, since poor districts were unable to provide educational opportunities to their children comparable to those provided by rich districts. The U.S. Supreme Court did not agree.[38] The issue has in the meantime been decided differently in other states and will come to the Supreme Court again in another form, but at the present time, "the law" of the U.S. allows unequal school financing, as it allows unequal welfare benefits, grossly unequal housing and public services, and wildly unequal incomes, all supported to some extent and in various ways by "the laws." But if, as we reflect on these more general and more particular judgments and on all the intermediate ones connecting them, we hold that a constitutional provision requiring equal protection of the laws and a particular decision allowing unequal public school financing are incompatible, we can judge the legal reality now existing to be defective; either the constitutional provision must be modified or the Supreme Court decision is mistaken and ought to be reversed. I suspect that most readers who agree on the incompatibility will agree that the constitutional provision ought to be maintained and the Court decision changed, rather than the other way around, not only because the Constitution is the more central provision in the law, while the Court decision is closer to the periphery and more easily revisable, but because it has the greater moral standing.

But there would surely be for everyone some proposed particular judgment requiring some form of equality—such as that every person in a publicly funded agency should have the same job as every other—that would be thought to be mistaken. It would then be concluded either that the particular practice, of different jobs, say, was not incompatible with the requirement for equal protection or that it was the constitutional provision that needed modification rather than the practice of what only appeared to be inequality. Limits to the principle of equality and its interpretation would thus be discernible.

Certainly we need some sort of distinction such as Ronald Dworkin's between *equal treatment* and *treatment as an equal,* [39] a distinction that was also made by Aristotle. To *treat someone as an equal* does not always mean providing *equal treatment* in the sense of giving each the *same* amount: a large adult should be provided with a different amount of food than a small child, a healthy person should not be given the same medicine as a sick person, and so on. But the significant problems for social choice remain after we recognize this distinction: we have to decide when and how treatment as an equal, which is what human beings have a right to, *does* require equal treatment, or, if it does not, how much of a departure is morally allowed or required and on what grounds. If treatment as equals does not require that persons A and B receive equal amounts of income, though both work as long and as hard, what departures from an equal income are compatible with treatment as an equal? And so on. If treatment of two children as equals with respect to education does not require that the same amount of money be spent on their education, what does it require? Does it require that they be given an equal degree of educational development of their capacities, which will usually require that more be spent for children from families already economically disadvantaged than for those from families in wealthy school districts?

Answers to such questions will have to be sought in actual legal, political, economic, and educational contexts. Certainly we must look for principles to guide us, and Rawls's difference principle and requirements for equality of opportunity would be possible candidates. (See chapter 10.)[40] But the principles will have to be applicable, and to be applicable they will have to connect with an existing context of law, of politics, of economic development, of education, and so on.

How a change in a situation created by a Supreme Court decision should be brought about, if it should, is yet another question to which morality should address itself: new cases and arguments may be presented with a view to a new decision, pressure may be mounted for the enactment of new legislation, or more radical measures of protest may be recommended. But the consideration of these ways of dealing with an injustice would depend, in the approach I am here developing, not on the prior judgment of ideal theory, but rather on the prior judgment of a theory constructed in the actual context of the partial compliance reflected in an existing legal system such as that of the United States.

Constructing Valid Theories

This does not mean that we are limited, in constructing moral theories, to considering moral principles already reflected in any given institutional structure. We arrive at our own particular considered judgments, and for us to consider them valid may well require, to achieve equilibrium, the adoption of general moral principles radically different from those already recognized in an existing social system. But we would thus choose the moral principles on the basis of actual experience lived within an existing social system, not on the basis of a hypothetical position outside reality.

What is needed in the area of moral inquiry seems to be something comparable to but not the same as the encounter with experience by which scientific theories are tested. Moral theories must be subject to refutation by *moral* experience. And if morality is to connect with real moral experience, it will have to do so as part of the process of *developing* its theories and working out their validity, and not only in terms of *mere* application. The kind of application where a theory developed with no confrontation with experience is simply "applied" with the help of logical inference to a given problem is of little use. This sort of attempt to "deal with the real world" does nothing to improve our moral theories and often makes "applied ethics" look foolish.

Because ethics is prescriptive rather than descriptive, it is helpful to work, in ethics, with the notion of validity rather than truth. Then, we need a way of distinguishing what is valid in experience and what is valid by assumption in a moral theory. This distinction would be com-

parable to but not a form of the distinction between the observational
and the theoretical in science. A moral decision "I ought to do X here
and now" should be tested in experience and found valid in experience.
(See chapter 15 for further discussion.) So should the judgment that
anyone like me in like circumstances ought to do so, and I take the requirement of universalizability to be a necessary reflection of requirements for rational coherence that any true or valid judgment in any domain must meet. But if I ought to do X because X would be the action
that would respect the equality of persons, I will be invoking a judgment concerning the *meaning* of equality, which judgment should be
valid by assumption. The two judgments should coincide if we have an
adequate understanding of the moral issues, as would an empirical finding that crows are black and a definition that they are. But we should no
more build into our moral theories the impossibility of divergence than
we should in our scientific theories.

Moral theories should, I am arguing, be thought of as analogous to
empirically interpreted scientific theories rather than as analogous to
mathematics. Only thus can we have a chance of developing moral theories adequate to the purposes for which we seek them. On this account, having an aspect of validity in experience and not only validity
by assumption would be a requirement for anything to count as a moral
theory. And moral theories will then be, primarily, partial compliance
theories.

This is emphatically not to suggest that moral theories can be construed as a type of scientific theory. Critics of naturalism in ethics have
provided arguments that I here take to be sufficient to require avoid-
ance of the subsumption of ethics under science. Moral experience is not
empirical experience, and moral theories are normative, not empirical.
Still, the methods of moral inquiry and of scientific inquiry may be parallel in important respects. And the further distinction between an empirically tested scientific theory and its application in, say, engineering
could have its analogue in the distinction between a moral theory tested
in moral experience and the application of that theory in, say, public
policy.

Inquiry in ethics by even eminently sincere persons with a wide
range of experience and moral understanding will undoubtedly lead to
the development of rival theories. But this need not disturb us. If, in
ethics, we would progress from the chaos of the present to the relative
order of rival theories connected with actual moral experience, there
would be cause for celebration. At present, a multitude of persons make
unconnected moral judgments, while a few philosophers construct

moral theories of such abstraction as hardly to touch on experience. To move from this to rival theories developed through the use of the method of experimental morality I have outlined would be a significant advance. We could then choose between rival theories with some hope of achieving a coherence that would not have been bought at the price of banishing actual experience from the conduct of moral inquiry.

Chapter 5

The Grounds for Social Trust

IF WE BEGIN our search for moral progress from where we are here and now, we must ask questions about what we ought to do from within societies that may be dissolving. And we must consider how to develop morally better societies from the points of view of persons already in the societies we are in. What in the way of social cohesion and cooperation will make it possible for us to move forward rather than sink lower? Can the societies of which we are part sustain themselves long enough for improvement to occur?

We live at a time when many observers fear their societies may be falling apart, when it seems that, in that once wonderful phrase of Yeats's which has become by now a cliché, "the center cannot hold."[1] To understand how a society can cohere or crumble, we need to explore the question of trust.

For cooperation among persons to be sustainable, trust must be present. At the level of a society, there must be the possibility of social trust. At the level of persons in their immediate interactions with those close to them, there must be the possibility of personal trust. In a society in the process of dissolution, mistrust and suspicion grow, as everywhere persons pursue their own self-interest, expecting full well that others will do so too. People increasingly become resigned to a society in which taking advantage of others when one can is standard and accepted behavior. All seem to feel they must take part in the struggle to advance their own interests, or others will do so at their expense. Many worry that American society is in such a process; a U.S. congressman remarked a few years ago that in over thirty years in public office he had never been so aware of an "every man for himself" atmosphere.[2] Since then, trust in the basic structures of the society has decreased rather than increased.[3]

The teachings that students and citizens absorb frequently extol rather than question egoism: the liberal tradition asserts that government is justified only if it serves individual self-interest; the myth of Adam Smith, on which capitalism and market economies rest, asserts that if all pursue their own selfish interests, this will add up to what is best for everyone; the novels of Ayn Rand and the theories of libertarians carry the excesses of egoism to new heights of popularity. And the practices of business societies, of which the United States is the foremost example, are built on the motivating forces of the egoistic pursuit of economic self-interest. But trust and cooperation cannot be built on egoism.

Morality, whether religious or secular, has long recognized the dangers of egoism and has often advocated altruism. However, against the weight of existing behavior, pleas for altruism have appeared to be little more than deluded longings for impossible ideals or, to some perceptive critics, positive contributions to the passivity of the weak and exploitable. As we shall see, trust and cooperation do not require altruism. More recently, the case for or against egoism has been made in terms of its rationality or lack of it. But rationality as usually understood cannot, from where persons are here and now, offer strong arguments against egoism. For those with existing privileges may rationally seek to hold on to them, even if their privileges are unjust and immoral.

It is frequently thought that the solution to the problem of generalized egoism is coercion. It is suggested that if everyone is forced to consider others and to act cooperatively in a common venture, all will do so.[4] But the problem is deeper. For if mistrust engulfs government, or whatever agency would carry out the enforcement, there is nowhere to turn to supply the pressure that will keep those who think only of themselves from pulling society apart. In such a society there will never be enough inspectors, investigators, police, and prisons.

Any mechanism for enforcement constitutes just another area of joint activity where all the problems that led to its creation recur concerning it. For instance, it will be in the interest of each person that others are forced to cooperate but that he or she is free to be egoistic. It will be in the interest of any given person for others to pay the costs of the enforcement mechanism, for others to assist it in punishing those who cheat, for others to fear being caught though the probability is low, but it will be even more in the interest of this given person to freeload on this system of enforcement.

If enforcement is seen as a mechanism to apply to a recalcitrant minority, the arguments in its favor may be quite strong. But in the view considered here it is seen as a mechanism to apply to us *all*, and the more rationally self-interested we are, the more we need it. However, since the enforcement apparatus adds a very large expense to the original cost of accepting collective decisions, it would be collectively better to have as little of it as possible, since it is as vulnerable to the arguments in favor of freeloading as are the rules or agreements it is designed to enforce. And if there can be as much compliance without a given enforcement mechanism as with it, it would be advantageous to do without it, since it has in itself no utility and merely adds to the cost of compliance with cooperative policies the further cost of enforcing compliance. Voluntary cooperation would be ever so much better, and a severe lack of voluntary cooperation may even engulf whatever means of enforcement are offered as a substitute.

Sissela Bok, in her widely read book *Lying*, has examined the implications for trust of a lack of *truthfulness*. She aserts—correctly, I think—that "trust is a social good to be protected just as much as the air we breathe or the water we drink. When it is damaged, the community as a whole suffers: and when it is destroyed, societies falter and collapse."[5] And she discusses the damaging effects on trust of the high levels of untruthfulness and deception that pervade contemporary society.

My concern in this chapter will be more with advantage and interest than with lying. People can betray and take advantage of others through deception, yes, but also openly. It will be the issue of trust in the context of interest and advantage and power, rather than specifically in the context of truth-telling, which I shall address.

A number of political scientists have concerned themselves with trust as an aspect of political culture, noting the difficulties a lack of trust may cause for national development.[6] Trust needs to be examined in the context of social dissolution as well as in that of political development.

What Is Trust?

The *Oxford English Dictionary* defines the verb "trust," when transitive, as "to have faith or confidence in; to rely or depend upon."[7] Webster's definition of "trust" is "the assured reliance on another's integrity."[8] In these senses, trust is a disposition. But we do not know from these definitions whether we *ought* to trust.[9] Often, trust is misplaced, misguided, foolish. Like faith. We ought to trust those who are worthy of trust. But we ought *not* to trust those who are not.

Trust, then, is not a virtue. It it not only not a virtue, it may be a vice. To be trusting, naive, or innocent may *help* others to take advantage of one, it may *contribute* to wrongdoing, and may thus, at various times and places, be a bad rather than a good characteristic. But to be willing to take a chance on trust, when others are willing also, is a virtue and may be the only way to break out of a climate of suspicion and fear. This, however, should be a willingness based on understanding, not simply naiveté.

The virtue that we ought to promote may be trustworthiness. We can probably say that it is always a virtue to be trustworthy. But we may have to admit that it is often an empty virtue if it does not lead to relations of trust. It is the relation of trust between persons which is important. It is this that societies need, that persons need.

All this is not to say that the relation is always and invariably a good one. "Trust between thieves" or price-fixers or war criminals may contribute to wrongdoing rather than to a good society. But relations of trust between persons trying to bring about a better society are good relations. Trust between trustworthy and virtuous persons is a social relation that we all ought to seek and, in those rare instances where it exists, that we ought to sustain.

Trust seems to be a willingness to respect and to rely on another person or persons. When it is mutual, it is based on mutual respect. Persons who trust one another agree somehow not to take advantage of one another, not to advance their own interests at the expense of the other's interests. As trust develops they are able to act cooperatively toward one another, to work together and not in competition with one another. Or, if they compete, they cooperate at a higher level in "playing by the rules" if the rules are fair. And they trust each other to respect rules they have voluntarily agreed to and not to cheat or bend them to their own advantage. Persons who trust one another count on each other to keep their agreements, if agreements are made. A relation of trust is, then, a mutual willingness to cooperate.

Of course, there is infantile trust, which is quite different, and possibly much trust between adults is merely an extension of such infantile feelings of blind trust.[10] But the trust I am talking about is voluntary trust, the trust that is possible between conscious, autonomous persons who are able to trust or not trust and able to betray or not betray. To trust is not merely to rely on and to predict accurately the behavior of another. Trust arises in situations of uncertainty more clearly than in situations of certainty. We trust another person who *could* betray us not to do so.[11]

In many cases, agreements do not need to be explicit because people who trust one another know what to expect and count on each other to give reasonable interpretations, no matter the changing circumstances, of the requirement not to take advantage of the trusting attitude of others. But when agreements that become explicit are called for, persons who trust each other count on each other to keep them.

Most of the achievements that human beings are able to bring about require some degree of cooperation. It takes cooperation to create relations of friendship or love, to bring up and educate children, to produce and distribute food and clothing and dwellings and transportation, to govern and to live under government, to make and uphold laws, to build cities, to have peace between nations, to have plays produced and paintings hung and novels published, and to conduct scientific inquiries. But cooperation is usually not spontaneous. It must be created, nurtured, appreciated, developed, and protected.

What Is Cooperation?

Cooperation does not require altruism. But it cannot be based *merely* on egoism. To be altruistic is to put the interests of the other person or persons ahead of one's own, to defer, to sacrifice oneself. To be egoistic is to act on self-interest above all, to put one's own interests ahead of the interests of the other person or persons, to be selfish, inconsiderate. To cooperate is to act with others but not against oneself.

Efforts are sometimes made to interpret cooperation in terms of rational self-interest—the efficient pursuit of a person's own gain.[12] It may sometimes be the case that a given course of action will be in the self-interest of both or all persons and that both or all, in *simply* following their own self-interest, will act together. For instance, to use an example made famous by David Hume, if there are two of us in a rowboat, and if I want the boat to go and you want the boat to go, and if the boat will go only if both of us row, then I will take an oar and row, and you will take an oar and row, and together we will make the boat move through the water.[13]

However, we might contend that what is going on here is only the easiest and most favored kind of joint activity, since both of us want the same objective *and* the same way of reaching it. We do not need to agree on who will do what or trust each other to keep the agreement, because if either of us fails to row, neither of us will get what he or she wants. Cooperative activity need not exclude joint activity based on no more than self-interest, but it must include much more than this.

Many cases of what is taken to be cooperation are no more than activities based on coinciding self-interest: if you and another person both want to play Ping-Pong, you may play together, or if you both want to make love you may do so together. But if such seeming cooperation should at any time run counter to the self-interest of either person, joint activity based only on coinciding self-interest will cease. It is only in situations where conflicting interests are *absent* that this model can be applied. And those situations may be rather rare.

We can *try* to follow Rousseau's advice, offered in what he refers to as "one great maxim of morality, the only one perhaps which is of practical use: to avoid situations which place our duties in opposition to our interests, and show us where another man's loss spells profit to us. . . ." Exploring his motives, Rousseau says, "My sincere wish has been to do what was right, and I have strenuously avoided all situations which might set my interests in opposition to some other man's, and cause me, even despite myself, to wish him ill."[14]

Certainly we can *try* to turn more social situations into ones resembling those Rousseau recommends and to avoid, where possible, requiring people to choose between their own interests and the interests of others. But our success in simply *avoiding* all conflicts of interests will inevitably be modest, at least in the short run.

What we will usually need will be ways of *handling* conflicts of interests, not of sidestepping them. We will want to be able to cooperate even when our interests do *not* fully coincide. And so, cases in which interests partially coincide and are partially in conflict are better cases with which to consider cooperation, because the life of human beings seems to present us with so many versions of them. When both of two people cannot have exactly what they want, it may be that no basis for cooperation will exist until, for both, some solution to the conflict seems better than no solution. But they will usually still have *some* conflict of interest about *which* solution to choose and about *how* to achieve any goal selected.

Let's consider a hypothetical case in which some interests conflict and some do not—the usual situation between persons. Suppose one person wants a truck to carry grain from west to east, and the other wants a truck to carry cloth from east to west. Neither can afford a truck alone. Both have the resources for half a truck, and neither one can impose an agreement concerning a truck on the other. Typically, such situations lead to bargaining, and often to a deal. In our example, the persons may agree to buy and use a truck together, cooperatively. They may agree to take turns using it and to share expenses. But let us suppose that at any moment in their cooperative enterprise benefiting both it would be *more* in the interest of either person to make off with the truck, take it to a new part of the country, and start a new life. Let us suppose they would have little to fear from being caught and punished or from the wrath of the wronged partner. In this situation, if the two persons have agreed to share the truck, cooperation requires them to keep on using it together or to ask openly for, and obtain agreement to, a change in the arrangement. But their own self-interest, simply interpreted, would be furthered by secretly breaking the agreement and taking for themselves what they have cooperatively achieved.

This situation is a model for an infinite variety of actual social relations between human begins generally. In such situations, policies based on cooperation and policies based on straightforward egoism recommend *different* courses of action, and people must choose between them. Unlike the case of the two people in the boat who both must row or the boat will not move—where their own self-interest is enough to "enforce" or "police" an arrangement requiring each to do his or her fair share—now, self-interest is not enough to bring about cooperation. Now, cooperation requires trust and mutual respect.

To enter into cooperative relations where interests conflict, trust is needed or neither person will be willing to risk losing what he or she will put into the relations. To keep on cooperating, and sharing, in such situations, trust is required because—and this is important—if one person has strong reason to believe that the other will use their common venture for self-advancement at that person's expense, he or she would be a fool not to do so first, even though he or she would like to go on sharing. The worst outcome of all for a given person would be that the other person appropriates the whole of their common venture, leaving the unsuspecting innocent with nothing. And so if trust breaks down and suspiciousness develops, both persons will be strongly tempted to avoid being taken advantage of and left holding the bag. In our example, each might refuse to let the other use the truck for fear the other would abscond with it, and both would be worse off than in the cooperative venture.

In sum, joint ventures for mutual benefit between persons will not get started without trust. And continued cooperation, which is better for both or all than not having what it makes possible, will become impossible unless the persons involved trust each other enough to count on the cooperation remaining mutual.

Notice, however, that cooperation does not require altruism. Neither person in our example is being expected by the other to sacrifice his or her interests in the sense of giving up his or her share of the common enterprise. When they entered into the cooperative venture, they did so because it would be, for both, in their own self-interest to have a truck to transport their goods. Neither even wanted the other to be altruistic.

When people offer to do us a pure favor, to do something that will be in our interest and directly contrary to theirs, we may feel uncomfortable or suspicious. If one person in the above example had nothing to transport and no use for a truck, but offered simply to give the other the money for it with no expectation of return, the recipient might wonder with some anxiety, unless there were ties of friendship or family to explain the action, what favor the donor would ask in the future and how to refuse it. Normally, we do not want to be indebted to others. We would rather act cooperatively in ways that serve the interests of others as well as of ourselves than to accept charity. To accept charity may be demeaning in a way that entering into relations of mutual respect and cooperation is not. But, as explained, cooperation requires trust, because if one person in a cooperative arrangement can get away with betraying the other, it will be even *more* in his or her self-interest to do so than to go on cooperating. However, if the other one, reasoning in the same way, does so first, the person betrayed will be worse off than with the cooperative arrangement. As long as both cooperate, both benefit over the situation that would exist without the mutual venture. But trust is needed to resist the temptation to betray. And even after patterns of cooperation have evolved, if self-interest is the basis for decision, cooperation may at any moment break down, for the more trusting others are, the easier they are to take advantage of.

The issues we have been considering are true at the level of a whole society as well as between two persons with a joint enterprise or relationship. To work with others in relations of mutual respect for goals that we share, we need to trust and be trusted.

Rational Decision

To depict situations of partial conflict in a formal way, we can look to the game-theoretical model called prisoner's dilemma.[15] At the level of a group, rather than of two "players," the issues can be formulated in terms of the "free-rider problem," seen as an *n*-person prisoner's dilemma.[16] In these situations, a solution does not seem to be posssible with either an egoistic or altruistic approach, and morality and advantage may conflict here or may be compatible. The prisoner's dilemma model has gained increasing acceptance as a way of representing a wide range of human situations in which some interests are in conflict and some interests coincide, and in which choices must be made in uncertainty. Since other persons can intentionally choose to disregard our interests and we can choose to disregard theirs, human beings acting with and toward one another face not only risk but uncertainty.

When human beings act upon the natural world, the outcomes may be difficult to predict, but the natural world cannot intentionally take advantage of us. Other persons, however, can. But we, too, can calculate what rational self-interest recommends and what other persons guided by it would be likely to do. We can learn to thwart others if they try to take advantage of us. Hence, for many social contexts the theory of games is more appropriate than theories that assume we can predict how others will behave and then maximize expectable utility.

The choice in prisoner's dilemma situations is between competition and cooperation rather than between egoism and altruism.[17] Choices between competition and cooperation abound in social situations. There should be no mistaken impression that such choices can be understood only in the abstract representations of a game-theoretical model or that they are rare and isolated dilemmas. Notice, however, that cooperation should not be equated here with collusion. In contexts where competition is the *right* relation—for example, honest competitive bidding rather than price-rigging, or honest playing of a competitive game—the "cooperative strategy" would be to play by the rules and compete honestly rather than cheat.

But notice also that when the rules are themselves unfair, "playing by the rules" may be the competitive strategy, and cooperation may require a willingness to *change the rules*, to make them such that those subject to them would agree to them if not coerced. Persons forced by economic necessity to enter into economic transactions against their will should not be coerced by a set of unjust rules to contribute to their own exploitation; those willing to cooperate will not use existing rules as just another weapon with which to defeat opponents.

When we speak of cooperation versus competition, we mean a cooperative *strategy*, which may include upholding competitive rules instead of breaking them or being willing to change unfair rules instead of insisting on maintaining them. The choice between cooperation and competition arises in situations in which the pursuit of self-interest at the expense of the interests of others will yield a potentially greater gain for a given individual than the cooperative pursuit of mutual value, but if both or all players choose the competitive self-interested course of action, both or all will share an outcome that will be *worse* for them than if they had shared the results of cooperation.

The dilemma is most acute when the players cannot communicate with one another and it is a one-shot decision, so there is no record of interaction on which to base an estimate of what the others will do. Life-and-death situations often are of this kind, along with some of the most crucial decisions persons face in their lifetimes, decisions that cannot be defused into repeatable choices where patterns and trust can evolve. However, even after a pattern of cooperation has developed, in a sense nothing changes, for at any later stage the parties are in effect choosing whether to keep or break the pattern. Breaking the pattern would be recommended on grounds of self-interest. After a certain amount of trust has developed, it would then pay one party to take advantage of this and choose the competitive strategy while the other continues to cooperate. If a given party chooses competition while the other continues to choose cooperation, he or she will achieve the higher payoff this outcome makes possible. If the other follows suit, they may soon be back with an outcome worse for both. But sometimes the gain from "breaking faith" may be very significant, especially if there is reason to believe that once a large gain has been realized, a player can get out of this particular game. This is often a plausible assumption in business, politics, or traditional marriage.

In such cases, if one party has solid grounds for predicting that the other will adopt the competitive policy, then not to do so as well amounts to altruistic self-sacrifice, which is not recommended. In the case of a group effort, if most others will try to freeload, the efforts of a given individual to be cooperative may simply be futile and foolish. However, when we can expect others to cooperate or when we have no grounds to predict that they won't, ought we not to cooperate? Standard definitions of rationality will not recommend that we do so, since rationality is defined in terms of the efficient pursuit of self-interest. But it would certainly be *reasonable* to cooperate when we can expect others to, and to take a chance on cooperation when the chances that it will be mutual are at least even. And if we must conclude from such reflections that, from a human point of view, the "rationality" of economics and decision theory and all the thinking they have influenced is in need of drastic revision, we had better acknowledge this.

Reasonable policies are those in which some mutual respect and concern are needed beyond self-interest. [18] The importance for society of reasonableness, in this sense, is very great. As a sociologist writing recently on exchange theory has put it, "what makes society possible is a solution to the prisoner's dilemma."[19] Are people in a society characterized by much mistrust, then, generally unreasonable?

American Society at Present

Let us turn to the question of the reasons there may be so little trust in American society at present. A great deal has been written about this paucity of trust, from descriptions of the dissolution and alienation characterizing our society in its loss of community[20] to analyses of the ramifications of narcissism.[21] An ever-shrinking percentage of Americans eligible to vote actually do so.[22] And polls consistently show an extremely low level of trust in U.S. institutions and a low level of confidence that much can be done about it.[23]

But many analyses focus on generalized features of our individualistic social condition. In doing so, many of the discussions of mainstream political scientists, sociologists, philosophers, and others may distract us from more direct explanations. Such explanations may be less intriguing conceptually, but in fact more plausible. In his study of the political culture of Italy, LaPalombara points out that the critical events in Italian history have been divisive events.[24] Sidney Verba, writing on this subject, notes that "such divisive political events which teach groups to distrust each other are probably a prime source of a political culture low in a sense of political integration."[25] Although the United States may have suffered fewer divisive events, it has recently had such notable contributions to mistrust as the war in Vietnam and the Watergate scandals. Furthermore, many groups in American society have good reasons to mistrust other groups. Greater understanding of how well founded is the mistrust of various groups might tell us something about the climate of mistrust that threatens to engulf us.

Consider the situation of the disadvantaged in American society. Poverty has not been overcome, and the poor continue to suffer severe deprivation. Their share of the national income has remained unfairly small throughout this century, and there has been virtually *no* significant redistribution to narrow the gap between rich and poor in the entire period since World War II.[26] In terms of wealth and corporate stock ownership, the picture is even less egalitarian than in the case of income. The top fifth of households owns almost 80 percent of the total wealth.[27] A study by the Joint Economic Committee of Congress found in 1976 that 1 percent of the population owned almost 26 percent of the total net worth of the United States. Half of this 1 percent owned 50 percent of the total value of all corporate stock outstanding in 1972.[28] And given the political climate of the Reagan years, these figures will undoubtedly be worse from the point of view of social justice in succeeding years than they have been in the 1970s.

American society fails dismally to provide equal opportunities for its children, desite its proclaimed commitments to at least equality of opportunity if not to more substantial forms of equality. Poor children suffer much higher rates of infant mortality and bad health; their parents are burdened with high risks of unemployment, which correlates strongly with mental illness, family breakup, and child abuse. Among children of comparably high ability, those from wealthy families are five times as likely to go to college as children with as high ability from poor families.[29] The poor, and all who fear being poor, have very strong reasons to be mistrustful.

Or consider the situation of women and nonwhites, many of whom are also poor. They routinely do the worst-paid, most tedious, least satisfying work in the society and do enormous amounts of unpaid and underpaid work throughout their lives. Power and cultural influences have been used to persuade many of those of whom advantage has been taken to accept their subordinate roles as "natural" or inevitable. Women have been socialized to have weak egos, losses of identity, and stunted ambitions. They have been taught to be altruistic so that others could more easily benefit.[30] Women have very good reasons to mistrust the parents, educators, psychologists, preachers, and writers, along with the more obvious architects and builders of the social structure, who have brought this about. Unemployment rates for blacks have remained almost twice as high as for whites throughout the period since 1970, with the gap widening for youths until half of black youths can find no work.[31] That this is not the result of educational differences can be seen from the fact that white high school dropouts recently had a 22 percent unemployment rate, while black youths with a college education had a 27 percent rate.[32] And to now interpret the movement to liberate women as a form of narcissism,[33] or the efforts of nonwhites to redress past wrongs as demands for unfair preference,[34] is further cause for mistrust.

The mean earnings of fully employed white males are already almost three times as high as the mean earnings of all others in the labor force.[35] Many policies and programs of the Reagan administration will make these disparities even more pronounced.

Given such facts as these, the poor, the unemployed, women, nonwhites, and many men who feel closer to them than to their rulers ought *not* to trust their privileged fellow Americans. To do so would be to contribute to the ability of the privileged to perpetuate their unfair advantages. But ought they to trust one another?

There can often be considerable trust among the members of groups deprived of power. In reform movements, there is often a high level of spontaneous reliance on one another among members, even when they hardly know one another. This is possible just because those in the movement can know that others in it are probably participating not merely to advance their own interests, but out of some dedication to a larger cause. Those active in the women's movement, for instance, or in the antiwar movement during the Vietnam war or in the disarmament movement, have often experienced this easy trust. Of course, there are exceptions: some people in such movements clearly *are* largely concerned with their own status and with personal gain at the expense of others. But the very disgust often felt for such people indicates the extent to which they depart from the expected standard of trustworthiness. The expected standard in this context requires that self-interest be restrained by a concern for the good of the movement.

In an unjust but very stable society, although there may be great mistrust between an oppressed group and the group that oppresses it, considerable trust may develop between fellow members of a disadvantaged group who may help one another to bear the burdens of discrimination, exploitation, and lack of power. At times, some groups in American society seem to show these characteristics. At other times, the society seems to succeed in undermining trust among the opponents of existing arrangements.

A society that skillfully practices tokenism, that cleverly buys off selected members of the groups it exploits, preventing large-scale upheaval, is in some ways even more insidious than one that is consistently unjust. If the only way members of an oppressed group can move ahead in a society is to distance themselves from the groups they leave behind, this increases mistrust between the members of such groups, who never know which of their members will betray them to serve their own ambition. And so, while trust is sometimes considerable among those who recognize the need to work together to overcome the injustices to which they have been subjected, the legacy of mistrust—mistrust for those who have exploited them *and* for each other—is very great.

The Grounds for Justifiable Trust

If we look beyond a conflict between the overprivileged and the relatively powerless, we can ask whether there *could* be any basic understandings underlying existing societies such that *all* their members might begin to trust one another. In asking this we might ask not for a causal explanation of cohesiveness or its absence in existing societies, but for an examination of the justifiability of trust in society. What would a society have to do to *deserve* to be trusted? This question has been reflected in a long line of social contract theories, from Hobbes and Locke to Rousseau and Kant, and now John Rawls. A "social contract" can be thought to represent what we might all agree to if we had no governing institutions and were freely choosing the principles on which to set them up. Most social contract theories of the past were marred by the crucial though unstated assumption, false for most people, that the persons who would enter into such contracts would be male, adult, economically self-supporting, and psychologically self-sufficient. The model invoked was that of the independent farmer or craftsman who, if he had no property already, could find some unoccupied land or useful trade and, through his own toil, provide for his needs and enter into Adam Smith's free market on his own terms. Such persons as these would, according to these theories, want a government that would keep the peace, assure freedom from interference as they went about their business, and aid their pursuit of their private interests.

Such views led to the development of western liberal democratic systems of rights and liberties in which the wrongness of taking away from someone what was rightfully his—his life, liberty, or property—was recognized. But the wrongness of failing to respond to the needs of those persons who had no property to protect and no way to acquire any, who were thus unable to be economically self-sufficient, was sadly ignored. (See chapter 8.)

The myth of the self-sufficient, self-employed individual voluntarily entering into whatever exchanges take place continues to operate to deflect criticism from our economic system. But the picture it presents is obviously fanciful. Today, almost everyone who works to earn money works for someone else. And we are forced by economic necessity as effectively as by threats of physical harm to do business with corporate enterprises. We can no more escape their power than we can escape the power of government, and so we sell them our labor, we buy their products, we live in an environment shaped by their actions, while they, among the most undemocratic of all modern institutions, pursue the interests of the corporation. We would be naive indeed to trust our corporate Leviathans.

An acceptable social contract for a contemporary, developed society would have to guarantee that when the society had the resources to do so, it would meet the basic needs of all its members. The means to acquire enough to eat, to obtain medical care, education, housing, and employment, would have to be assured. And these would have to be assured as a matter of *right*, not as a matter of governmental charity, which can be withdrawn, and certainly not as a matter of mere private charity, which can dry up at the whim of the rich.

It makes no sense whatever for a society to see the terms of its "social contract" or the task of its government to be the protection of those who already have what they need from having their excess taken away by others, unless it also sees these terms and this task as the provision of what is required for a decent life for those who lack it. *Rights to live one's life must include rights to what one needs to live one's life.*

At any given time, the existing set of legal and economic and political and social arrangements makes it possible for some people to succeed in earning incomes, in owning property, in acquiring what they seek—none of which they could do without the assistance of government and law. The police protection that enables the fortunate to hang on to their property is a service provided by government, however unwilling conservatives are to acknowledge this fact. At the same time, the existing set of arrangements may make it impossible for many others to acquire what they need.

Those who would sincerely consider that they themselves might be destitute would never agree to a social contract that enables the fortunate to hang on to what they have, but fails to provide a decent life for those unable to be economically self-sufficient in a given set of economic conditions. (See chapter 10.)

A first requirement for general trust to be justified would have to be, then, a recognition, as a fundamental principle underlying social and political arrangements, that none of the members of the society should be denied what is needed for a decent life and for adequate self-development while the society makes it possible for others to have far more than they need. Deciding on the level of what would be adequate for a decent life would be a task for collective decision, just as it is now a task of collective decision to determine how much protection of the property of those who already have property is adequate.

For trust in the societies in which we actually live to be well founded, the basic economic and social rights described above must be seen to be just as important as traditional civil and political rights. (See chapters 8 and 10.) Rights to basic necessities should be honored and assured, by the actual arrangements of the society, as adequately as are civil and political rights.

U.S. society now protects by law fairly well many civil and political rights—rights to free speech, to a fair trial, to vote in democratic elections, and to make contracts. But it has not begun to recognize adequately that people have rights as well to such basic necessities as food, shelter, medical care, and employment. Though these economic and social rights have been proclaimed in various international documents, such as the Universal Declaration of Human Rights of 1948, and they are formally recognized as fundamental rights by most other countries, they are not yet acknowledged even formally as fundamental rights in the United States.[36] The Supreme Court has held on many occasions that *if* Congress or a locality decides to provide funds for various necessities such as food, housing, medical care, or education, it must do so in ways that meet what the Supreme Court sees as constitutional requirements of equal protection. But the Supreme Court has never recognized that persons have constitutionl rights to such necessities in the first place. Thus, if Congress were to decide to end the food stamp program or Medicare or any "aid" of this kind, this would not be unconstitutional on the basis of any decision made so far. Even if a locality were to decide to do away with welfare payments or public education, those denied these services could not look to the Constitution as so far interpreted for help, because it recognizes no such rights to what would enable persons to have what they need rather than to hold on to what they have.[37] A more obvious basis for *mistrust* in the American social system would be hard to imagine.

Just as such traditional rights as the right to free speech and to a fair trial put limits on what persons can do in pursuing their own advantage, so must rights to basic necessities put limits on the pursuit of economic gain. These economic and social rights should protect the vulnerable from the coercion of the economically powerful, they should provide the deprived with the chance to acquire what they need to live and develop, and they should provide those who lose out in the hustle and scramble of economic pursuits with a decent floor of sustenance beneath which they need not fall. It is ironic that many Americans are willing to agree, at least in principle, that even those who break the law are entitled to a fair trial, yet they are not yet willing to agree, even in principle, that those who are unlucky in the economic marketplace are still entitled to a decent life.

In putting limits on the extent to which economic conflict can proceed, arrangements guaranteeing a decent minimum for all would facilitate the development of rules on which all could agree for the conduct of economic contests. If persons have a genuine alternative, then those entering such contests may be thought to be doing so freely and may more justifiably be expected, if they turn out to lose rather than to win, to accept the consequences. If a person's freely purchased lottery ticket turns out to be worthless, we need not suppose that society has failed to meet its obligations. But we should never suppose that a society has no more responsibiity toward a member who can find no job than it has toward a person who loses a lottery. It is especially important in an economic system that promotes risk-taking and competition that those who will be losers be assured against disaster.

What Rate of Progress?

Another requirement for trust is that when a relation is seen to be unjust, it must be transformed into a just relation at some reasonable rate of progress. At any given time, social relations, in varying ways, fail and will continue for the foreseeable future to fail to reflect a full respect for rights. The ways in which relations are unjust become visible at different stages of history under different conditions. It is rarely possible to eliminate quickly an injustice built into a society—racism, for instance. Established interests resist losing the advantages the injustice provides. But once a commitment has been made to end what may be generally agreed to be an injustice, there remains the issue of the *rate* at which this will be done.

The victims of an injustice cannot be expected to wait *indefinitely* for a redress of their grievances. An important question is, What is a *reasonable* rate of progress? Only if some such reasonable rate can be decided on and lived up to can there be any hope of trust between those who have been unjustly treated and those who have benefited from such mistreatment. For instance, courts in the United States have wrestled in the decades since *Brown* v. *Board of Education* in 1954 with the question of how fast schools must be desegregated. The problems have been enormous, and blacks have had many occasions to mistrust those who have declared themselves in favor of equality but have delayed its realization.

A policy not requiring the privileged to suffer losses while the deprived catch up is only possible when an expansion of jobs and income creates gains that can go to the previously disadvantaged. When an economy is relatively stagnant, the only way some can gain is for others to lose.[38] Contention over existing rewards becomes more acrimonious, those in danger of losing privileges dig in their heels and become more resistant to change, and those realizing they have been cheated by unjust social practices have less reason than ever to be patient. Yet for environmental and other reasons, growth should not always be promoted, even if it could be achieved.

The possibilities of trust between advantaged and disadvantaged can be developed only if both agree on a reasonable rate of progress. When expansion is absent, it is not the rate of progress that ought to yield, but the privileges of the advantaged.

Although of course the privileged will not surrender their advantages without protest, a society meeting the requirements for trust among its members will have to see that they do so at a reasonable rate. Otherwise, those suffering from an absence of justice will be justified in refusing to accept the rules of the society. If we abandon the illusion that justice can be attained with no loss to anyone, we have to ask who should be asked to lose how much, and what interests must be taken into account. Justice does not depend on calculations of interest; justice confers moral rights. But in a transitional period, we have to contend with the interest of one group in preserving a system that denies the rights of another, and with the interests of the latter group in alternative ways of achieving their rights.

Such a conflict ought not to arise; where it does, it ought to be settled on grounds of rights, not interests. And yet where it is not being so settled, those whose rights are being thwarted must choose, if they can, justifiable courses of action to take in such circumstances. On what grounds can such a choice be made? In considering this question, it may be helpful to try to delineate the requirements of self-respect. Self-respect requires that one not acquiesce in the disregard of one's rights.[39] We should not and usually cannot trust those who ask us to violate our self-respect.

Interests, Rights, and Self-Respect

Where persons have acquired their positions as a result of unjustifiable procedures, we can conclude that although they may have interests in maintaining these positions, they do not have moral rights to do so. And if their maintaining these positions prevents the realization of the rights of others, we can conclude that the rights of these others are being avoidably denied.

Avoidably to deny to persons their rights is an affront to their self-respect. To acquiesce in the avoidable denial of one's rights is to lack self-respect. As between forms of nonacquiescence, it is reasonable for persons whose rights are being avoidably denied to act fully in accordance with their interests, without regard for the interests of others in denying them such rights; then, for them voluntarily to yield their own interests in securing their rights to the interests of others in thwarting them is incompatible with their self-respect.

If progress toward ending injustice is not actually taking place, or is occurring at such a snail's pace as to provide no prospect of benefits within an actual person's lifetime, that person certainly has no interest in maintaining the social arrangement that brings about this result, and no obligation to be considerate of the interests of others in maintaining it. To accept "gradual improvement" of this kind would be to accept defeat of one's aspirations for justice and would be incompatible with one's self-respect.

However, to act without regard for the interests of those with superior power is to court disaster and to risk various aspects of destruction on both sides. If anything less is incompatible with self-respect, could any alternative be acceptable? Are there moral obligations, perhaps, that supersede self-respect? Perhaps the victims of injustice have an obligation to future generations to temper the pursuit of their interests in realizing their rights and to avoid the risks of destruction and institutional breakdown. But this consideration seems balanced or outweighed by the wrongness of allowing the present beneficiaries of unjust privileges to continue to violate the rights of others. What course of action should those committed to improving society adopt?

Let us consider the issue in a more specific domain, since such decisions arise in specific contexts rather than in some abstract choice between "reform" and "revolution." Let us focus on the issue of equality of opportunity for occupational attainments. This is not to say that equality of opportunity is an adequate conception of equality if the structures to which equality of opportunity is being offered are themselves unjust, but equality of opportunity is *one* aspect of an adequate structure of rights.

Let us imagine a change under which all positions based on privilege in a given institution would be suddenly vacated and refilled through selection procedures providing genuine equality of opportunity, including the opportunity to acquire the necessary qualifications. Let us label this change "immediate equality." If one could suppose that the institution, and the positions within it, would remain virtually intact and that the only change would be for the persons now in privileged positions to face competition on a basis of equality, every victim of past discrimination seeking equality of opportunity would have an overwhelming interest in "immediate equality." In justifiably pursuing interests in attaining respect for rights, the only issue for them in this hypothetical example would be to weigh large gains immediately against the same gains postponed, and the solution would be obvious. The sooner we gain that to which we are entitled, the better. And those who *rightfully* hold the positions they do should have little to fear from "instant equality" because they would regain these positions.

We would have little basis, however, for assuming that the institution in question would remain intact. Very few people are, or would risk testing whether they are, rightfully in privileged positions. Privileged classes and groups can probably not be expected to yield to even the most just demands without resistance. Hence, a more plausible assumption would be that many of the privileged would resist the sudden overthrow of the organizational supports of their positions, perhaps even to the point of the destruction of the institution and of the organized activities within it, and that many others would be willing to accept the risks of such resistance.

So we might have to suppose that the immediate realization of equality of opportunity would lead to the breakdown of the institution and its positions. In that case, opportunities for the formerly privileged and the formerly victimized would be equal only because they had become empty for both. And in that case the former victims would gain nothing from "immediate equality," as they would gain nothing from a "gradual improvement" too slow to be of benefit to them. The history of disregard for rights would not have been overcome in either case.

And yet there is a difference between the two forms of defeat as here outlined. If the victims of inequality choose "immediate equality" and strive for it through organized boycotts, strikes, and disruptions, they *risk* defeat; if they accept "gradual improvement" as described, they acquiesce in certain defeat. Given such a choice, the former seems compatible with self-respect in a way in which the latter does not.

Alternatives to the two forms of defeat outlined earlier should be considered. Instead of supposing certain defeat through "gradual improvement" and a risk of defeat through "immediate equality," predictions of our actual situation might be such as to indicate certain defeat through "immediate equality" and only probable defeat through "gradual improvement." This is the picture that established organizations have an interest in promoting: they suggest that if those who have suffered injustices will be patient, attitudes and the rate of improvement will increase. But for this assertion to be plausible, there would have to be evidence of an increase in the rate of equalization, and there is often no reason to suppose any such increase to be likely. Clarity about the actual yields to be produced by given rates of progress can do much to dispel illusions on these matters.

For trust and cooperation to be possible in a society, *some* rate of progress must be developed that is not incompatible with the self-respect of those who have suffered a denial of their rights. "One generation" is sometimes thought to be the maximum length of time any group should be asked to be patient.[40] Rates will understandably vary from context to context, depending on conditions, and justifiably so. But the general point that a reasonable rate of progress is a precondition for social trust should be understood by all members of society.

The trust that would be made possible by respect on the part of the society as a whole for the economic and social rights of its members and by a willingness to end injustice at a reasonable rate of progress would not automatically affect trust between individuals in their personal relations with one another. But much of the mistrust that now exists between, for instance, a black student and a white student, or between a woman and a man, is aggravated by their membership in groups between whom mistrust is all too appropriate. We need not await the lowering of mistrust between groups to try to form bonds of trust between trustworthy individuals, but we can be impatient for the assistance that would be provided in this effort by public policies that indicated a decent regard for human rights and a willingness to move toward ending the disregard of the rights of many at a determined pace.

Reasonable Solutions

Societies cannot transform themselves instantaneously. But they can make progress. However, if we assume that moral progress will be made as a result of the goodwill of the privileged, we may, again, be naive and foolish. Perhaps those who benefit from disregarding the rights of others will have to be led, again, as throughout history, to recognize that in the long run the mistrust that they make inevitable will bring it about that they, too, will be seriously hurt. *They* may be the ones left with no society to inherit. But this will be true only if they "succeed" in preventing trust from developing among those whose rights they fail to respect. If, alternatively, those who have been denied their rights join with those who are willing to move at a reasonable rate toward a decent society, then trust and cooperation are possible in developing such institutions as a genuinely democratic state, a just rule of law and a beneficial economy.

The issues can themselves be depicted in prisoner's dilemma terms, as some seek to maintain their privileges against any challenge and others to overthrow institutions that make this possible. Both would do well to cooperate in accepting policies that would bring about progress at a satisfactory rate, progress toward a better society more respectful of moral rights.

In situations of partial conflict, we should consider the collective or social as well as the individual outcomes and the ways in which reason should take this into account. From a collective or social point of view, the shared values of alternative relations are just as important, and just as relevant to what reason should recommend, as the gains to individuals.

In prisoner's dilemma situations, cooperative strategies clearly yield results that are collectively better. Sometimes we can see this by summing the values to the various parties that cooperation makes possible, instead of asking only what outcome will produce the highest payoff from the point of view of a given individual. But if we go on to consider the social value of a social relation such as that of the mutual choice of a given policy, we would have to consider other aspects of the relation than the sum of the individual values it achieves.

We seem clearly to need a concept of the "reasonable" and ways of arriving at the "recommended policy" that will take collective or social values into account as well as individual values. In the whole area of partial conflict, as most social interactions in most contexts seem to be, we need to move beyond the mere maximization of individual utility, or minimization of individual disutility, for either self or others in isolation.

Cooperation is not always the best policy, from the point of view of either morality or reasonableness. If a situation is such that the gains—both social and individual—of a given cooperative arrangement are small, whereas the individual gains of noncooperation might be much greater, perhaps the cooperative arrangement, and the policies and activities that comprise it, is confining or obsolete and should not be maintained or entered into. But cooperation has social value as well as value for the individuals who take part, and the former must be recognized and taken into account.

We can learn to estimate the social values of the outcomes of our mutual choices and to deal routinely with them. We now concern ourselves largely with individual gains, utilities, pleasures, satisfactions, and interests, and strive for precision and insight in our discussion of them. We could come increasingly to concern ourselves also with such questions as whether various social relations between persons, as embodied in their joint choices of policies and in their common activities, are trusting, affectionate, mutual, open, respectful, and supportive or, on the contrary, suspicious, exploitative, envy-inducing, hateful, and mutually damaging. And we could strive for rigor and insight into these matters comparable to what we expect in dealing with individual values. To sustain a society threatened with dissolution, we will have to pay attention before everything else to the relations between persons.

From where we are here and now, rather than from such a purely hypothetical condition as the "state of nature" or the "original position" of ideal social contract theories, we can try to agree on the outlines of the basic moral positions on which our societies can be justifiably built. In Chapter 8 we will see, for instance, how we might agree on the requirements of equal liberty. These positions can enable us to live together without violence, to respect one another's fundamental rights, and to get on with the challenges of making our societies better and more joyous.

Individual Responsibility

It is often as individuals that we begin to become aware of the deplorable state of our societies and our world, as our sense of what ought to be is offended by our observation of what is. But our individual glimmerings of discontent and outrage are difficult to sustain without support and confirmation from the perceptions and attitudes of others. It is important to seek communities of understanding as a condition for acting.

The supposition, however, that there will be collective action on the part of the critics of existing social arrangements to bring about change is often overly optimistic. The more likely prospect is often individual defiance of the institution denying various moral requirements and defeat of the defiant individual by the institution's privileged members. But even at the individual level, to risk defeat in behalf of what is right or good is compatible with self-respect in a way in which acquiescing in certain defeat is not. And recognition of this among various members of groups that have been treated unfairly can often bring the argument back to a consideration of the collective effort which would be justifiable and which would, if anything could, reduce the likelihood of defeat.

Often, change is possible only through collective action, and the individual who challenges injustice alone courts futility. But individuals are always ultimately responsible for making collective action possible or impossible. An individual may often best discharge that responsibility by trying to *bring into existence* the collectivity that can act successfully, rather than in acting alone against corrupt authority when the outcome may achieve little.[41] Determining whether the action to take should be to organize others for future collective action or to defy the forces of injustice alone requires a consideration of various factors to be discussed in later chapters. In any case it can be said that morally responsible persons ought to join together to establish the grounds for justifiable trust that will make possible the development of decent societies.

Chapter 6

Acceptance or Rejection
of the State

LET US TURN next to what reasonable persons might or might not agree to in the way of fundamental institutions. Those institutions in the legal-political-economic-social system which can coerce compliance and which can be thought of as underlying or surrounding or permitting or overseeing all the others in a given society can be thought of as the "state."

We all face such questions as whether to stay where we are or to emigrate, whether to obey the law or not, whether to participate in the political process or go around it, whether to try to succeed in or to rebel against the economic system we are in. Dealing with these issues involves us in innumerable actual actions that imply acceptance or rejection of a network of basic assumptions and intermediate theories about what we ought to do and what goals are worth seeking.

The Reality of States

We can *try* to imagine what it would be like without any state, but our ability to do so is extremely limited. We have grown up and developed our thoughts and outlooks within national entities organized in such a way that among the most massive determinants of our lives and experiences has been the nation-state.

Many social contract theorists have speculated on what a hypothetical "state of nature" without any state would be like. Hobbes's vision provides a haunting and central model of the "war of every man against every man." But it is apparent that he read back into his imagined state of nature various assumptions about the egoistic, aggressive, possessive, insatiably desiring nature of men which may have been more nearly characteristics of the type of individual presupposed by the authoritarian state making room for the development of capitalism than they were universally necessary characteristics of human beings in general.[1] Locke's depiction of the "state of nature" was more benign, but he imagined that human beings in it would have the attributes we can now recognize as those of man in the "bourgeois state." John Rawls does not posit the state of nature as a hypothetical but empirically describable condition; he depicts his "original position" as a set of assumptions we might make from which to imagine choosing the basic principles and institutions of society. But these assumptions incorporate those of the liberal, bourgeois state: that human beings are motivated by rational self-interest and that democratic political institutions should serve the interests of acquisitive individuals.[2]

I shall not even try to speculate on what a "state of nature" would be like. Nor shall I consider what we *would* choose from a hypothetical original position. I shall try to deal with the issues of what we should choose here and now, surrounded as we are by the nation-state in which we find ourselves, which is itself, in turn, surrounded by other nation-states. If the state in which we find ourselves is stable, its internal order probably rests on an enormous amount of force being used against either internal dissidents or external threats. If it is in a condition of civil war, force will be used to determine the kind of state it will be. In any case, an enormous amount of force relative to any individual will affect the position of the state in which the individual is located in relation to other states. The individual may be a member of a state with an advanced, developed economy making possible a high standard of living, or a member of a state in which mere economic survival is an everyday doubt.

Actual persons are born or brought into societies in which a whole set of institutions is already in place to help or hurt them, in which laws and enforcement officers either protect or constrain them, in which political processes facilitate or impede their pursuit of their interests, in which economic arrangements allow or prevent them from obtaining what they need.

Considering what one would agree to from a hypothetical state of nature may be an interesting exercise of the imagination. But if there is no connection between the actual state we are in and the state we would agree to from such a hypothetical situation, we may get little help from such theories for the dilemmas of acceptance and rejection that confront us every day.

Every actual state is the outcome of patriarchy, racial oppression, economic exploitation, force, and war, *not* of a social contract. The questions we face are whether to consent or not to be members of the state systems that surround us here and now. If we accept, what ought we to do, and if we do not, what ought we to do? These are among the most basic and pervasive moral questions we must answer. In no way can we avoid answering them by our actions. We can consider emigrating, but by the time it can be a free choice even to attempt to leave the state in which we live, we are already enmeshed in a language, a culture, a set of ties. We have received a certain kind of education and preparation for work, and finding a state that will be more acceptable and accepting than the one we are in, given the situations in which we are already placed, is rare.

Often there are few alternatives. The threat of war and violent death are worldwide in the nuclear age, and no country offers immunity from their dangers.[3] And in any state whatever, power is the crucial determinant of decisions, and there is nowhere to go to avoid the rule of power. Underground groups within existing states may sometimes offer more promising alternatives than other states, but their chances for survival, let alone growth, are often very low. And for the poor and uneducated the chances of escaping their present surroundings, even when the bars to doing so are weak, are even worse than for those born with advantages of resources and talent.

Despite all these obstacles, however, we must make moral decisions about whether to consider ourselves members of a given state system. If we reject membership, we may stay where we are, unnoticeably navigating the restrictions and requirements of a given society, rejecting it only in our hearts. Or, with only slightly more courage and commitment, we can choose to act on our rejection: to speak out at the very least, to try to change the system on its own terms, or on ours.

Our stance toward any actual social system will of course be mixed. We may accept most of its laws prohibiting violent crimes against persons, for instance, but reject the way it distributes economic benefits. Or we may accept its arrangements for the selection of legislators, say, and reject the ways nonelectoral power subverts the workings of that legislature to which they have been elected. And so on.

The issues that present themselves to us as actual persons faced with the realities of actual states have to do with the acceptance or rejection of given states' claims to impose their will on us. If we find a given state acceptable, we may freely agree to accept membership within its political system or agree to abide by its laws. The status of citizen is one to which we may give consent if a state is of sufficient acceptability for us to freely agree to do so. Most of us are born into and become capable of free choice within a given state. Hence, if we seem to "do nothing," we are citizens of the state into which we are born. But of course, "doing nothing" is nothing of the sort. If we do not leave a given state, or renounce our citizenship, or at least at some internal level "reject" our citizenship or repudiate our membership in the political system or resist the claim of the law of the state, then we accept this state and must accept moral responsibility for so doing.

The Dilemmas of Acceptance

Enormously serious issues are hidden within the notion of "freely choosing" to accept or reject the state in which we find ourselves. I shall not try to deal with many of them here. Suffice it to say at this point that I am concerned with the internal decision to "consent" or not, to accord our will with or not, to consciously oppose or not at the level of will and thought. How we decide to act on this consent or nonconsent is a different question.

A state that is relatively open to discussion, criticism, and influence for change is far more worthy of acceptance than one that is not. We may in such a state make what efforts we can to move it in directions we can approve of. Using the procedures and mechanisms made available by the state, we can make our decisions on membership in it partly in terms of our expectations for improvement and our chances to affect that improvement, even if we are seriously discontented with that state's present requirements and results.

To try to change a state from within its own rules, as in speaking out where free speech is allowed or trying to apply political pressure where the avenues for doing so are open, may be to accept the state at deeper or higher levels or to accept it on the whole. Doing so may involve no violation of its existing laws.

But when we consider that we cannot, on moral grounds, accept some outcome of the political process that we accept in general, but whose outcomes we have no ability to change, or that we cannot accept a particular law or legal decision within the legal system that we accept on the whole, we may consider acting on moral grounds in violation of the law and in nonacceptance of·a political outcome.

These issues well illustrate the levels of moral decision and commitment that we make and the way the method of experimental morality is suited to developing theories about morally acceptable state arrangements. Once we make a moral judgment at the level of a state or subsystem of a state, such as its legal system, we can talk about the possibilities of its being compatible with the particular moral judgments we make about particular actions. If compatibility is not possible, we must either revise our acceptance of the system-level judgment, or revise our particular judgments, or discover how the particular judgments thought to follow from the general commitment do not do so.

Consider the highest-level legal commitment we can make: we accept the legal system and membership in it, and we take the judgment "I ought to obey the laws of this legal system" to be a valid moral judgment. What follows from this? Does it follow, as Socrates argued in Plato's *Crito*, that if we accept a legal system, we must accept *all* its laws and decisions in our actions, though we must also continue to speak out on grounds of conscience against those laws we consider wrong?[4] It seems that even within the range of commitments by which we submit to law, we must seek an equilibrium between our general higher-level commitments and the particular judgments we make about particular actions, and that even if we consider ourselves bound by acceptance of the legal system as a whole, it may happen that our actions ought sometimes to be against the law rather than in accord with it. We should not argue in strict deductive fashion that if we accept the judgment "I ought to obey the laws of this legal system," then we ought to obey every particular law and legal decision within it. The deductive inference seems to follow from "I ought to obey the laws of this legal system" and a second premise that can be added to it stating, "This is a law of this legal system." But the conclusion "I ought to obey this law" may come into conflict with other moral judgments that we hold, and although we will know from this that we must revise our commitments somewhere, the decision about where will be open.

Consider the following familiar case: in the 1950s and early 1960s, segregation statutes were still considered legal throughout the South, and blacks were required by law to sit in the back of public buses and to stay out of white restaurants. Prior to the overturning of these laws as unconstitutional by the Supreme Court and the enactment of civil rights statutes, "the law" in Montgomery, Alabama, required blacks to obey these restrictions. A given person might well have refused to obey these laws without rejecting "the legal system" of the United States, even though in general to accept a legal system involves accepting local statutes as well as a nation's constitution and the decisions of particular courts as well as of the Supreme Court.

At the time that Rosa Parks, a black on a bus in Montgomery, Alabama, on December 1, 1955, refused to move to the back of the bus when ordered by the bus driver to do so, she was violating the law as so far developed in the United States. Her action was a good example of a spontaneously taken moral stand, the judgment about which could even more appropriately be made after than before the act, when the developments to which it led could be assessed.[5]

Those considering this action might well judge that she did the right thing, as did all those who decided to support her refusal and who, in organizing and taking part in or supporting the Montgomery bus boycott following her arrest, turned this issue into a national cause, contributing to the changes in the laws that later took place. Thus a significant transformation of the legal situation for blacks in the South occurred, brought about by particular refusals to accept legal decisions. The equilibrium thus upset was restored and morally improved through changes at the level of local statutes. Theories about morally acceptable legal arrangements concerning relations between blacks and whites had for most people been ahead of the actual legal provisions, though not as clearly as one would have hoped, since most moral theories had little to say on such questions. Moral theories should have guided and anticipated the actual decisions. In any case, particular judgments rather easily deemed to be valid claiming that "this black person should not be required to sit in the back of this bus" could be used to invalidate moral theories favoring legal arrangements allowing such segregation practices.

The framework within which these issues are best considered can be represented as follows.*

An individual person's network of commitments with regard to matters of public decision includes various possible judgments. The variables are particular decisions, laws, policies, etc., which we can designate X, and decision methods—however simple or complex— which we can designate M. We may then have the following judgments: "Individual I accepts (or rejects) X"; "Individual I accepts (or rejects) M"; and "M yields X (or not-X)".

---

*Certain passages in this and the following section of this chapter have been drawn from "Civil Disobedience and Public Policy," by Virginia Held, from the book *Revolution and the Rule of Law*, edited by Edward Kent. © 1971 by Prentice-Hall, Inc. Published by Prentice-Hall, Inc., Englewood Cliffs, New Jersey 07632. They are used with permission.

A problem arises, and the equilibrium in a person's judgments is upset when the person tentatively espouses a set of commitments such as these:

(a) Individual I rejects X
(b) Individual I accepts M
(c) M yields X

because it would seem to follow that from (b) and (c) together we would get

(d) Individual I accepts X,

and of course an individual cannot reject X and accept X at the same time.

A simple model of the problem would be a case where a given person is opposed to having a voluntary association of which he is a member hire a given administrator, A, knowing the direction in which A would be likely to take the organization. Hiring A would then substitute for X. But the person accepts the method of majority vote by board members for deciding such matters, and let us suppose a majority of board members vote in favor of hiring A. What should the person then do? Should he change his earlier view that the association should not hire A, or is he really not committed to the decision method of majority vote of board members on the issue?

It would seem that the totality of our political and legal and economic and social commitments are complex versions of the above problem. We have a set of views on what we are for or against. We accept in general various component methods of, say, "the democratic process" or "the rule of law." These methods yield outcomes in conflict with our views. And we face moral dilemmas about what to do: should we change our view, give up on the component methods, or go along, grudgingly and with misgivings, with the decisions the methods produce?

The usual solution that has been suggested is that when the methods yield a decision of which a citizen disapproves, the citizen does not change her *judgment*, but does change her *conduct*. Thus Rawls says that "the right to make law does not guarantee that the decision is rightly made; and while the citizen submits in his conduct to the judgment of democratic authority, he does not submit his judgment to it."[6]

But this does not answer the question of whether the person accepts or rejects the decision at a moral level. She still must meet the question of whether the judgment "I ought to act in accordance with the decision" is valid or not. The possibility of separating thought and action, judgment and consent, seems to evaporate at this point. For if an individual sincerely subscribes to a given method of decision, then presumably she must accept what the method yields. But then again, if she is sincerely committed to a position contrary to this outcome, then presumably she must reject it.

What to do about such acceptance or rejection is a separate problem. Clearly, a moral rejection of a political or legal decision should not always lead to civil disobedience or rebellion protesting it, for the consequences of such actions might often be worse than those of doing nothing. But moral rejection of a legal decision does yield at least one good reason for actions that violate the law: it is an essential first step. Before the individual can decide whether the good reasons are conclusive for acting upon his rejection, he must settle for himself the problem of moral acceptance or rejection of the decision in question.

The problem is not resolvable by locating the process of decision in time, and suggesting that the citizen accepts, say, (a) and (b) *until* he finds out (c), and then he changes his mind (or his will), because the problem is one of logical incompatibility.[7]

What must be concluded, I think, is that—importing a well-known metaphor—the fabric of our commitments faces the tribunal of experience as a corporate body.[8] We can reevaluate the interconnected judgments within it where we choose, and furthermore, the weave we are willing to accept at any point is our responsibility.

Although most political and legal decision methods are complex and vague, it may be helpful to examine the issues being discussed through examples of a precise decision method such as a majority vote, without assuming that the vote has, itself, the force of law.

Consider the following political possibilities within the framework outlined above in (a) to (d). Suppose someone were to take seriously a proposal for national direct democracy and to assume a commitment to this method (M) of decision. Then suppose a majority of voters did in fact approve a plan (X) to wipe out poverty in their nation-state by expelling all those with incomes below the poverty line. Presuming that the person had an original judgment (a) rejecting such a plan, could we suppose that when faced with such a decision as an outcome of M, he would now, because of his commitment to M, abandon (a) and accept (d)? In all probability, one hopes, he would hang on to (a) and revise the network somewhere else, such as in restricting M when basic rights are at issue.

But consider another case. Suppose someone were opposed to the building of a playground in a nearby park, thinking trees more beneficial, yet was committed to a majority decision of affected citizens on the matter. If the latter then yielded a decision to build the playground, the person might well at this point abandon (a) and hang on to (d).

Most of the interesting issues in the network of our political and legal judgments seem to fall between these two kinds of cases: we know we must revise our commitments somewhere, but it isn't at all clear where.

When a person has satisfied herself that a legal or political decision method has not been misapplied, but that it really does yield an outcome that on moral grounds she cannot accept, she may consider acting in ways that are condemned by the state as in violation of its authority, even though she accepts membership in that state. The range of possible actions extends from nonviolent civil disobedience to organized resistance and violence.

Let us consider now some of the major forms that the rejection on moral grounds of aspects of an existing state's arrangements may take.

Civil Disobedience

Acts of civil disobedience are violations of law on moral grounds. They are designed to appeal to the consciences or political sense of those in power or of potential supporters in order to change the arrangements protested against. Of the various kinds of actions to change a state that go beyond what are allowed by the laws of that state, acts of civil disobedience are the easiest to justify.

There are three kinds of civil disobedience. First, there are acts violating currently valid laws taken by persons who claim and can reasonably expect that such acts will be found legal by higher courts within a decade or two. These acts are sometimes tests of whether the more particular laws really are "the law" or are unconstitutional. This kind of civil disobedience can be considered to be defiance of the law only in a very technical sense, but if those performing such acts are unwilling to wait for the test to work its way up to the highest court—often a matter of several years—and violate existing law on a significant scale, the acts become more than a mere test of a law's legality. In the civil rights struggles of the early 1960s, massive defiance of segregation statutes that were only later overturned constituted civil disobedience of the first kind.

In a second category of acts of civil disobedience, the person violating or protesting a law acknowledges fully that the law is currently valid and will not soon be found unconstitutional. In these cases, because he considers the law to be morally wrong, he intentionally disobeys, or acts illegally to protest, that which clearly *is* law. Examples of this may be found among young men who did not challenge the *legality* of the draft but refused to comply with it on moral grounds. In such cases, the act of civil disobedience may be an attempt to get the legal system itself to change the legal reality through new court decisions. Or the act may be performed with the purpose of influencing the political system to change the law, either the law violated or some other law that the civilly disobedient considers legally valid but morally unacceptable. This can be achieved through the passage of new legislation or through new administrative regulations.

Finally, in acts of civil disobedience of a third kind, the violation of law as such is entirely incidental. Acts of this kind are forms of political protest. Such acts are intentionally and primarily directed at *political decisions and policies* rather than at *laws*, either the one directly violated or some other law, and may therefore be justifiable or unjustifiable on quite different grounds than acts of civil disobedience protesting laws.

The most compelling examples of widespread civil disobedience that we have had in recent years were those in connection with protests against the war in Vietnam. In some cases, various component acts, when directed at specific political policies and decisions, were acts of civil disobedience of the third kind. But protest against the war was so deep and so general that it involved all three kinds of civil disobedience, its acts ranging from attempts to have pursuit of the war declared unconstitutional, and to have Congress curb the war through legislation, to application of pressure to policymakers and presidents and to passionate outcries against war in general.

The distinction between the second and third kind of civil disobedience is not altogether easy to maintain, since an effort to apply pressure within the political system to change a law is a political act, and acts of civil disobedience designed to do so might be classified as acts of the third kind rather than the second, or a new category might be set up. But, as I shall argue in later chapters, we can usefully and plausibly make a distinction between a political system and a legal system as recognizable subsystems of a society, and we can distinguish different forms of justification that seem especially characteristic of and appropriate for each. Although the systems overlap, they are distinguishable, and acts of civil disobedience may be classified in terms of whether they are directed primarily at affecting one or the other.

Consider, as an example of a political decision, the establishment by a president, on the advice of his Budget Bureau and with the pressures of various interest groups upon him, of budget priorities and of appropriate sums to be spent on the various activities of the government. Such decisions are among the most important that government can make, yet they are not legal matters in any primary sense. Of course, the president is such by law, but to consider every decision of a person legally holding an official position a "legal decision" is to collapse politics into legal formalisms. And, of course, the executive makes its decisions within certain legal constraints. It is required by law to fund programs already mandated by law, such as veterans' benefits and agricultural subsidies. And what Congress does about the president's recommendations will later be law. But the crucial decisions are primarily political rather than legal decisions. And so on down the line to decisions of the president's advisers, of department heads, of members of the bureaucracy and of regulatory agencies, and so on. Many such decisions have the force of law, but many have *political* rather than legal force. This is true also of many of the decisions of political actors such as parties, interest groups, rich donors, and powerful individuals; they may be of great political significance, though largely beyond the reach of legal attention.[9]

It may be that the citizen's objection to a given political decision is not an objection to any of the relevant laws surrounding it, but entirely to the political decision made within these laws. And just as most writers on civil disobedience have rejected the argument of Socrates that whoever accepts a system of laws must accept every law within it, so the time seems to have come for us to move beyond the view that every political decision made within a "framework" of acceptable laws is itself acceptable.

If, in protesting various political decisions, or trying to, protesters violate a *law*, this may well be thoroughly incidental, yet it may be the only or the most justifiable way for them to register or to act upon an unwillingness to consent to such decisions. Accordingly, the requirements that some writers have suggested for acts of civil disobedience of the first two kinds to be *justifiable* may require reinterpretation.

One suggestion has been that the act of protest should be directly related to the law that is objected to, so that the law being protested is the one that is violated. Thus, if the draft law is thought immoral, an act of civil disobedience that violates it rather than some other law would be thought to be more justifiable. In some cases we may agree that such a direct relation contributes to the justifiability of the act;[10] as a general requirement, however, a demand for a direct relation makes little sense when the object of protest is a law difficult or impossible to violate, or is the absence of a law. It obviously makes no sense when the object of protest is a political decision or policy, for an individual simply cannot *violate* a budget priority, or an executive decision not to press for a poverty program, or a foreign policy, or a party nomination. But these may be just the things she is most inclined to be civilly disobedient about in the sense of *rejecting*, on moral grounds, the decisions of the political system of which she is a member.[11]

Another suggestion frequently made is that an act of civil disobedience is justifiable only when that which is being protested is remediable by a legal or constitutional change.[12] The kinds of issues in what I am calling acts of civil disobedience of the third kind, however, frequently are not issues that can be remedied by constitutional or legal provisions, or issues that the courts could or would adjudicate; they are often not even maters of legal rights or basic liberties, unless the term "rights" is so broadly construed as to lose the clear core of its meaning and erase the useful distinction between legal rights and political interests. Questions of whether citizens should be provided with a wiser political appointee or more efficient public services or defense policies with more foresight or a less insensitive foreign policy in a given area are frequently issues that cannot be appropriately dealt with on legal or constitutional grounds. They are often not justiciable issues.

Clearly, citizens should not expect the courts and the constitution to make all their decisions for them, and those performing acts of civil disobedience of this third kind might sometimes justifiably choose to bypass altogether the attempt to make a legal defense or to have new laws enacted. Their purpose would be to act upon their nonacceptance of particular political decisions and policies, and their acts could be justifiable on other grounds than if they were acts of civil disobedience of the second kind. In time, ways may be developed to act upon such nonacceptance without actual violations of law, or with some assurance that the political system will not prosecute certain kinds of civil disobedience. Hannah Arendt has suggested, for instance, that groups of civilly disobedient persons be accorded a recognition within the political system comparable to that accorded to organized pressure groups whose lobbyists are permitted and expected to influence Congress.[13] At present, short of illegal action that is subject to prosecution, there is often no way for persons to refuse to accept political decisions.

The grounds for the justifiability of acts of civil disobedience of this third kind would be straightforwardly teleological. The arguments here would not be, as they might well be for acts of civil disobedience in conflict with the legal system, that an individual has a deontologically based prima facie moral right not to obey an immoral law, even when the consequences of such an act are unknowable. (See chapters 3 and 7.) Nor would the arguments be that the citizen may have a moral obligation to protest a legal situation that is immoral on deontological grounds—for example, a denial of basic human rights—even when the actual chance of bringing about change through such an act is insignificant.

The questions that would now be most relevant would have to do with whether the act of civil disobedience is likely to bring about good consequences, what values to attach to its possible outcomes, what the probabilities of its effectiveness actually are, and whether the effects that will be produced by it will be more beneficial than burdensome in terms of the general good.

In distinguishing sharply between civil disobedience and crime, as most writers on the subject have done, it has usually been assumed that the criminal wanted only to benefit himself at the expense of others and had no legitimate complaint against the law as it stood and no serious intent to change it. This view may be increasingly inadequate for a certain kind of crime technically involving theft of property, but motivated, like other violations of law that clearly count as civil disobedience, by moral considerations. A morally principled rejection of prevailing arrangements, in this case those of economic systems yielding grossly unjust distributions of wealth and income, could result in an act of civil disobedience. Where a person protesting economic injustice takes only enough to satisfy the basic needs of himself or others, and takes from those, including collective entities, who profit excessively from the economic arrangements in question, where harm to persons is avoided and an intent to increase economic justice present, there seems to be as good reason to consider such acts to be acts of civil disobedience as there is in the case of many other violations of law on moral grounds.[14]

Political Strikes

When civil disobedience becomes an organized and collective action protesting a political arrangement, it may be thought of as a special kind of strike.

The first characteristic of a strike that must be noted is that it is a *collective* action. An individual acting alone cannot conduct a strike. A strike must involve significant numbers of persons acting together. If a nonviolent protest involving civil disobedience and directed specifically at a political target is a collective action, its collective nature may distinguish it from civil disobedience, or even resistance, as frequently understood. Civil disobedience is a violation of law on grounds of conscience; resistance is a refusal to accept the legal penalties of such violation. Both are associated with individual action and individual conscience. Of course, many persons can together perform such actions, but they are acting as individuals, and the participation of others is in no way required for the acts in question to be acts of civil disobedience or resistance. Nonviolent collective protests, on the other hand, may well be such that their collective nature is essential to them. They may involve no intentional violation of *law* as such, as when large numbers of persons block streets or passages; and the question of whether a resulting penalty is accepted or rejected may be quite incidental to them. Their purpose may be to exert political pressure rather than to seek legal redress.

After a period of frequent, nondisruptive demonstrations, demonstrations may come to be seen as ordinary parts of the political scene, so ordinary as to be of little significance and less effect. Violent revolution may continue to appear to most of its potential recruits as either unnecesary or impossible, and isolated acts of individual civil disobedience often seem futile, however justified. What may be more effective are intermediate forms of action: collective, frequently but not necessarily in violation of law, and capable of exerting real pressure on the political managers the way strikes are capable of exerting real pressure on the managers of corporations. Perhaps the term "citizens' strike" could appropriately be used for such collective political interferences with the normal activities of the political system, even though a withholding of the participant's own work would not necessarily be a feature of such "strikes."

The political system, like the economy, is broken up into units or subsystems of varying dimension: there is this city agency, that federal department, this armed forces unit, that county office. And just as corporate management determines the conditions under which the worker must either labor or go elsewhere, so, in important respects, political management determines the public conditions under which the citizen must live or go elsewhere, if he or she can.

In a cohesive system, many persons translate the sentence "X has authority" into "What X commands ought to be done"; for political decisions to be authoritative in almost any sense, however, they must be accepted at least grudgingly by those affected by them. And just as the corporation cannot turn out products unless the workers put up with the working conditions, so a political system cannot turn out authoritative decisions unless its members put up with the conditions it provides.[15]

If groups of members of a political system or a subsystem of it refuse to accept the conditions they are offered, and if this refusal is organized and substantial, an appropriate description of the situation might seem to be: *The citizens are on strike.* If such occurrences were to become more frequent, the political managers, to avoid them, might begin to bargain in earnest with those whose grievances could not be met by a suggestion that they take their problems up with "the voting public." All too often, the voting public reveals itself to be a reflection of the selfish interests of the regnant majority rather than a collectivity concerned with the requirements for social justice or aware of the minimal responsibilities a political system must meet to assure its own future and the possibilities of international peace. With the development of political strikes, citizens of conscience could avoid being at the mercy of electoral largesse or judicial innovation. To the extent that their actions might be coercive upon those in power, this coercion should be no less justifiable[16] than that already employed by the political system. But evaluations along these lines should lead to recommendations for restraint, not to immobility.

To be effective, such political strikes should be organized, collective refusals to accept specific political decisions, such refusals being registered through an impeding of the work of the political unit being "struck" and, sometimes, through disobedience of various of its legal requirements. Familiar forms that may be improved upon are the blocking of entrances to governmental buildings, deliberate interference with military or defense-industrial activities, nonpayment of kinds or percentages of taxes, refusal to move from an official's office, and so on. Certainly, new forms may be imagined and developed, but with the growing awareness of the purposes of such strikes and the grounds for their justification, the particular form adopted may be less important than the organization of large numbers of persons to go on strike against a unit of the political system, or against the system as a whole, when they consider it appropriate and justifiable to bring about specific and genuine good consequences.

For such persons, the citizens' strike, even when it involves civil disobedience, will not be thought of as a rare and extreme response, appropriate only for the most outrageous or tyrannical of governments or laws or the most blatant violations of fundamental rights. It can be directed toward decisions and policies that the political managers faced with it can change, and can come to be thought of, perhaps, by participants and observers alike as no more outlandish than a labor union strike. To be out on bail or in jail as a result of such activities may come to seem rather like refusing to work—uncomfortable, costly, and sometimes painful, but hardly cause for much more righteous fury than a banker now expends on a striking hard hat.

Of course, the worker's right to strike against a corporation is now acknowledged by law, while the citizen who commits an act of civil disobedience is by definition acting illegally. But prior to 1921, labor picketing of any kind was held by some courts to be unlawful, and for almost two decades afterward, judicial definitions of the kinds of picketing that were legal and the kinds that were not were confused and contradictory. Until the mid-1930s, an employer could fire an employee for union activity and require workers to sign contracts binding them not to join a union, much less strike. Both arrangements are somewhat comparable to ones the political system thinks it has with those for whom it makes authoritative decisions.

Which sorts of political strike activities may be justifiably coercive and which sorts may not will have to be worked out in detail, just as the lines between acceptable and unacceptable union "coercion" have had to be worked out. The lines for labor have obviously shifted from pre-1914 conceptions allowing injunctions to be issued forbidding even attempts by unions to persuade, and from the days afterward when a single picket for "communication and persuasion" was allowed at each gate, but mass picketing was prohibited. The uses made by the courts of injunctions in the 1920s, when any union action that intentionally interfered with interstate commerce could be interpreted as an illegal "restraint of trade," belong clearly to the past. Similar shifts may be appropriate in our conceptions with regard to political strikes.

By the time legislation was enacted requiring employers to bargain collectively with workers, the strike was a familiar occurrence. Various forms of what is now thought to be civil disobedience might begin to be worked out such that some obstructions of the production of authoritative governmental decisions might similarly be permitted by law, and some could by agreement go unprosecuted, while enforced restrictions against violence remain. Since decisions to prosecute or not prosecute are frequently political decisions, the threat of political strikes by citizens' groups could come to be seen as calling for negotiations rather than for a rigid enforcement of law.[17] The tradition of the general strike, familiar in Europe and elsewhere, in which workers withhold their work to achieve political objectives, should also be learned from.

Most citizens have come to take it for granted that in attaining an acceptable level of wages, workers may be justified in going on strike against a corporation. It is not much more difficult to argue that, under actual conditions, in the process of gaining morally acceptable political decisions, citizens may be justified in going on strike against a political system or a unit of it. Unless forms of political action that exceed the present bounds of electoral and interest-group politics are developed, and in time given legal scope, much discontent among conscientious citizens with the political conditions they live under may have no outlet through which to work for fundamental political change.[18]

Violence

Acceptance of a state is not an all-or-nothing matter. We may recognize appalling moral deficiencies in the state in which we find ourselves, and yet want to stay there, prefer it for any number of irrational reasons to any other state, decide on balance to put up with it, and so forth. The crucial feature in acceptance of a state is our recognition that it is legitimate for the state we accept to require us to renounce the use of violence to try to destroy it. We may use many other means to register our nonacceptance of any number of features of it. We may disobey its laws in acts of civil disobedience while still accepting membership in its legal system. We may try to exert whatever political pressure we can to transform its political system. We may engage in potentially violent confrontations that may cause those who have refused to listen to us to pay attention to a grievance or point of view. And, of course, we can speak out, demonstrate, or assemble in protected ways where these are permitted or in unprotected ways where doing so may be much more costly to us.

If we engage in full-scale armed resistance, in acts of violence designed to destroy the state, in attempts to overthrow it by force, at this point we no longer accept the state in question. We deny its right to exist as a state.

We can have moral grounds on which to accept citizenship in a state, or membership in a legal or political system, even if the state in question is to a high degree unacceptable to us. We need only decide that we should not use force to try to destroy the state. If one renounces the use of force to destroy the state in which one finds oneself, does this mean that one renounces the use of all forms of violence? Not necessarily. Let us consider the arguments surrounding violence. Can the use of violence ever be justified?

If we judge that there is no possibility for us to effect improvement in a state because the state's arrangements render us powerless and, worse yet, voiceless, we may be justified in acting in such a way as to force the state at least to take notice of our arguments. Civil disobedience appeals to the moral sense and views of those in power, but if they are so deaf as not even to hear such appeals, civil disobedience will have no chance of effectiveness. Political strikes depend on having some actual power to marshal in this form; if those who protest have none, they will not be able to conduct a protest that will *be* a strike.

If a state is so corrupt as to be unmoved by reasonable argument, so blind as to render invisible those bearing such arguments even when the arguments are clearly significant, some violence may then be justfied. [19] Colonized peoples, members of racial minorities, and women have at various times had the experience that their arguments for some form of justice have simply not been allowed by those in power to register upon their minds. Those making these arguments have been looked through or looked at as if they were inanimate objects or animals or mere pieces of flesh rather than human persons. Acts of violence may sometimes jar into awareness those who have failed to recognize that those performing these acts are human. An act of violence may sometimes cause those with excessive power to acknowledge that those they oppress are capable of providing arguments which must be answered and not simply ignored.

But such acts as these are limited efforts to force an opening in the political process for reform through political means. They are not threats to the very existence of the state. If we renounce the use of violence to overthrow the state, we commit ourselves at a very general level to treat various ranges of issues through the avenues of more specific contexts such as the legal, the political, the economic, and the cultural.

Chapter 7

Law and Rights

IT IS NOW time to consider in greater detail the components of the "state" that we may agree, or not agree, to "accept" in the sense discussed in the last chapter and the reasons for our choice. The most salient feature of the state in terms of formal visibility is its legal system. We can distinguish within a society a number of domains of activity and think of them as organized in terms of relations and interactions. How to conceptualize the relation between them is highly unclear and disputed. I shall argue for a conception that sees the legal system, the political system, and the economic system as separate but overlapping areas of activity organized by distinctive ways of doing things. Different forms of moral argument are characteristic, I think, of the way moral issues should be addressed in these different domains.

The State and Its Subsystems

If we decide that we ought to consider ourselves members of a given state, there will obviously be issues involving moral concerns that the state will decide. The state will make claims that its decisions are justifiable. Sometimes and perhaps even often in some matters, these claims

104

will be valid. Although we may often conclude that what a state decides is based on only part of the arguments that would be relevant if we were making a moral judgment that the decision is morally valid in a comprehensive sense, we may make a moral decision to allow various ranges of issues to be decided in these partial ways. For instance, if we agree to the moral validity of a law forbidding armed assault, and if we agree to a jury system to decide on the guilt or innocence of a person charged with this specific crime, we may agree to accept the verdict of the jury as an adequate approximation of the moral judgment that we think we would come to if we ourselves inquired into all the aspects of the case, including the justifiability of the law and the justifiability of all the procedures employed by the legal system leading up to the verdict and all the particular facts relevant to this case.

Within the state are, in my view, subsystems that do and should employ forms of justification differing from one another and from total moral justification in its most developed form. We can make moral judgments that a given range of issues ought to be handled in a given way, using those more limited justificatory procedures appropriate to that sort of issue. Using these procedures and the institutions and processes they require, we can constantly try to approximate the best possible moral answers to questions such as how various violent or coercive actions ought to be handled or prevented, how the products of industry and labor ought to be distributed, how the power to decide who will occupy what governmental offices ought to be organized, and so on. It is my claim that different approaches for different sorts of issues will have a better chance of furthering the objectives of morality and of reflecting the requirements of moral concern than if people try to leap over all the institutional constructs and more specific norms and to apply the totality of morality directly to every particularity of responsibility.

Let us look first at the legal and political systems. Even if we are interested entirely in description, there are reasons to consider the legal and political systems to be conceptually distinct. Once we turn to prescription, there are further reasons for judging them separately, but let's begin with the case at the descriptive level.

It seems plausible to hold that not only can there be actions and decisions that belong primarily to one system rather than to the other, but there may even be cases where one system could exist without the other.

Since my concern here is with actual advanced societies having both well-developed legal and political systems, I shall concentrate on distinguishing some characteristics of each in a social system "containing," in some sense, both. But since my concern will also be with justification (refer to pages 32–33), and its irreducible normative content, I shall also be concerned with an ethical system—which may or may not be embodied in a social system—as that within which a legal and a political system may be thought to be "contained," in the sense that we have made a higher-level moral decision to treat certain issues in certain ways that we can now refer to as legal or as political.

What can it mean for an act or decision to "belong to" a system, and what is the relation of a system to what goes on "within" it? I shall not try here to deal more than cursorily with these difficult questions, but a tentative case may perhaps be granted.

Let us turn first to the suggestions made by Giovanni Sartori in a careful exploration of the problem of what politics *is*. He claims that "in order to find our way in the differentiations among politics, ethics, law, economics and so forth, it is necessary to refer to the structural differentiation of human aggregations. . . . Only the field of ethics, which is the most ancient and the most developed, escapes reference to a structural underpinning."[1] Then, with the exception of the term "ethical," characterizing behavior as "political," "economic," "juridical," or "social" specifies a locus, a site of behavior. "The behavior observed by the economist belongs to the site 'economic system,' which is a constellation of structures, roles, and institutions,"[2] Sartori writes. And so on for the other terms.

The Legal and the Political

Different writers, however, perceive or interpret the structures of society very differently, and so Sartori's suggestion may be at best a starting point. It appears to be tempting, for instance, for writers on legal systems, as they gaze beyond the borders of their own territory, to picture political systems as subsystems of or wholly dependent upon those systems to which their primary professional attention is attached. Thus Alf Ross writes that "political power . . . is the power exercised by the technique of law, or, in other words, by the apparatus of the State—an apparatus for the exercise of force. . . . The power of those in control of the apparatus of the State depends on the fact that they occupy the key positions which, according to the Constitution, afford the legal competence to hold power. *All political power is legal competence.* A 'bare' power, independent of the law and its basis, does not exist."[3] And Kelsen writes that "one of the distinctive results of the Pure Theory of Law is its recognition that the coercive order which constitutes the political community we call 'state,' is a legal order. What is usually called 'the legal order of the state' or 'the legal order set up by the state,' is the state itself."[4]

And it appears to be tempting for writers on political systems, as they gaze beyond the borders of their own territory, to picture legal systems as subsystems of those systems to which *their* primary professional loyalties are attached. According to two representatives of this tendency, one of the subprocesses of *the* political process is the quasi-mechanical kind (others are the intellectual and the social), and *one* of the quasi-mechanical subprocesses is the legal one. "Law and constitutions," they write, "can be considered as established decision guidelines, intended to provide a framework for 'programming' in a 'quasi-mechanical manner' certain substantive types of decisions."[5] In Morton Kaplan's more precise formulation, *"Law is the consequence of past political decisions. Constitutions are laws which specify hierarchical relationships within the political system and methods for changing these relationships."*[6]

It is surprising that neither group seems to have read the books of the other: writers on legal systems seldom mention writers on political systems, and writers on political systems seldom refer to writers on legal systems.

The view I recommend is that political systems and legal systems be seen, in some sense at least, as subsystems of ethical systems, or of what ethical systems would be if they could be said to "exist." As Sartori notes, ethical systems do not normally have the sorts of structures, roles, and institutions that prevail in the other systems, but this does not mean that something constituting a "locus" for ethical decisions could not be developed or has never been present, and perhaps Sartori underestimates the extent to which ethical systems might be comparable to the others. But in any case, political and legal systems may be thought to be subsystems of social systems, whatever the relation between social systems and ethical systems may be. And in any case, I think, neither the legal nor the political system is best construed as a subsystem of the other; they are more or less equal, and more or less independent, although they frequently overlap in very significant measure.

Let us turn to some decisions that we might classify as legal *or* political but not both. Since among the issues being confronted is the structural differentiation, if it exists, between the political system and the legal system, we cannot appeal to these structures to allow us to recognize the system in which these decisions are located, and thus the appropriate characterization of the decisions. We must try, then, to establish their properties on independent grounds, just as we would try to establish that a certain entity is a crow and is black on the basis of our observation and of our understanding of the terms "crow" and "black" independently of one another, and not because we have derived this view from the general statement, which we believe, that all crows are black.

I think that by appealing to our usual meanings of "legal" and "political," and without assuming that the structures within which legal or political decisions are located are either the same or different, we can recognize that there may be acts or decisions that belong to one system but not to the other. If this is the case, at least we can know that the two systems are not coextensive, nor is either located wholly within the other. A question may arise as to whether the existence of acts that are legal but not political, and of others that are political but not legal, indicates anything about the distinctiveness of legal and political *systems*. I take it that it does, since systems are composed of elements in relation to one another, and if an element is present in system A and not present in system B, the two systems are not the same, although of course there may be other elements present in both.

Consider the following two hypothetical cases.

1. Individual A deliberately carries out the killing of individual B and, as planned, makes off with a material object in B's possession and valuable to him. There are no mitigating circumstances, such as A's poverty or social discontent, B's wealth or insulting behavior, etc. A is caught and tried. The legal decision is straightforward and simple: A is guilty of murder.

We would have, in such a case, a clear violation of law and an unproblematic application of a legal rule to a particular case. We can say that no political factors were relevant to any significant degree. Any normal legal system would have included a prohibition against murder and would have yielded a comparable result, no matter how its judges were selected, no matter what were the particular characteristics of the persons involved, and no matter what importance or unimportance private property or public status played in the social system. Furthermore—and this is especially significant—it would have yielded such a result no matter how adequate or efficient the enforcement mechanisms of the legal system were, and even if there were no enforcement mechanisms. If it is asserted that a legal system cannot exist without sufficient political power to enforce its decisions, we may respond that we are dealing not with a question of causal prerequisites, but with a question of discerning what properties such a decision has if we take its existence as given. It would seem that to call the legal decision in this case a kind of political decision would clearly be to misunderstand its nature.

2. A potential leader, C, of a group of persons gathered in a public place is considering whether to favor in his speech a controversial local proposal to build a new road. One group of potential supporters strongly favors the proposal. Another group of potential supporters strongly opposes the proposal. The speaker decides to declare himself in favor of the position of the group with greater political influence *because* it has greater political influence and for no other reason. The political influence involved is independent of the legal standing of its possessors, depending only on such factors as the relative strength of the numbers of the two distinct groups.

In terms of the factors that almost any recent political science text would recognize as making an event "political," we could easily classify this decision as political. But in this case a political decision is made in which no legal factors have played any significant part. C is a *potential* leader occupying no position distinguishable by the legal system from that occupied by any other members of the political system; in making his decision, he appeals to no legal factor; his decision would be what it is no matter what legal provisions or legal mechanisms also touched the persons involved in the situation. Again, it may be hard to imagine anything that could qualify as an existing political system that did not include legal rules conferring powers to decide and to act. But, as in the previous case, we are trying to establish what properties the decision described has apart from its causal prerequisites. Then we can say, I think, that to consider the political decision made in this case a special sort of legal decision would clearly be to misunderstand its nature.

If we acknowledge, then, that conceptually there are decisions that belong to legal systems and not to political ones, and that conceptually there are decisions that belong to political systems and not to legal ones, we may conclude that conceptually, at least, although the two systems overlap in large and important areas, and may perhaps be causally dependent upon each other, neither is the subsystem of the other and they are not coextensive. A separate argument may then indicate that the conceptual separation of the two systems allows for a better understanding of real systems than do its alternatives. But let us consider further how these two systems may be characterized.

The Legal System

To try to depict a legal system, let us turn first to what H. L. A. Hart has to say. What "any educated man" would be able to identify as salient features of a legal system, Hart contends, are the following: "(i) rules forbidding or enjoining certain types of behavior under penalty; (ii) rules requiring people to compensate those whom they injure in certain ways; (iii) rules specifying what must be done to make wills, contracts, or other arrangements which confer rights and create obligations; (iv) courts to determine what the rules are and when they have been broken, and to fix the punishment or compensation to be paid; (v) a legislature to make new rules and abolish old ones."[7]

It is interesting to note that a legislature to make and change rules is mentioned *last* among the five features and that there is *no* mention at all of all the *political* processes and forces that go into making and changing legislatures and that result in their being composed of one set of persons rather than another. Hart makes no mention of political parties or organizations or groups, and no mention of what we can roughly identify as the executive-administrative branch of government. I do not quarrel with Hart's picture, if it is meant to represent what is only a legal system; it lends support to the view that it would be a gross distortion to consider the political system a subsystem of or coextensive with the legal system.

Nor am I suggesting that the distinction is merely that between the judicial branch of government and other branches. Of course, the judicial system is institutionally distinct, but I am concerned here with more basic characterizations than this institutional differentiation. Clearly, the most central aspect of the legal system is the judiciary, but it would be misleading to call the system I am discussing "the judicial system" because of the extent and importance of the overlap between it, whether we would call it legal or judicial, and the political system. I am including the *making* of law by a legislature within the legal system, as do most writers on legal systems, but also within the political system, since political processes go into the making of law, so that lawmaking must be found in an area of overlap between the legal and the political. There is no doubt, I assume, that legislating occurs within something that can be called the political system, but if we were to label the other system "judicial," the suggestion would be that the making of law fell outside this other system, whereas the system I am concerned with is one in which the functions of courts are central but in which legislative functions are also included.

That various political officials hold the positions they do "by law" sometimes leads to the conceptual amalgamation of the two systems. And there is a tradition, of course, of assuming as meaningful the observation that the legal system somehow "includes" or "covers" anything anyone in a social system does because whatever is not forbidden by law is permitted. (The formula "What the sovereign permits, he commands" goes even further.) But both of these positions seem more misleading than helpful, rather like asserting that the universe is composed of those things which are chairs and those things which are not chairs; the statement is not false, but it is certainly misleading.

Consider the influence of a leader of environmental dissidents in recent years. If large numbers of supporters accept her appeal and descend upon a capital, can it be denied that she has some political power, however short of her hopes it may be? Yet she may have *no* official position or "legal competence" relevant to this capacity. And what of the political influence of someone who has merely written a book or become known as an actor or "personality"? Surely the line between influence and political power can be crossed long before such a person acquires an official position with *legal* competence.

There is also the political power sometimes gained by law*breaking*, as in notable acts of civil disobedience. It can hardly be the legal status of "defendant" that gives the young man who refuses to register for the draft his political power to affect the actions of others.

There is a way in which the attempt at the conceptual level to incorporate the political system into the legal one may lead to undue servility toward a given status quo. We may recall what Franz Neumann said in criticizing "the liberal attitude":

> Its sole concern is the erection of fences around political power which is, allegedly, distrusted. Its aim is the dissolution of power into legal relationships, the elimination of the element of personal rule, and the substitution of the rule of law in which all relationships are to become purposive-rational, that is, predictable and calculable. In reality, of course, this is in large measure an ideology tending (often unintentionally) to prevent the search for the locus of political power and to render more secure its actual holders. Power cannot be dissolved [into] law.[8]

Legal Justification

A position for which I am arguing in this book is that deontological justification is especially characteristic of and appropriate to legal systems, whereas teleological justification is especially characteristic of and ap-

propriate to political systems. Legal systems ought to concern themselves primarily with the domain of rights and obligations; political
systems ought to concern themselves primarily with serving human interests.[9] The first half of these claims will be defended in this chapter,
the second half in chapter 9. Although within either system departures
are in fact often made, I think these are the primary forms of justification and concern within each. And I expect that as awareness increases
of the forms of moral argument available to each, the distinction will
increasingly be observed.

Among issues that legal theorists have debated extensively in recent
years are the following: Does a legal system consist of rules, or of rules
and principles?[10] To what extent do judges exercise or not exercise discretion?[11] Must judicial decisions be principled or not?[12] Are the
moral principles to which judges appeal extralegal or already within the
law?[13] The question of whether legal justification is deontological does
not depend on answers to these questions. If I am correct in my contention that it is, this will in some ways strengthen the view of law attacked by Ronald Dworkin in his claim that no clear distinction can be
made between legal and moral standards. But it will support his view of
law as a system of rights and duties in which decisions should be based
on what he calls principles and not on what he calls policies.[14]

One way to examine whether legal justification is deontological
may be to consider cases where the good and bad consequences of a decision are thought to be exactly equal or completely unknowable. Consider a case of preventive incarceration in comfortable surroundings in a
context of high crime rates. It is calculated, let us say, that to incarcer-
ate a given person who is shown by tests to be prone to crime but who
has not as yet committed any crime will probably have the beneficial result of a reduction in crime. This benefit is calculated to equal exactly
the burden of dissatisfaction for the person himself and for others who
are troubled that they themselves, or persons for whom they have affection, may undergo similar incarceration. If a judicial decision in such a
case or on the validity of a law providing such treatment were to be
made on teleological grounds, it would be an even choice—as apt to go
one way as the other. Although this may well be what we could expect
from a purely political decision—of a politician trying out the popularity of an idea, for instance—we can hardly suppose that this would be
the way the decision would be appropriately made in a legal system.
There would instead, almost surely, be some assertion of the deontological position, whether embedded in the relevant constitution or not,
that persons ought not to be punished for crimes they have not

committed. The judges involved might be expected to offer a deontological argument, including presumptions concerning the priority of the relevant considerations, and would claim their decision to be justifiable on these grounds. If they did not do so, they would appear to be deciding in a political rather than a judicial manner. To decide in a judicial manner here would just be to decide on grounds that respected rights apart from calculations of consequences or regardless of the inconclusiveness of such calculations.

The Range of Legal and Political Justifications

If we consider the range of judicial decisions, is it not especially the sort of factors that a teleological ethical theory would leave inadequately dealt with that we rely on legal systems not to overlook? It would seem that, despite the good consequences that might be expected from sacrificing the basic rights of some to increase the welfare of others, a legal system would restrain such choices, as it would curb *ex post facto* legislation or the uses of fraud, even though they might increase the general happiness.

It is often thought that in easy and routine cases a judge employs a more or less deductive approach. As Rolf Sartorius describes it, "The occupant of the office of a judge, depending of course upon his specific office and its place within a judicial hierarchy, will be under an obligation to apply certain legal rules merely because of their formal origin, irrespective of their content and regardless of the consequence of applying them."[15]

The issue of justifying a decision becomes more apparent the more difficult the case is. In difficult cases, the judge must choose between competing plausible grounds for decision. It is sometimes thought that in such cases the judge seeks the decision which will achieve the greatest coherence between the elements of the legal system and that, although judges in such cases do in some sense make new law, the grounds to which judges find it acceptable to appeal may not be those to which legislators find it acceptable to appeal in enacting new law.

On the interpretation being defended in this book, even if it is thought that in difficult cases the judge is free to reach beyond the existing legal system to moral principles not yet incorporated into it, these principles ought primarily to be principles based on deontological arguments. Thus, if the existing rules of a legal system do not provide grounds for a decision, and if appeal to those principles that have already been the basis for prior judicial decisions is still inadequate, a judge may appeal to such deontological moral principles as that no person should profit from his own wrongdoing or that the courts ought not to allow their decisions to be inequitable or unjust. But appeal to a utilitarian prescriptipon for the maximization of happiness would usually not be appropriate.

Richard Wasserstrom has given a different account of legal reasoning. He would have the judge decide, among the rules of law he might choose to apply to a given situation, that one which best promotes the function of the legal system as a whole, which Wasserstrom takes to be a utilitarian function.[16] But, as Ronald Dworkin has pointed out, this assumes a question Wasserstrom needs to be concerned with: "Why *must* evaluation of techniques of judicial decision proceed in terms of some ultimate *goal* to be reached by a legal system[?] There *are* other sorts of criteria, and the question of why these are inappropriate is the real question we should face."[17] The theories of precedent and equity, which Wasserstrom would like to see replaced by the one he recommends, are alike, Dworkin has argued, "in that the appeal of each depends upon the claim that some standard which is not a forward-looking standard (such as the principle of fair play that rules be announced before they are applied, or that it is unfair to surprise one who has relied upon established rules . . .) lies among the most fundamental standards to which judges ought to be subject."[18]

In his more recent work, Dworkin has—mistakenly, I think—moved away from the implications of this insight.[19] Many theorists have hoped to find in a rule-utilitarian approach the non-forward-looking standards so often recognized as needed in law. However, because of the inability of rule-utilitarian standards to withstand any contrary judgments on act-utilitarian grounds, this hope is in my view vain. (See chapters 2 and 3.) Law and the assurance of rights require deontological foundations.

Alternative Views

Let's consider further how it is that many writers on law and interpreters of law can suppose that law should be judged and structured on utilitarian, not deontological, grounds. It is suggested by such writers that people have interests, that people seek, and appropriately so, to maximize the satisfaction of their interests, and that law is a mechanism by which individuals and groups can settle disputes that arise between them and regularize the ways in which people pursue their interests. In this view, rights are no more than especially strong or compelling interests that people choose to have recognized by the law and enforced by the courts. Judicial decisions routinely refer to the "interests" of the parties, to "compelling state interests," and to questions of whether various interests are "fundamental." According to this view, such terms are quite appropriate.

Such language appears to conflict with my claim that the primary concern of the law ought to be the assurance of rights and *not* interests, and that judicial decisions ought to be based on deontological rather than teleological arguments. But the language of legal discussion can often be reinterpreted into the language of rights with a gain, not a loss, of clarity and meaningfulness and an improvement in the extent to which law can be thought justifiable. That vast numbers of legal decisions have been written by persons influenced by the utilitarian traditions of Anglo-American legal thought is no reason to suppose that judicial decisions *must* employ that particular form of moral reasoning. If there are good reasons for thinking that utilitarian forms of moral reasoning are defective for the kinds of issues that characteristically arise in the contexts of judicial decisions, these forms of argument should not continue to prevail merely because they have done so in the past. Language should be modified accordingly.

A good example to consider may be the area of tort law, where utilitarian influences have been very strong and especially so in recent years. A court may decide on holding an agent liable or not depending on whether doing so can be thought likely to decrease the risk of similar accidents in the future.[20] The basis for the legal decision may thus seem to be the utilitarian one of increasing safety.

But there is another way of understanding what is at issue. Persons can be thought to have rights not to be harmed unnecessarily, or rights not to be put in the position of having to risk unnecessary harms involuntarily. These rights flow from deontological principles about respecting persons, and avoiding the causing of harms to persons, just because they are persons worthy of respect and not for any further reason that such harm will produce a decrease of happiness or utility. (See chapter 2.) The courts, in seeking to interpret these deontologically based rights, will try to find ways to assign obligations to avoid harm to those who may cause it inadvertently as well as negligently. The growth of strict liability and especially of activity liability can be assessed within a framework of obligation to avoid harm, on the grounds that persons have rights to personal safety, rather than in the utilitarian framework of maximizing the social utility of a judicial decision one way or the other.

But to the extent that merely financial interests are at stake in a legal dispute and that the courts are called on to resolve a dispute in an area of economic activity clearly above that needed for the respect of the rights of all citizens to a decent life, the courts may here be acting in a quasi-legislative fashion rather than in the ways characteristic of judicial structures. (See chapter 10.) That they act uncharacteristically in some cases does not undermine my claim concerning what ought to be the *primary* concern of the legal system.

Legal Rights, Moral Rights, and Enforcement

The primary function of the legal system is the assurance of those rights which ought to be the object of legal concern. Rights are stringent entitlements yielded by valid rules or principles. At a high level of generality, we can decide that certain moral rights ought to be turned into legal rights that are upheld by law and defended by lawyers.[21] Not all moral rights should be thus transformed, since transforming them thus would so overregulate and overlegalize a society that the solution would be worse than the problem it was supposed to solve. For instance, we can recognize that we have moral rights to be treated with respect by our friends and acquaintances, but that we often should not bring in the *law* if these rights are not respected. And we have moral rights not to be the object of malicious ridicule, but unless this reaches a level of actual slander, we should regard it as no business of the law to police our every insult or instance of wounded pride.

Many moral rights ought to be guaranteed by laws specifying what these rights are, and they ought to be upheld by the institutions that assure compliance with law. To have only moral and not legal rights would surely be inadequate for many of our most basic rights.

The question of enforcement, however, is a separate question. Legal systems as so far understood include coercive mechanisms as normal features; some theorists even hold that enforcement is a necessary feature of law.[22] But whether particular laws or even whole systems of law are coercive is in my view a different issue from their validity as law. Morality may demand that an institution make its requirements explicit, and then the law ought, morally, to be obeyed. Those who fail to obey it ought to be judged as at fault. But it is *compliance* with law that ought to be sought, not punishment or enforcement. If the *same* degree of compliance could be achieved with the use of force and without it, not using force to compel compliance would clearly be morally better. That legal systems now have no better way to ensure compliance than by using force, and punishment that restrains liberty in the cases of persons convicted of violating law, may indicate a failure of imagination and a lack of effort on our part to bring about respect for law by other means.

One way or another, it is a feature of law that it demands compliance and that its rules are binding. In the absence of better ways of achieving compliance, it uses compulsion. If one consents to be a member of a given legal system, one is *required* by the law to obey its laws. An analogy with the rules of games is helpful in some ways: if we agree to play baseball, we have to accept the rules, otherwise it is not baseball we are playing. The analogy is also misleading, since we can choose not to play games in a way that we cannot choose not to be subject to law. But at the level at which we are deciding whether to accept or reject membership in a given legal system, the decision is up to us.

Some theorists hold that it is part of the meaning of a "right" that force may justifiably be used to uphold it; others that the capacity to enforce the right must already be in place before we can meaningfully say that the right exists.[23] But these views seem, again, mistaken. We can meaningfully speak of moral rights that ought never to be made the object of legal enforcement. And we can most certainly speak of moral or human rights that are not yet given recognition or are not yet enforced in a given legal system, but ought to be.

Law and Morality

What is the relation between a legal system and morality? According to positivist theories of law, there is no necessary connection between law and morality. In John Austin's well-known formulation, "The existence of law is one thing; its merit or demerit is another."[24] Nonpositivist theories of law are usually some version of natural-law theory of law, according to which there is a necessary connection between law and morality.

One of the motives for holding a positivist position on law is that we want to be able to criticize on moral grounds a given law or legal system that in any realistic sense "exists" because it is functioning and effective. But if we hold, as natural-law theorists do, that law can only truly be law if it is not contrary to morality, then we will have to say of what looks like an existing but immoral law or legal system either that it does not after all "exist" as law or that if it really *is* law, it must be morally acceptable. This seems unpersuasive.

But a positivistic view of law has drawbacks of its own. If what appears to be a legal system does not in *any* way reflect the requirements of morality, and not just of the procedural kind, we may want to acknowledge the existence of a tyranny or center of power with the capacity to issue commands and compel compliance, but we may conclude that it is *not* really a system of *laws*. For something to count as law it would seem that it must have *some* connection with what can be morally justified, or it will be indistinguishable from a mere exercise of power. And if we hold this, we must defend a nonpositivist theory of law.

We can discern, I think, between positivist and natural-law theories, room for a new category of theories of law. These would maintain a necessary connection between law and a part of morality, but not the whole of morality. What David Richards calls "stingy natural law" comes close to this. He defines "stingy natural law" as the view that "the legal system may incorporate only some subset of the relevant moral principles, and thus lack a full repertoire of moral choices."[25] But in addition to there being no reason to consider what he calls "methodological natural law" (the view that in fact the moral beliefs of a society influence its legal system, a view to which any positivist can easily agree) a natural-law theory, there may be little reason to consider what he calls "stingy natural law" a natural-law theory. We can have separability between morality as a whole and legal validity even if we hold that we cannot have separability between legal validity and legal morality. This requires a somewhat different view of the relation between moral principles that are to be appealed to by the legal system and those that are not to be so appealed to, than Richards suggests for "stingy natural law." The distinction, I think, should not be made in the way he suggests, in terms of kinds of particular situations, such that some will bring in moral principles, and that subset will be included, and some will not—for instance, to use Richards's example, in cases in which the sovereign is a party. The distinction should be made, rather, in terms of the kinds of moral principles that should appropriately be brought in for any legal decision where morality is in any way at issue. Some sorts of moral principles, namely deontological ones, should be brought in, and some sorts of moral principles, namely teleological (or consequentialist) ones, should not.

In some situations, morality is indifferent, as when a decision might uphold a regulation permitting a right turn at a red light. But if there are situations in which morality will not be brought in at all, even when morality is not indifferent, because law in these cases disregards what morality would require, then "stingy natural law" should not be considered a type of natural-law theory, since the law could on this view exclude morality whenever it pleased.

Richards thinks that Ronald Dworkin's theory should be characterized as what he calls "sporadic natural law" because morality is only brought in sporadically, in hard cases, not all the time.[26] I do not accept this characterization. Dworkin seems to be arguing not that easy cases have nothing to do with morality, but rather that in easy cases the morality is already contained within the applicable legal rules, whereas in hard cases judicial decisions must reach beyond the legal rules already in place to certain moral principles. Richards suggests that for "sporadic natural law," morality "only figures in hard cases, the easy ones being free from any internal systemic morality".[27] The point, I think, is not that a legal rule against aggravated assault is "free from" morality, but that applying the moral principles the legal rule reflects in easy cases requires no further appeal beyond the legal rule.

The theory for which I am arguing seems to me more plausible. Such a theory should not be called a kind of natural-law theory, but if someone insists on classifying it this way, it could be called a "partial natural-law theory." It is a kind of role-morality theory of law.

If one imagines a system of rules *all* of which are incompatible with valid moral principles, it is doubtful that any of us would be willing to call it a legal system, though a straightforward legal positivist might be able to offer few arguments for not doing so, as long as the system was effective. A view of law such as the one for which I have argued would allow us to claim that there is a necessary connection between law and part of morality. Thus we could say of a given law or legal system that it exists as valid law if it reflects deontological moral requirements, even if, when judged on comprehensive moral grounds including an evaluation of its consequences, it would be judged morally defective.

The argument I have outlined requires us to assume that a moral theory including both deontological and teleological considerations satisfactorily joined is possible. Whether we call general teleological recommendations "principles," as utilitarians would, or adopt Dworkin's term "policies" for them, requires a choice. In view of the usual association between "policy" and institutional context, we might use the term "policies" to designate those teleological recommendations which political and other organized systems adopt, and continue to use the term "principles" to formulate general deontological or teleological moral considerations. This would allow us to agree with

Dworkin that judicial decisions should be based on principle, not policy, but we could add that they should be based on deontological principles or legal rules, not on either policy or teleological moral principles. And we would allow deontological principles to yield decisions concerning both individual and collective rights, teleological principles to yield recommendations concerning both collective and individual interests.

I am convinced that only a moral theory that does satisfactorily join deontological and teleological considerations, and individual and collective concerns, can be a moral theory worthy of being assumed and capable of standing up to the tests to which we ought to subject our moral theories. Such moral theories, I believe, can be developed and progressively improved.

Among the ways in which we can argue for the possibility of such theories is to show how we are sometimes already doing what they would allow and require. We are sometimes already, I think, in our legal system and elsewhere, working with such moral theories, though we may not yet be more than dimly aware of it. It is possible to use the English language very well, even to be a poet or a scientist in it, without being able to formulate the rules of grammar, much less being able to understand or choose between complex theories of language. That we are not yet adequately aware of the moral theories for which the workings of, and especially the strivings within, our legal and political systems provide evidence, is no definitive argument against them. The legal system already contains within it a complex and worked-out theory about the moral rights for which human beings should demand respect and about the obligations that human beings have toward one another. That in any given system it is a theory in need of improvement goes without saying.

We must decide for ourselves whether to accept the legal system of any state of which we are a member. We may decide that although we disagree with many specific provisions of its laws and many decisions within it, we accept the fundamental moral principles underlying the legal system. We can then try to improve the extent to which this and other actual legal systems reflect these principles and to increase the actual respect for human rights that actual systems offer.

Chapter Eight

Rights to Equal Liberty

THE PRIMARY moral and human rights that the legal system ought to assure are the rights of persons to life, liberty, justice, and equality. Often these are not separate rights but intersecting ones. I shall consider at some length the right to equal liberty, which results from combining rights to liberty and rights to equality.

Almost every theory of law recognizes in some form that among the fundamental rights that a legal system should be called on to assure are rights to liberty and equality. Either these will be declared in a general formulation in a constitution, or they can be taken to underlie at a very deep level the very ideas of law and legal system. To have a system of laws rather than of arbitrary commands is in part to treat persons with the respect due to them as persons. A commitment to law implies that we ought to treat persons justly, or fairly, as they deserve to be treated. Among the ways in which persons deserve to be treated is in accordance with the requirements of equality and freedom, though how these requirements are to be interpreted is often in dispute.

The Principle and the Reality

Freedom is accorded high regard by almost every society. It is often thought to have the highest priority among moral considerations. No one wishes to take a stand against liberty, though different persons may interpret it very differently and may consider very different limitations on it to be justifiable. But principles endorsing liberty or freedom are high on almost everyone's list of principles to which he or she subscribes and according to which he or she believes societies ought to be organized.

Equality is also high on standard lists of proclaimed principles. Persons are to be treated with equal respect and concern, it may be said, whatever further arguments are still open. Combining such principles (though not all principles can be combined this way) should allow us to proclaim that persons are entitled to equal liberty. And we usually do find people willing to subscribe to this judgment at the level of principle.

The reality, clearly, is very far from what such a principle would require. One of the reasons, I shall argue, is that the conception of liberty often accepted in the thought and institutional foundations of many societies is faulty. And this unsatisfactory conception of liberty has significantly contributed to a denial of equal liberty to many in ways that are often unrecognized.

In what follows I shall use the terms "liberty" and "freedom" interchangeably, as do most writers. Although there may be reasons for moving toward distinguishing "liberty" and "freedom," usage has not yet sorted them out sufficiently to make doing so other than a stipulation which I shall refrain from here.

Were one to develop such a distinction, it would suggest, I think, that liberty is a part of freedom, that part to which we have rights which ought to be guaranteed by law. Liberty is something the law could assure us, though it often fails now to do so. Liberty is something we have or don't have, depending on law and its effectiveness. Freedom, in contrast, is something we can go on having more and more of. Law can assure part of it, but freedom as the creative development of the self and the society goes far beyond what law can provide. But as I say, in this discussion I shall use the terms interchangeably without trying to make a distinction.

The idea that a right to liberty is a right to be left alone, not interfered with, not forcibly coerced, has a long and familiar history. In the seventeenth century, Hobbes provided, as he so often did, a classic formulation: "Liberty, or Freedome," he wrote, "signifieth (properly) the absence of Opposition; (by Opposition I mean externall Impediments of motion). . . ."[1] Thus, for Hobbes, we are free to walk down the road if no one interferes with us, if no one subjects us to external impediments, and if no law forbids it. Locke has been interpreted as having a similar conception of liberty, though there is room for argument about this. In any case, the conception of freedom as the absence of interference has become a rather standard part of the Western liberal tradition, at least in its theoretical formulations, if less so in some of its more recent practices.

The assumption underlying this conception was that a man left alone could fend for himself. He could till the soil or ply a trade and make a living. If he had no soil or trade, he could go off into unoccupied territory somewhere and begin. (Locke suggested that he could always go to America.) If others would only not interfere and force him to do things he did not want to do, he would be able to live his life, earn a living, acquire some property, and be his own man. Of course, law would restrict some liberties—people would not be free from legal restraint to murder and steal, for instance—but only for the sake of the superior liberty that would ensue as people were left alone, free from attack, to live their lives in civil peace and safety.

How limited this assumption was can be seen immediately if one includes, within the picture, women. A woman was never imagined to be able in a comparable sense to fend for herself and was not permitted the chance. A woman could not choose to be a "free man" in the sense provided by this conception of freedom. All others who were incapable of becoming economically self-sufficient, such as servants, were also excluded.

The conception of freedom as the right to be left alone was unsatisfactory when it was formulated and is even more unsatisfactory today. Yet it continues to be the standard conception accepted by many contemporary philosophers and most economists. The conception is severely deficient for all those not favored by current economic, social, political, and legal arrangements. The assumption that a person not interfered with can adequately acquire what he or she needs to live is obviously false in a modern society where we find ourselves with an earth and an industrialized economy that are already fully appropriated and that others often have no willingness to make available in any way to us. The traditional conception of freedom serves to camouflage the degree to which some persons are favored by the status quo and others denied the chance to be free. It allows those who already have privileges and property to hang on to them without interference, while preventing those who lack such privileges and property from acquiring them. It allows those who call themselves libertarians to claim to be concerned with enlarging freedom when in fact they are all too often concerned with enlarging the economic privileges of those whom their favored economic arrangements would permit to be overprivileged. And it often allows those who call themselves liberals to be irresponsibly unaware of the extent to which their policies fail to work toward greater freedom for those disadvantaged by current arrangements: women, members of minorities, the poor, the sick, the unemployed, the young and old.

Despite its patently misleading nature, the myth of the self-sufficient farmer or tradesman continues to underlie the work of many contemporary thinkers one would think would be more often criticized for spreading it than they are. The libertarian economist Milton Friedman, for instance, writes that "since the household always has the alternative of producing directly for itself, it need not enter into any exchange unless it benefits from it. Hence, no exchange will take place unless both parties do benefit from it."[2] What, we may wonder, does Friedman imagine a household in Harlem to be able to produce directly or for itself? What can an urban mother with small children to care for, when she has no property and can find no employment, do to produce? Most persons in contemporary society are, on the contrary, forced into the economic exchanges in which they take part, or are forced to stay out of them, by economic need and the lack of alternatives. Only about 7 percent of nonagricultural workers in the United States lucky enough to have jobs are self-employed.[3] There are almost no other ways to make a living than to sell one's labor. The myth that anyone selling his or her labor does so "voluntarily" merely masks the reality for those who prefer not to see it. And unless there are means by which we can "produce for ourselves," mere noninterference can hardly provide freedom. If we lack the means to stay alive and act at all, we cannot act freely.

Negative and Positive Freedom

The conception of freedom standard in the Western liberal tradition deriving from Hobbes and Locke is often described as "negative freedom." The distinction between negative and positive freedom was made familiar to many by Isaiah Berlin in his essay "Two Concepts of Liberty," published in 1958.[4] Negative liberty or freedom is freedom *from*: freedom from interference, from being pushed around, restricted, locked up.

We are free in the negative sense if we are free *from* being arrested for speaking our minds, being attacked as we walk in the street, being forcibly prevented from meeting with others. Positive freedom, in contrast, is being free *to do* various things. As Isaiah Berlin interprets it, basing his view of positive freedom on the Hegelian and Idealist tradition rather than the tradition of Hobbes and Locke, we are free in the positive sense when we are guided by our better, rational selves rather than by our passions, free *to do* what we ought to do. We are, for instance, free to serve the common interest when we overcome our selfishness and take part in a community project.

Berlin discusses the dangers of the positive conception of freedom: it leads to the view that we give people freedom by making them do what they ought to do. If, for instance, we prohibit the drinking of alcohol, people will be free to choose soberly and act rationally, hence the prohibition of alcohol might not be seen as an interference with freedom. Berlin would insist that we be able to say that prohibiting people from performing some action, such as drinking alcohol, *is* a restriction on freedom. Then we can consider whether such an inteference with freedom is or is not justifiable, or worth it, in terms of other considerations, such as health. But we must first be able to recognize it for what it is: a loss of freedom.

Recognizing the dangers to which a positive conception of freedom has often led, from Rousseau onward, Berlin argues for the negative conception as the more satisfactory and more basic.[5] But, it can be argued, his formulations of negative and positive freedom are misleading. He seems to set up a disparity between the contexts for negative and positive freedom such that negative freedom has to do primarily with *physical* impediments to and interferences with action, and positive freedom with essentially *mental* aspects of willing and rationality and morality.

If, instead of accepting Berlin's two contexts, we try to give as fair an account as we can of these matters, we seem to be able to make good sense of negative and positive freedom in both the physical, material sense and in the mental, rational sense. And it seems an unfair formulation to see negative freedom as physical and material, and positive freedom as mental and rational, despite the fact that the traditions in which the two conceptions have developed have had these different emphases.

For instance, we can be free *from* physical assault as we sit in the park and free *to* eat a lunch while we are there. The former requires that police protection against assault be provided by the society; the latter that the society has provided a park and made it possible for us to acquire food. Or we can be free *from* our urge to watch inane entertainment on TV and free *to* follow the intellectual interest of our better selves. The former requires that our will resist an impulse, the latter that it freely choose a goal to pursue.

Freedom in the rational, willing sense involves the question of free and rational choice at the mental, psychological level, and it seems to
X be a different sort of freedom than the kind having to do with action and the material, physical hindrances to it or incapacities for it. Social arrangements may facilitate or hamper both kinds of freedom, but these two kinds of freedom seem distinct quite apart from the negative/positive distinction. If we agree with this, we would have to recognize four kinds of freedom: negative-physical, positive-physical, negative-mental, and positive-mental.

A much more satisfactory conception than this multiplication of categories may be that offered by Gerald MacCallum in his article called "Negative and Positive Freedom," published in 1967. Freedom, he argues, is always a triadic relation: *We are free from X to do Y*. He writes, "whenever the freedom of some agents is in question, it is always freedom from some constraint or restriction on, interference with, or barrier to doing, not doing, becoming, or not becoming, something. Such freedom is thus always *of* something (an agent or agents), *from* something, *to* do, not do, become or not become, something; it is a triadic relation."[6] *All* cases of freedom, he thinks, can be fitted into this format. Disputes will be over what can be substituted for the Xs and Ys.

To take our previous examples: we can be free *from* assault *to* eat lunch in the park; we can be free *from* the impulse to watch TV *to* concentrate on more worthwhile pursuits. And so on. Some would insist, and I would be among them, that to be free in the mental, willing sense, we must be free *to* follow the dictates of reason *or*—contrary to the Hegelian tradition—*to* disregard them. But that is an issue we need not pursue here.

Not everything can count as a limitation or enlargement of freedom. We should not, for instance, substitute for X conditions over which human beings can have no control, or for Y actions beyond the range of possible human action. It would not be helpful, for instance, to say we are not *free* from the tendency to fall if we walk off a high ledge, or that we are not *free* to live to be one thousand years old. Of course, we cannot escape the laws of nature. But they are not limitations on *freedom* in the sense in which we are concerned with it when we speak of rights to freedom. We should restrict the application of terms such as "freedom" and "coercion" to what results from the actions—or inactions—of other people, not natural events, and to humanly possible actions—or inactions. Thus, if a person lacks shelter because of an earthquake, this does not necessarily deprive him of freedom. However, if others prevent him from entering intact buildings, or fail to come to his aid by sharing their surplus shelter with him, these actions or inactions may well do so.

An alternative view to Gerald MacCallum's is to maintain the concept of liberty as the absence of external impediments, but to include within the notion of impediments the lack of access to what we need to be free. This is the approach of C. B. Macpherson. He writes, "Liberty is the absence of humanly imposed impediments . . . these impediments include not only coercion of one individual by another, and direct interference with individual activities by the state or society (beyond what is needed to secure each from invasion by others), but also lack of equal access to the means of life and the means of labor."[7] This view recommends including within the notion of negative liberty the lack of a capacity to do various things when this lack results from the actions of other human beings, as when people retain property and laws protect it in such a way that others are denied access to what they need.

I think the arguments in favor of MacCallum's approach are stronger, since it often seems strained to think of absences as the kinds of impediments we want to be free *from*. It is not strange, however, to think of such absences as limiting freedom or liberty, and MacCallum's format allows us to say this. Thus we could say that we are not free *from* a certain legal impediment maintaining another's property *to* occupy an empty building and obtain shelter. We could also say we are not free *from* the weakness of hunger *to* walk to the village, if others who could supply food fail to do so, even though it might be difficult to count such weakness as an "impediment" or "interference."

In his Tanner Lectures, Rawls amends his view of the principles to which, in an original position, we would all agree. (See chapter 10 for further discussion.) Instead of requiring "the most extensive total system" of equal basic liberties, he now formulates his first principle as requiring "a fully adequate scheme" of such liberties.[8] He continues to see liberty in the traditional negative sense. His list includes freedom of speech, political liberties, liberty of conscience, and freedom of association, but excludes the material resources necessary to exercise any of these. However, his theory now requires that the *worth*, or usefulness, of the liberties provided by the first principle be equal for all. What he calls the "fair-value" of political liberties must thus be assured. This should lead to restrictions on the way greater wealth might otherwise be able to influence the political process or dominate cultural expression. It thus removes a problem, which did affect his earlier formulation, in according the first principle priority over the second. And the second, the difference principle, will assure the material resources with which to exercise the liberties required by the first principle, since it only permits inequalities that will benefit the least advantaged.

This way of understanding liberty would prevent, as would Macpherson's also, the gross misuse of principles of liberty to support unjustifiable social and economic inequalities. But it still seems to me more plausible to recognize that liberty itself requires capacities and not merely an absence of interference. And it seems to me essential that rights to adequate sustenance be understood as rights belonging to individuals as individuals and not only to persons as members of the least advantaged group, which is the most that the difference principle would recognize.

Stanley Benn and W. L. Weinstein, in their article "Being Free to Act, and Being a Free Man," accept MacCallum's basic format. They agree with the linking of freedom from and freedom to do, and try to go on to characterize the sorts of things we can be free from and free to do. They argue that the conditions of unfreedom "restrict choice by making alternatives unavailable or ineligible."[9] For instance, the person threatened with death if he does not raise his hands over his head is rendered unfree by having the choice of not raising his hands made ineligible. Similarly, the worker who has to sell his labor for an exploitative wage or face starvation is also rendered unfree because the choice not to sell it is not really open to him. Benn and Weinstein hold, as I have elsewhere argued, that such denials of liberty can occur through offers that persons in need cannot resist as well as through threats to make their lives worse than they are already.[10] Thus a person in very great need may be unfree to turn down an offer as well as unfree to resist a threat. Benn and Weinstein agree that to interpret freedom as negative freedom only is mistaken.

More recently, the respected economist Amartya Sen has developed for economic contexts the notion of freedom as capacity rather than as mere absence of interference. In this view we are more free when we have more attractive and feasible alternatives to choose between and when we have the capacities actually to choose them.[11] The case seems to me clear: rights to freedom are rights to the enablements to be free and not only rights to freedom from interference.

Rights to Freedom

Sometimes it is suggested that the means of acquiring what one needs to live and be free should be considered an aspect of what it would be in the general interest, on utilitarian grounds, to provide, not an aspect of liberty. This is not, in my view, an adequate solution to the problem. To be concerned with equal freedom, we must include among the aspects of freedom the acquisition of the means to be free as well as the maintenance of such means for those who already have them. Otherwise, concern for rights to freedom will relegate the provision of even basic necessities to something that can be achieved only at the *expense* of freedom and of rights. It will unfairly profit those who benefit already from the status quo.

Certainly our own interests and the public interest are values to which we all have some commitment, but these are different from freedom. Sometimes our interests in various goods must be weighed against our rights to freedom when the two conflict, and sacrifices of one or the other may be necessary. But normally, rights take priority over interests, even general interests, and the tradition that limits freedom to the right to be left alone cannot adequately take into account the *rights* to freedom (and not only the interests in various goods) of those who do not already have the means to be free. To be free, the man of property may need only to be free from interference, but the person without property or the means to acquire it needs more in order to be *free* than to be left alone with nothing. [12]

It may be helpful to think of freedom in terms of independence, a much wider notion than the freedom from interference of standard negative freedom, and yet a notion traditionally associated with freedom in a way that the components of interests in goods are not. It is then clear that for human beings to be independent in a developed, industrial society, and for independence to extend to groups previously excluded from it such as the poor, minorities, and women, human beings must be assured of much more than an absence of interference. They must be assured of access to the means to live: decent jobs, minimum incomes, medical care, housing they can afford, and child care. Such provisions should not be imposed on people, but made available for them to choose.

A worker, for instance, cannot be free and independent if he or she is at the mercy of an employer who can give or withhold the job without which the worker would be destitute. Persons who can find no employment no matter how hard they seek, and are accorded no more than public or private "charity," cannot be free and independent. And a woman cannot be free and independent if she is at the mercy of a man who can give or withhold the sustenance she needs to live. What will contribute to their being free and independent is assurance of an adequate minimum of what they need, in the form of a guaranteed income or a right to a decent job. And these are just as essential for freedom and independence as the police protection traditionally associated with assuring freedom from attack, the negative freedom of noninterference.

Whether persons *feel* themselves to be independent or not is a somewhat different question. The capacities for self-deception are great and often widespread: employees of corporations imagine themselves independent because they can leave one job and find another equally damaging to their freedom; technicians and intellectuals imagine themselves at liberty, not acknowledging that the institutions which pay their salaries only do so to serve their own interests and can cease doing so at will; women imagine themselves free because their husbands are generous or famous. But self-deception is at least challenged in times of high unemployment, institutional cutting back, and marital tension.

Of course, we cannot all be independent of others. We need one another economically, politically, emotionally. And we should not try to do without the benefits that can often be gained by mutual dependence freely accepted by equals. But there now exist enormous differences in the degree of independence some of us are privileged to enjoy and others of us are systematically denied. It is ludicrous to suppose that those privileged and those deprived in terms of such independence both enjoy equal liberty because both enjoy rights to free speech, to vote without interference, and to be left alone. To assure that persons in contemporary society truly have equal liberty, we cannot interpret liberty only in the traditional negative sense but must enlarge it to include the freedom to live, to work, and to develop.

Freedom and U.S. Law

Despite the distorted picture it presents, the negative conception of freedom continues to exercise enormous influence. It underlies, for instance, a whole area of U.S. legal decisions in which the equal protection clause of the Constitution is applied to certain legal freedoms but not to any kind of economic independence. The Constitution requires in the Fourteenth Amendment "equal protection of the laws." This has led to Supreme Court decisions that find various interferences unconstitutional—for instance, a poll tax restricting voting, the statutory exclusion of blacks from juries, the exclusion of aliens from the bar, and the compulsory sterilization of habitual criminals—but the Supreme Court has not interpreted the constitutional provision as requiring equal protection of any kind for what we need to live or develop.[13]

The Supreme Court does not interpret the provision of equal protection as protection of our rights to be equally free to acquire even the essentials of what we need to live. And it allows the law to support in all sorts of ways gross disparities in wealth and income, in public services and benefits, and in financing for education. The Supreme Court has for many years had a double standard, applying the constitutional provisions of due process and equal protection to certain personal rights but not to basic economic rights, continuing to see economic rights as essentially rights to noninterference. As one writer states, "by virtue of the application of the double standard, the Court has for the past generation abdicated any constructive role in resolving this major issue of our time, the relationship between economic independence and individual freedom."[14]

And Congress has not yet recognized the *rights* of citizens to jobs or to a minimum income or even to various necessities that would allow them the beginnings of independence. When governmental assistance is provided, it is thought to be the result of governmental generosity or largesse, not a recognition of fundamental rights. This failure should be recognized for what it is: a denial of the rights to equal liberty of large numbers of citizens.

Libertarians and Anarchists

Contemporary libertarians claim to be the champions of maximal freedom and minimal government. Though they claim affinity with the American pioneer tradition and invoke those aspects of Locke that suit their purposes, they occasionally gain support from the suspiciousness of government characteristic of anarchist writing.

Reformers are often drawn to socialism because of its concern for human welfare rather than private profit. But they are also wary of extending the socialist approach, past and present, beyond what is definitely necessary in transforming certain basic structures of industry and society. For the socialist approaches often require bureaucracy, and bureaucracies may turn out to be run by men of small sensitivity along with the managements of giant corporations and the structures of government in capitalist societies. Reformers may predictably be drawn to anarchist proposals. They may subscribe, with libertarians, to ideals of minimal government and of maximal freedom. These ideals are expressions of the goal of *liberation*.

However, sincere reformers can never, in my view, be libertarians in the contemporary sense, for no reformer could consistently subscribe to the libertarian conception of freedom.

An example of the unsatisfactoriness of the libertarian conception of freedom can be found in Robert Nozick's widely noted recent book, *Anarchy, State and Utopia*. Nozick considers how something equivalent to state power might justifiably arise in a hypothetical state of nature without infringing on anyone's rights and without coercing anyone. Nozick claims to be trying to assure above all our rights to freedom. He does not claim to be arguing for equal freedom, since equality is for him only something governments can impose on people, not something to which we have moral rights. He does claim to be defining rights that should not be infringed, that are not to be sacrificed for other objectives, and that include our rights to freedom. The only kind of freedom he considers, however, is the standard negative freedom of freedom from interference.

For Nozick, economic transactions are never coercive. If a poor person sells her lifetime labor for a pittance, even if she sells herself into slavery to stay alive, she has in Nozick's view made a free choice to do so. As long as the rich man buying up the poor person's life or labor does not threaten to make the poor person's life worse than it already is if she does not sell, such buying up of the lives of others is not, in Nozick's view, an infringement on anyone's freedom. For Nozick, if we leave people alone we respect their rights, even if they are starving and we refuse to share with them any of our surplus.

Unlike Locke, whom he likes to claim as his philosophical ancestor, Nozick does not recognize the rights of anyone to have others, no matter how wealthy and powerful they are, share with her anything of what she needs to live and to develop. Locke had written that "God . . . has given no one of his children such a property, in his pecular portion of the things of this world, but that he has given his needy brother *a right* to the surplusage of his goods; so charity gives *every man a title* to so much out of another's plenty, as will keep him from extreme want."[15] Locke recognized full well the coercive possibilities of economic power. He warned, "A man can no more justly make use of another's necessity, to force him to become his vassal, by withholding that relief God requires him to afford to the wants of his brother, than he that has more strength can seize upon a weaker, master him to his obedience, and with a dagger at his throat offer him death or slavery."[16]

For Nozick, in contrast, freedom for the rich and powerful requires that they be free from interference in hanging on to their holdings. An interference such as taxation to provide for those in need is in Nozick's view an unjustified attack on their freedom: "taxation of earnings from labor is on a par with forced labor."[17] The poor and powerless will likewise be free from attack and from having their holdings taken away. But if they have no holdings, if they lack what they need to live, they are left with the freedom to nothing. The deficiencies of a purely negative conception of freedom have seldom been more striking than in Nozick's depiction of what he takes to be a free society, where some persons will be free to sell themselves into slavery in exchange for food and others will be free to buy them.

A further consequence of the negative conception of freedom is the direction it suggests for appropriate governmental action. Again Nozick's discussion illustrates the problem. Given his view of freedom, not only is that government best which governs least, but the *only* functions of government that are justified are those of the traditional night-watchman state, protecting citizens against murder, assault, theft, and fraud.[18] These are the functions of government that protect a traditional conception of negative liberty. They suit the interests of those with ample property and power, protecting the fortunate from losing what they have. They do little for those who lack what they need to live and grow, who have not been able to acquire even basic necessities. To be protected against attack when one is already overwhelmed by the difficulty of caring for children for whom one cannot provide food, shelter, and medical care, is hardly to be a free person.

This emphasis on the night-watchman functions of government leads, according to Nozick, to a minimal government. But it may instead and as easily lead to a police state in which vast resources are devoted to preventing those in desperate need from acting to improve their situation. If no other chance to avoid extreme deprivation is open to a person except taking what he needs, he will doubtless be inclined toward such action. Nozick's theory justifies the use of the power of government to prevent him from, and punish him for, theft, but it does not justify the use of the power of government to provide him with what he needs to live, by, for instance, providing him with a job. So the supposedly minimal state favored by Nozick could well develop into a vast police apparatus protecting the privileged few from the hungry and desperate. Any such apparatus would, even more surely than any bureaucracy, be dominated by ruthless men. It would of course be a threat to freedom, as anyone but an ideologically blinded libertarian would see. And it would negate the anarchist intention even more cruelly than more ordinary governments.

Further, it would certainly encourage the development of a comparable situation on a world scale, with the rich nations spending ever-greater proportions of their resources to arm themselves against the poor, guarding their hoarded wealth while deprivation rages ever more frightfully elsewhere. A state that would concern itself with the needs of the hungry and desperate might be far more minimal than would the night-watchman state in terms of numbers employed, expenses, and obtrusiveness. And it might go far further in assuring our rights to freedom in a full and satisfactory sense. [19]

As recently as 1971 the U.S. Supreme Court characterized welfare payments as "charity."[20] Thus a woman who expends her labor taking care of small children, but who is not paid by anyone for this labor, nor even given an allowance by a husband on whom she is dependent, is thought to be receiving charity in merely being accorded the freedom to eat and be sheltered. Similarly, much popular sentiment regards the provision or subsidization of services by government as an unnecessary gift to those who, it is thought, should instead provide for their own needs. According to this view, all persons should meet their own needs by themselves and without governmental "assistance." This would include their needs for decent and paid work, for medical care, for housing, for transportation. But many persons *cannot* do this. To be *capable* of doing so is to be already a privileged holder of a job or of substantial property. And to regard the night-watchman functions of government as legitimate, but the provision of the means to live as not legitimate, is merely a reflection of a traditional but unsatisfactory negative conception of liberty and our rights to it.

What conservatives have long recognized is that a defense of freedom against illegitimate governmental interference depends on economic independence. What conservatives and neoconservatives[21] fail to recognize is that this kind of independence could and should be extended to all persons. The aristocrat who defends his honor and stands up to a political bully is often not rich. He bears slight resemblance indeed to Nozick's entrepreneur and may well be subsisting on a very modest income. But he knows that he can count on a floor of assured economic and social sustenance being there if he challenges the power of government. A right for all to a satisfactory floor is what neoconservatives and libertarians fail to provide, and in this they miss the most important point of the conservative tradition. And though libertarians fail to see this, a floor that will stand firm against the attacks on our self-esteem endemic to bureaucrats and officials *and* to the wielders of economic power is what is needed to protect liberty in the welfare state, not the destruction of governmental sources of sustenance for those who would otherwise have none.

Comparative Perspectives

Even when we consider negative freedom only, we should weigh the relative amount of freedom permitted by corporate economic power as compared to that permitted by governmental power. We should become accustomed to recognizing as present interferences with our freedom many conditions and actions we have been induced not to interpret this way. Laws concerning property *interfere* with our liberty to take what we need from the goods society and its members have produced. And the *interferences* with our lives caused by those with economic power are limitations on our negative freedom. The power of the allegedly "private" corporation stands in our way and intrudes on our privacy and coerces us as does the power of government.

Economic power assaults our senses with commercial messages, economic power coerces us to work on its terms or lack the means to feed our children, economic power pollutes the environment in which we live, and economic power decides that we will be a nation of automobile-driven people. Let us never be deluded by the libertarian myth that only the power of government can interfere with our liberty. The wielders of economic power can do so as effectively. Among the most obvious threats to our liberties are modern supercorporations, because they, of all the various concentrations of power around us, are the least subject to democratic checks and the least accountable to citizens. Citizens' representatives can impeach a president of the United States but cannot touch a president of General Motors. Citizens can vote a governor and his policies out of office but can do almost nothing to change the policies of Mobil Oil. In the political arena, one person has one vote, but in the realm of business, one person with economic power has many votes and one person without economic power has none.

So even when we consider only negative liberty, we must always ask whether our liberty will be interfered with *less* when an issue is decided by government rather than by industry, or interfered with more. Consider the case of the pollution standards cars must meet. If we recognize polluted air as the interference with our healthy breathing that it is, we will in sum be interfered with less if government sets such standards than if industry is free to avoid doing so.

If we recognize the power of corporations to interfere with our lives by their decisions—on when to close down plants, on what to produce, on what to charge for their products—we may conclude that although the laws and regulations of government are also interferences, they often increase the sum total of interference less than would otherwise occur without them. If we understand the issues this way, we will not always imagine that in increasing the power of government to control business we are surrendering the present freedoms of noninterference for some lesser and more distant possible benefit, but will see that we are arguing over *freedom itself* and how to assure it. Those arguing for a sane ecological future do not need to yield the banner of even negative freedom to their opponents.

It is *law* that gives to corporations and people the power to accumulate and use property. And just as a society can choose laws that will protect the negative freedom of persons from physical attack by those who threaten their physical safety, so it can choose laws that will protect the negative freedom of persons from economic coercion. And we can choose laws that will limit the power of property to responsible uses. There is no absolute right to use property as we wish, no matter the harm or interference with others it causes. And there is no absolute right to have whatever a person now holds continue to be considered *his property*. Property is what we, as a society and as responsible moral persons, decide it is. (See Chapter 10.)

The Future of Freedom

The arrangements that now exist in the United States do not remotely embody the ideals of negative freedom, of the night-watchman state. Government now provides enormous subsidies for corporations and individuals through tax benefits and expenditures for defense, highway construction, housing mortgages, and the like, along with large amounts of expenditures for social programs. But the reforms sought by many who claim to be the champions of freedom aim to bring about an entirely unsatisfactory libertarian model of government that will protect the negative freedom of the fortunate only.

We should in a transition period, at least, put these vast powers of government to work to assure the positive freedom of the unfortunate at moderate levels of adequacy. However, it is possible that in the long run the growth of individual responsibility will be a more promising source of progress than the multiplication of bureaucratic and governmental mechanisms. If individual enterprises would take responsibility for providing safe working conditions, there would be less need for governmental regulation. If local businesses would put the good of human beings ahead of the scramble for profits and ahead of mere growth for the sake of growth, the structures of social control at more centralized levels would often be unnecessary. If larger agglomerations of economic power such as giant corporations would transform themselves into truly democratic institutions, serving the genuine human needs and interests of those their activities affect, instead of serving the selfish interests of stockholders and managers, there might often be few demands for increased political and legal control of their activities. The distant goals of both libertarians and anarchists might at such a point coalesce. And those most concerned with equal liberty might take the lead in developing the theory and practice of such forms of economic activity. Individual firms cannot often make such transformations alone, for reasons explored in chapter 5 in connection with the free-rider problem. But voluntary cooperation between firms would be better than governmentally imposed restraints on profit-making, harmful working conditions, and irresponsible production.

Were we to take freedom really seriously, we would reorganize the structures of work so that production would be aimed at enlarging human freedom rather than maximizing profits and so that democratic self-determination would be extended into the organization of economic life. We would see to it that the activity of work would become as much as possible the source for everyone of free and creative expression, for we express our lives in our work as we express our thoughts in our speech, and for both we need freedom. Work should be shared far more than at present, so that enough jobs will be available for all who want to work. And work could routinely rather than only occasionally be organized in nonprofit enterprises that would seek to produce useful products and provide needed services in humanly satisfying ways.

More immediately we should insist on a much more modest advance—one that could be quickly brought about with a minimum of institutional transformation of American society—the assurance by right of the basic means without which we cannot have liberty. If freedom is given any sort of priority, or if a commitment to liberty is taken to be a primary source of our rights, then liberty must be understood to include what we need to live and to be free, and rights to liberty must include rights to basic necessities. Our liberty must not depend on whether we are already economically self-sufficient. And our liberty and its means should be assured to us as individuals, not only as members of a disadvantaged group. There is no more a moral right to be free to hang on to what one already has than there is a moral right to be free to help oneself to what one needs. All rights have to be developed with a view to the rights of others, and a proper concern for our rights to equal liberty requires an appreciation of and respect for both the negative and the positive aspects of freedom.

Equal liberty should be assured to everyone as a matter of right. This means that the legal system should guarantee a set of rights that includes such traditional freedoms as the right to free speech, to participate in the processes of government, and to be secure against threats of attack and incursion. The legal system should also guarantee as individual rights sufficient property and economic resources for each person to be a free and independent and self-respecting citizen.

Equal liberty does not require each person to have the same income or an equal share of the entire product of a society. (See chapter 10.) It does require that persons have adequate resources to resist coercion by those with economic power and by those in government. And it does require that *rights* to these resources be effectively assured by the power of law.[22]

Chapter 9

The Goals of Politics

IF WE ACCEPT membership in a given state, we find ourselves voluntarily enmeshed in a variety of institutions and practices. Among the most salient are those we can designate as political, as legal, and as economic. Politics and law are not the same, though a state contains both, and they are often confused. Economic activity is not independent of law and politics, though the conception of a "private" sector independent of government in capitalist states obscures the facts of political economy. But however much these domains overlap and affect one another, it is still useful to recognize that in fundamental ways they are distinct. Activities within them are interconnected in specifiable ways, and we can meaningfully speak of the resulting systems as the political system, the legal system, and the economic system, each of which is different from the others in important ways. It is helpful to then consider the normative grounds on which activities within them ought to be judged and evaluated. In occupying roles within these spheres, we ought, I have argued, to be guided by moral concerns that are different for the different domains.

What Is a Political System?

The political system is the arena in which political forces and interests contend. It includes much more than the formal mechanisms by which laws are enacted and policies adopted. It includes social "movements," dissidents who disobey the law, and influential "personalities" such as entertainers whose stands on political issues influence the public. It includes, of course, voters, potential voters, and agitators. In a system that is at least moderately stable, it includes the wide range of interest groups through which demands on the political system are made, and political parties. It includes the presidency, or some comparable office, and the executive branch of government. Finally, it includes the legislature, which we ought to see, I think, along with the administrative segment of government as occupying a position in the overlapping area between the political system and the legal system. (See chapter 7.) The legislature reflects and anticipates political pressures, but it makes law. In contrast, the courts ought not to reflect and anticipate political pressures any more than is necessary to maintain judicial independence. While we expect legislators to "sell" their proposals and decisions to the voters, we do not expect judges to seek popular support. We expect them to uphold rights, regardless of or even in the face of public disapproval and the opposing interests of individuals or the majority.

A political system[1] is that which authoritatively determines values, decides policies, and promotes goods in a society. The authority with which this may be done may be *formal*, such as that possessed by officials with governmental titles, or *effective*, such as that possessed by a commercial interest group that turns out to have the political power to get a policy accepted. Formal authority approximates previously established effective authority and makes it possible to predict future decisions on the basis of who occupies what offices. Effective authority approximates future power, which can only be guessed at until after the fact. A politician who has succeeded in gaining national attention on a given issue has more effective authority than another who has not, though their formal authority may be equivalent.

Political systems, like legal systems, validate claims as justifiable or nonjustifiable. The grounds upon which a judgment can be valid may be different in the two systems, but both provide a method of deciding between conflicting claims. The method of deciding between conflicting claims will be far more formalized in the case of a legal system, and will usually depend upon prior rules, even though legal decisions sometimes create precedents as well as follow them, and change rules as well as apply them. In a stable political system there will be practices (aside from or in addition to legal rules) for deciding between conflicting political claims, but they may be tacit rather than explicit and will prescribe far fewer of the issues that arise for decision than do legal rules. They will, however, produce authority for the making of political decisions. Sometimes this authority will be ascertainable before a decision has been made; sometimes it will not be recognizable until sometime after a decision has become operative and has been accepted.

Decisions within the political system will generally be formulated in terms of future consequences rather than merely by reference to prior rules, and practices will be justified by their consequences. A familiar political practice, for example, is that a mayor of a large city should effect a certain ethnic balance among his appointees corresponding to the ethnic groups composing the city's population. But if a particular mayor can gain political credit and accomplish results that are approved by ignoring this practice when it becomes confining, her decision may be found justifiable within the political system. And if a decision for which there is no practice but concerning which there are strongly felt conflicting claims turns out to have results that are generally considered to be good ones for the political system, the decision will be considered justifiable within this system.

David Easton, a leading theorist of political systems, suggests the following description: the political system "is the most inclusive system of behavior in a society for the authoritative allocation of values."[2] But "authoritative" is to Easton a purely descriptive term referring to psychological attitudes. A policy is authoritative, he contends, "when the people to whom it is intended to apply or who are affected by it consider that they must or ought to obey it."[3] Or, in the words of Almond and Powell, "force is 'legitimate' where this belief in the justifiable nature of its use exists."[4]

We can note that nothing in this conception of a political system precludes its decisions from being thoroughly extralegal as long as those affected accept them as authoritative. If a leader's decision, no matter how arbitrary or unrelated to specifiable rules, is accepted by his followers, it has political force that is called legitimate. But since a system of such behavior might function without including what is characterizable as a legal system, it would be a distortion to think of legality as necessarily present in the political system just because legal decisions are also "authoritative" or because both systems require "efficacy" or "acceptance."[5]

My concern in this book is with what is not only believed to be justifiable, but is justifiable. On either interpretation of what is justifiable, however, something can be politically justifiable without being legally justifiable, and politics can be engaged in without the presence of law.

Political relations can be based entirely on power, whether they are the outcome of balance and bargaining or of domination and submission. Even when such relations are widely accepted, to cloak them in the attributes of legality where no legal system is in place and no legal rules are upheld is to falsify the reality. And to turn law into politics is clearly unwise. In criticizing "political justice," which he defines as "the utilization of judicial proceedings for political ends," Otto Kirchheimer discusses the "basic cleavages" that ought to exist between political action and the apparatus of justice: "Whatever attempts are made at settling power relationships, the very nature of power defies limitation, calculability, and permanent obedience," whereas justice is intended to create and enforce an attitude of obedience toward legal rules that provide limitation and permanence. "These are basic cleavages to be kept in mind," he says.[6] And, we may add, maintained.

Political Justification

Political justification is not the same as moral justification. Political justification may fall seriously short of moral justification. But it does not fall short in the same way that legal justification may fall short of moral justification. The forms of moral argument appropriate in the two domains are different. It is my contention that political justification is and ought to be teleological. Those occupying roles in a political system ought to strive to do what will be justifiable. To be even politically justifiable, actions must be such that they can be recommended on some moral grounds. But those striving to do what will be politically justifiable should appeal to part rather than to the whole of morality. They should strive to do what can be recommended on teleological or consequentialist moral grounds.

Consider a situation in which picketing by a large number of persons is interfering with the passage of others in getting to their jobs, and a decision must be made on what to do. Let us suppose that the relevant deontological considerations in this case are deemed to be of equal stringency, with neither taking priority: persons should not be coercively prevented from getting to their jobs, and persons should be permitted to express their views through picketing. If a prediction in such a case could reasonably be made that to side with the persons picketing would have significantly better consequences in the long run than would siding with the persons whose passage is hampered, a political decision—a politician's declaration at a news conference of support for one side or the other, say—would almost surely be made in favor of those picketing. We could expect a judicial decision in such a case to apply some relevant statute if one existed, despite the consequences. If, at the moral level, the deontological considerations were approximately equivalent, it would not be of great importance whether the statute favored one deontological consideration or the other. But the political decision in the matter would appropriately be made on the basis of expected good consequences, and where deontological considerations were equal, it would certainly not as appropriately favor the decision with the worst consequences as the decision with the best consequences, as it would if political justification were a deontological form of argument.

The range of political decisions covers those which are predominantly concerned with results. Characteristically, political decisions are wagers on the expected good consequences their defenders hope to bring about, and deontological factors are often quite appropriately put aside. The concepts of welfare and public interest, essential for evaluations of political decisions, are probably best understood in teleological terms. The issues they raise cannot adequately be dealt with by reference to legal rights and obligations. As David Braybrooke has well expressed it, "the welfare of one and the same set of people is a consideration distinct from their rights. . . . Welfare and rights are logically such different subjects that the one may be invoked while the other (without inconsistency) is disregarded."[7] And, Braybrooke continues, the concept of welfare cannot be dispensed with, for advocates of a given form of political system must be able to argue "that the governments they would judge good will promote welfare."[8] The same points may be made about the public interest.

Among those considerations which might be recognized as good reasons for legislative but not for judicial decisions, Rolf Sartorius cites "political expedience, practical enforceability, and the desires of one's constituents."[9] For all those political decisions and actions not having even the semipermanence or generality of legislation, it would seem that such reasons may be even more easily appealed to. The decision to appoint one person rather than another to an executive or an administrative post should require good reasons, as much as any act, but the justification of the decision should normally, it would seem, be in terms of the appointment's good consequences, or the good consequences of appointments of this kind. Almost any competent politician learns early not to make genuine promises he will be under a moral obligation to keep no matter what the political and other consequences. And he is forgiven many reversals of prior positions and *ex post facto* condemnation of his opponents, if the results of such actions are in general good. Again, the decision of a president or governor or mayor to propose a program or not, or to exert pressure or not in behalf of a given policy, can well be justifiable on grounds of the political practicality, interest satisfaction, or contribution to welfare or general good of the consequences. There may in such cases be few deontological considerations relevant to the decision.

The legislature may seek to further both collective interests and individual interests and may in my view do so justifiably. In both cases an objective is sought, and teleological arguments concerning the consequences of the decisions to be made are appropriate. Political decisions ought to look to the future, estimating with utilitarian and other teleological calculations the probable effects of one policy or another. The pursuit of interest is not only characteristic of politics but fitting, though it ought to be conducted in justifiable ways.

A moral goal that ought to be sought by the political system is the public interest. This is not the same as justice. The public interest is an aggregating value; justice is not. Calculations for the aggregation or maximization of interest satisfaction are inherently incapable of taking adequate account of considerations of justice and of rights. This does not mean such calculations should be abandoned and all moral talk turned into rights talk. They should instead be limited, in a public context, to the sphere of politics, recognized as appropriate within that sphere, but not asked to do the whole job of morality.

Under normal circumstances, we should assign to the legal system the assurance of the rights and obligations of justice, equality, and freedom, and to the political system the pursuit of interests, the public interest, and the general good. We should not ask each segment of government to do the whole work of morality, but should expect them to complement one another and balance one another, as one segment employs deontological justifications assuring rights in a framework of justice and another segment employs teleological justifications to promote the interests of the public and its members.

The Public Interest and the General Good

The ultimate aim of the political system ought to be to pursue the general good, the way the most fundamental ground of the legal system ought to be to realize justice and equality and freedom by respecting moral rights. But the general good is a purely moral concept. A political system as a whole can have an interest in doing what is good for itself and its members, and this is the public interest. The public interest can be thought to be the interests of the political system as a whole that are claimed to be justifiable.[10]

To pursue what is good for itself and its members, a political system must consider the interests of other political systems. But the public interest of system A is not necessarily the same as the public interest of system B. The interest of a global community may conflict with the interests of states. The public interest is a more limited notion than the good of the world community.

The public interest is not identical with the common good, for the latter is best thought to include the interests that are the *same* for all members of a given collectivity, and the public interest must often be forged out of conflicting rather than coinciding interests. As members of the global human "community"—if we can call it that—we all share an interest in avoiding nuclear holocaust. *This* is an objective that is for the common good of all human beings and of a given collectivity of people. It is also in the public interest and for the general good. But many other objectives would not be the same for everyone in this way.

When goods are not fully sharable or the same for all, we need to determine which outcomes would be better and which worse. For a given "public" such as that of a nation, the best outcome would be what is in the public interest. But the good of one nation may conflict with that of another nation. It might, for instance, be in the public interest of Alania to build a canal linking two of its cities; this might divert water in such a way as to be contrary to the public interest of Bilenia. The general good is what would be best for all, not just for a given public that might be a small part of humanity.

We can perhaps accept the fact that the world is divided into national entities. At least for the foreseeable future, it may be morally permissible for us to belong to given national systems, though we should do our best to diminish the dangers to global peace that national divisions pose. If we accept the judgment that in the world we live in, we are more likely to achieve what is good for human beings by accepting the organization of ourselves into national entities than it would be, at the present stage of development, to refuse to do so, we can hold that nation-states ought to exist and to continue for the time being to exist. To do so they must pursue the interests of their members. A political system pursues the public interest when it counters damaging internal forces threatening to cause the system to crumble from within and strives to build a society out of limited resources of land, raw materials, labor, and so on. If it pursues its own interests against the interests of other states, it pursues the national interest. If all states pursue their own national interests at the expense of the interests of other states, the problems we examined in connection with mistrust (chapter 5) repeat themselves: states must learn to cooperate. The institutions that should be recommended for dealing with this requirement may be different from the governmental structures recommended for dealing with conflicting individual interests; we will consider some of these issues in chapter 14.

A state that meets the requirements of cooperation with other states can then pursue the public interest in a way that ought to contribute to the general good. If Alania's progress does not harm or threaten or unjustifiably withhold resources from Bilenia's, then the general good is increased by an increase in Alania's good, even if this is not shared by Bilenia. For one person or society to be better off if no others are worse off is a good outcome. Pareto optimality, thus defined, is recognized as an appropriate basis for preferring some economic outcomes to others. Pareto optimality is not an appropriate basis for deciding questions concerning rights, since rights should be respected even if this entails costs or losses or a decrease of good (though there are limits to how much good should be sacrificed for rights to be respected). But for calculating various aspects of the general good, Pareto optimality, once all relevant rights have been respected, provides a suitable conceptual foundation. Within the bounds of justice, politics should promote the public interest.

The legal system should ensure that as a matter of right each citizen is enabled to obtain the basic minimum of what he or she needs to live. Each citizen has a right to some of the goods that the society produces; the amount should accord with the requirements of justice. The amount may be enough for a decent life and adequate self-development, rather than any given proportion of the entire product of the society. (See chapter 10.)

However, beyond deciding what share of the goods of society citizens are entitled to by right are questions of making those goods greater or lesser. Political decisions should aim to increase steadily the benefits that political organization can achieve for a society. The political system should see that the economy allows for the production of as much more than is needed to satisfy basic needs as is compatible with the general good. This does not mean that production should be forever increased. On environmental and other grounds, efforts should go into improving quality rather than quantity after appropriate levels have been reached. The political system should also see that common goals, such as those involved in the relation of a given state with other states, are pursued. The political system should attend to the development of collective goods such as bridges, water supplies, transportation networks, parks, and artistic productions. Its goals should be pursued efficiently and responsibly. Within these considerations, however, *promoting* the interests of the public and its members rather than detracting from them is the primary responsibility of the political organization of a society.

The Maximization of Interests

A political system provides for power to be accorded to certain persons to try to decide how the public interest ought to be sought. Though it may often be appropriate for those persons to consider the preferences of majorities, they ought not to infer from "A majority prefers X" that "X is the morally best goal for the political system to pursue" or even that "X is in the public interest."

To a considerable extent, however, the goods that the political system should pursue can be evaluated in terms of the maximization of individual interests. For instance, congress may enact legislation to safeguard undeveloped land for recreational purposes. Sometimes this should be to preserve a natural phenomenon such as the Grand Canyon, concern for which should be a collective goal of the society as a whole. This collective goal would not be reducible to the interests of particular individuals. Preserving national treasures for future generations should not depend merely on satisfying the interests of a majority of present citizens. But often, facilities should be provided simply to supply swimming and picnicking areas for individual citizens. The public interest in recreational facilities in some of these cases can be reduced to some sum of individual interests.

In the latter kinds of cases, there are serious problems as to what we can mean by maximization. How can we combine judgments about production, say, and judgments about curbing pollution? Suppose producing more energy, which people want, will produce more pollution, which people do not want. Some people will benefit more from more energy and more pollution, other people will benefit more from less energy and less pollution. How can we compare these alternatives?

The question whether interpersonal comparisons of utility are legitimate[11] and, if so, how they should be made, has been debated inconclusively for many decades. On one side are those who consider that we can order our preferences, specifying our first, second, third, etc., choices, on an ordinal scale, but not attach to them cardinal values or numbers representing more than the order of our preferences. Then the problem is to derive some collective ranking from a set of individual rankings. This presents logical problems that are as yet unsolvable.[12] Other problems may be that even for a given individual, an ordinal ranking is a poor reflection of preference, since it does not indicate how much something is preferred to another thing, and such rankings may not be transitive.

On the other side are those who think that it is legitimate for us to represent what we value in cardinal terms. This allows for summing up the preferences of a set of people and allows for the result to reflect the intensity of their preferences.

I shall not try to explore these problems, but rather to deal with the political questions that would remain even if we assume satisfactory answers to them.

Once we have decided on the way interests are to be measured and assigned value, there is the problem of whether the basis for a choice between alternatives should be the maximin principle of avoiding the worst[13] or the Bayesian one of maximizing expected utility, calculated by multiplying the probability that an outcome will occur by the utility of it if it were to occur. In considering the principles that rationally self-interested persons in an original position would choose as a basis for ordering society, Rawls argues for the maximin principle. Since rights do concern the basic minimums to which every citizen is entitled and below which none should ever have to fall, there are good reasons why the maximin principle might be appropriate for the establishment of legal rights, if legal rights were to be founded this way on utilitarian considerations from an original position. I do not think this is the way rights should be construed; I have argued for deriving rights from deontological principles taken as valid from actual, not hypothetical positions.

For the range of political interests, however, utilitarian calculations are often appropriate. But here the maximin principle seems considerably less plausible than the Bayesian. As Harsanyi illustrates in his discussion of Rawls,[14] the maximin principle would in ordinary life lead to clearly questionable recommendations—for example, we would stick with a boring and unsatisfactory job in one city instead of taking an excellent and satisfactory one in another if doing the latter required a plane trip and there was a slight possibility of a plane crash, which would be the worst outcome. If we consider probabilities, taking a chance on a large gain that is highly probable would often be better than taking a chance on avoiding an even larger loss that is highly unlikely. But if we have a policy of avoiding the worst no matter how slight its probability, as long as it's greater than nil, we could not choose to pursue the large gain. In most political situations, as in ordinary life, this would seem irrational. Hence, for pursuing those interests which political arrangements should be designed to serve, it seems that what ought to be maximized are the expected utilities that alternative policies can bring about.

The Good of Society

The basis for individual political choice as for collective political choice should be not only self-interest, but an evaluation of what would be best. There may be sincere disagreement over whether, for instance, less inflation or higher wages (if ways cannot be found to avoid having to choose between them) is the more important political good—both for the citizen choosing and, in that citizen's view, for others. A citizen's decision to choose one or the other can legitimately be an amalgam of self-interest and interest in the well-being of others, as argued for in the chapter on social trust.

The effective way of representing the judgments citizens make about the actions that governments ought to take is in terms of interests. The interests citizens pursue may be largely self-serving, but they may also have interests in governmental policies that they deem to be best for the society.

In aiming to achieve the general good of a society, those in government should be guided by what they take to be the public interest. This includes the interest of the political system or polity as a whole, once a moral judgment has been made that a given political system's existence, incorporating as it must a given set of procedures, can be justified.

Just as a person's interest may be an amalgam of self-interest and what he or she believes to be best, so the public interest may be an amalgam of what those acting in behalf of a polity take to be necessary for the continued existence of that polity and what they take to be best in even wider terms. Any official of government must be concerned with the stability, health, and growth of that political system, at least in some measure. Certainly it may be for the best for a given bureaucratic structure to be abolished, though its members have interests in its survival. And it may sometimes be for the best for a whole political system to be overthrown or defeated and replaced by a different one, if, for instance, it pursues power with an utter disregard for the basic human rights its legal system ought to protect. But normally it is reasonable and morally justifiable for those acting in behalf of a political system to try to assure its continued existence, as it is reasonable and morally justifiable for any individual person to be concerned with his or her own interests and to expect to go on living and developing. But pure self-interest, for individuals and states, is not justifiable.

A moral judgment must be made about how governments ought best to aim at the general good. The assumption has often been made that allowing pluralistic groups to pursue their own interests, and expecting government to mediate, respond to, and provide a mechanism for reconciling conflicting interest-group pressures, is the best way for government to do so.

Criticisms that such a procedure favors those groups which already have the power to press their interests, and neglects those groups which may never acquire such power, are persuasive. Pluralistic politics are of advantage to many, but may be highly disadvantageous to those groups to whom political power has been denied through social and economic arrangements that regularly undercut their positions, often through cultural views that fail even to perceive their problems.[15]

Furthermore, the conception of government as a mechanism for reconciling pluralistic interest-group pressures may turn persons into egoistic demanders of what will be to their own interest far more than will some other conceptions, such as that government ought to pursue the public interest. The pursuit by both citizens and governmental officials of the public interest may be no more illusory than the pursuit of purported group interests and may provide the possibilities for trust and a modest sense of community without which, in the long run, political systems may not be able to ensure their own continued existence.

Another assumption of how government ought best to pursue the general good is that it ought to win support by being congruent with the political culture—the shared norms, values, and attitudes that exist in a society and that have been largely inculcated in childhood and adolescence.[16] Though normally presented as an empirical claim about what causes people to support government, it is sometimes offered as an answer to the normative question of what government ought to do. It suggests that government ought to win support and, given what is taken as the empirical requirement for doing this, ought to mesh with the political culture.

There is evidence, however, that casts doubt on the empirical claim. Perhaps, in fact, a shared political culture is not a necessary condition for support of a political system or its government's actions.[17] And there are strong reasons to reject this view as a normative recommendation. If the norms and values that a given group of persons happen to share are unjustifiable, government ought not to appeal to them.

Another empirical claim that some construe as a normative guide is the view that government receives supports and demands as inputs from its environment, that it responds by providing the outputs of authoritative decisions, which then feed back into the system as new supports and demands, and that doing this is what government ought to do. Demands are seen as motivated by drives over which people may have little rational control, but satisfying them is seen as a good outcome. In the words of David Easton, the primary author of this view, "We can expect that direct satisfaction of demands will at least generate specific support; and the longer such satisfactions are felt, the more likely it is that a higher level of political good will can develop."[18]

However, as Ronald Rogowski sums up the evidence, "diffuse support cannot always be built by the satisfaction of overt demands, neither will it always be destroyed even by severe value-deprivations."[19] Rogowski goes on to defend a rational choice theory of political support, arguing that people make political decisions, and decisions about support for government, on rational grounds.[20]

But even if it is empirically true that people tend to support government on what they take to be grounds of rational self-interest, we can certainly distinguish between choosing rationally and choosing what is in the public interest. And it certainly makes sense to ask whether government ought merely to respond to people's demands, even when they are rational, or whether those in government ought to consider, as well, the public interest and the general good of the society and of the globe.

Rational Choice and Representative Government

Rational choice theory has led to the normative suggestion that government ought to act to serve the rational choices of its citizens. The inadequacies of this view, on standard interpretations of rationality, can be seen from the arguments in chapter 5 on social trust. The egoism, conflicts, and eventual breakdown of mutual respect resulting from the pursuit by all of what rational choice theory would recommend may lead to the erosion of the political system. Even where cooperative patterns have developed, self-interest may recommend freeloading on rather than contributing to ongoing social arrangements.

However, for those decisions where conflict is not a threat to the basic trust on which a political system rests, theories of rational choice may well suggest those decisions which ought to be taken. This may be true in the following ways: an individual citizen may justifiably decide, on a given range of issues, to pursue rationally what he or she prefers. Some political issues are appropriately ones of no more than preference, once rights have been respected and it can be held that the activity or service ought to be provided by government rather than by persons acting individually or in nongovernmental roles such as that of a business manager or union official. For instance, once all the relevant rights had been respected, citizens might want a given service even though they had no right to such a service. They might prefer a governmental agency to provide it from tax revenues rather than wait—perhaps indefinitely—for such a service to be provided by a business that would charge individuals for it and expect a profit from it. Then, it might be an issue for decision whether to increase or decrease tax expenditures for such a service, and a given individual might be justified in favoring whatever policy he would himself prefer.

To pursue one's interests in a rational way will usually involve favoring certain positions, voting for certain candidates, contributing to certain interest groups. If the procedures within which the political process is operating are fair, and if the individuals in such a process pursue their interests from positions of political equality, the outcome may be in the public interest in the sense that it is in accordance with the position that has the greater support. This will be so if it has been determined for this kind of issue that having greater support is a sufficient reason for the outcome in question to be in the public interest.

However, this depiction of the political process suggests that finding out which outcomes would have this characteristic would be a merely technical problem, and that the office holders which people elect to "represent" them have no significant independent role in the process. This overlooks the best arguments in favor of representative government: that those elected often have the resources to arrive at better judgments than such a mechanical process of registering individual preferences (if the logical problems of aggregating them could be solved). For instance, it would be rational for any given individual to prefer lower taxes for himself. He might accordingly favor a decision to lower the taxes needed for the service for persons like himself while raising them for some other kind of person, if he thought the total level should remain the same. The decision could theoretically be made by direct democracy, with each citizen registering his or her preference through a mechanical device attached to a TV set by means of which the citizen might have been presented with a few arguments in favor and a few opposed. But would this be advisable? Almost surely not.

The representative should not think of herself as a mere substitute for a mechanism to register the individual self-interested preferences that citizens have at any particular time. The representative ought to inform herself as well as possible about the likely consequences of the alternative policies and ought to make her own evaluation of what would lead to a maximization of satisfaction for all those to be affected. She may well be able to have a more comprehensive view of what would truly be in the interests of all those affected than would be provided by any device to register the existing preferences of voters. For this kind of decision, the representative should employ a utilitarian calculation to bring about what the voters would choose if they were fully informed and if their rational preferences could be aggregated into a collective choice. There will be many difficulties, familiar to utilitarian theory, in ascertaining how such calculations should be made, but progress both at a theoretical level and in the application of the theory to specific cases is continually being made.

It should be understood, however, that the range of issues for which such a decision would be suitable would be rather narrow. The range should be bounded by the limits of rights already discussed, which should not be subject to such calculations. And there will be many decisions that can be understood and justified only in collective rather than individualistic terms. The collective good, or the good of the collectivity, may not break down into the goods of its individual members. What is in the public interest, or in the interest of the political system as a whole, may often be a collective interest that cannot be split up into the interests of individuals.

For instance, the value to a collectivity of having many shared facilities can often not be understood in terms of the value the facility may have to particular individuals, because the value to the collectivity may be a relation between the individuals, not anything that an individual can "have" apart from the relation. If there is a city park to which anyone and everyone can go to share green grass and cool shade, it simply would not be the same benefit if it was surrounded by a fence and admission was charged at the gate, even if the taxes that provided for its upkeep were reduced by an amount that gave everyone an equivalent sum to spend on admission. The shared and open quality of a public facility and the relation of cooperation and trust that ought to exist among those who enjoy it is lost if it is cut up into individual admission tickets that people may buy. This is true for many public goods. Some are more in the nature of attractive conveniences that representatives of the public do well to provide. Others are among the most fundamental institutions of the society, such as the type of economic system allowed or provided by the political system, or the type of educational system. A political system that promotes capitalist economic arrangements encourages the proliferation of individual consumption at the expense of more collective benefits, and this may often reduce rather than increase the general good. A system of higher education in which only those with rich parents can afford to attend many of the most desirable institutions promotes class divisions based on wealth and inheritance. Such divisions are contrary to the general good of the society, as well as contrary to the individual interests of those in disadvantaged classes.

Political decisions will be required to establish that range of choices where a political process influenced by individuals pursuing their own interests should determine an outcome. And political decisions will be required to decide for a society those issues on which collective political choices should be made by representatives in terms of collective, not individual, considerations. For instance, it is a political decision to allow individual preferences for single-family dwellings to determine that land in a given area will be approved for use for such dwellings. The political decision might instead be that the land should be used for the collective good of a community facility. Outside these two domains may be an area of economic activity that need not be subject to political decision. We will discuss this in chapter 10.

As voters, citizens should choose those representatives who will do best what representatives ought to do. This is different, for voters, from registering their preferences. When registering preferences is appropriate, citizens often may do so on the basis of self-interest. But their representatives will be in a position to decide which issues should be settled on the basis of serving individual interests and which on the basis of the public interest in a collective sense, or on the basis of the general good of human beings beyond the borders of the society or in the future rather than the present. When voters choose which persons they think will be best at making *these* decisions, they ought to do far more than register their preferences. And legislators ought to be guided by far more than the preferences of those who put them in office.

The Accountability of the Legislator

One of the best ways to evaluate the performance of politicians and legislators is through the notion of accountability. Legislators are accountable to those who elect them but also accountable in another sense. Legislators should weigh the claims of morality more heavily than they weigh the immediate desires of their constituents, though they can recognize that to continue to occupy the role of legislator, reelection is necessary. This problem is not entirely different from that facing any morally responsible person in any role. In order to continue to be employed in a given corporate position, or to be a doctor or teacher, one may have to do certain things that appear morally questionable. The judgment "It is morally permissible for me to continue to try to occupy this role" is always at issue and should be periodically reexamined. Sometimes the answer a morally responsible person will have to come to will be that it is not permissible and that he or she must step down or away from the role in order not to violate fundamental moral requirements. But once it does seem to the person to be justifiable to occupy that role, and this is often not especially difficult when the role offers possibilities for moral achievement that the person will give up in stepping out of the role, then the person will have to do certain things he or she might otherwise not do, in order to stay in the role.

Let us look more closely at the accountability of the legislator. Much of the discussion applies to anyone working in politics who aspires to be or to influence a legislator. It can also be applied to voters choosing legislators.

Consider the moral function of the legislature. The legislature has a special responsibility to seek the public interest, which often conflicts with private advantage. Once an estimate of what the public interest would recommend has been made, there may be, in addition, individual interests that conflict with it but are nevertheless justifiable. A legislature might legitimately take these interests into account along with the public interest. Hence, the policy interests of the legislature need not always be the aggregated interests Ronald Dworkin requires them to be.[22] Some individual interests are worthy in themselves. The method of experimental morality can be used to decide questions concerning morally justifiable interests as it can be used to decide questions concerning moral rights. The cultural interests of small minorities, for instance, often ought to be promoted even if they do not please the majority and even if their defenders do not have rights to support that the courts could assure as matters of principle. Legislative decisions to subsidize symphony orchestras or research in anthropology need not be justified in terms of their contribution to an aggregate good, but should be capable of being supported by sound, though not necessarily utilitarian, teleological arguments. But by and large, the legislature ought to seek to promote the public interest, and it can often do so best by maximizing the expected utility of those for whom it legislates.

Many of the individual interests to which legislatures respond are economic interests, which should *not* be valued in themselves, but rather subjected to scrutiny in the light of the responsibility of the legislature to assure the public interest. Some subsidies to some industries can be justified, as Dworkin suggests, on grounds of sound policies to pursue an important interest of a society's majority, such as when the development of a source of energy might have highly beneficial effects of various kinds and it is clear that public support is the best or the only way such development would take place. Most tax advantages and import quotas and favored treatment of most special interests cannot be justified and should be modified to accord with the requirements of the public interest. The appropriate arguments will usually be both teleological and utilitarian: among alternative policies, the greatest advantage for all those affected will be an adequate basis on which to seek a solution to the conflict of most economic interests above the level of the resources that need to be devoted to assuring rights.

A political system may decide to accord persons merely legal rights (as distinct from moral rights reflected in law) to engage in self-interested economic contests, and it may permit the winners of such contests to enjoy substantial rewards from them. The justification for such arrangements should then be utilitarian justifications of maximizing interests, not the deontological justifications that yield moral rights. (See chapter 10.)

It is the responsibility of the legislature to facilitate and permit and manage and control economic activity in such a way that it promotes the public interest. It is the responsibility of the courts to see that moral rights are reflected in the legal system as legal rights and assured of respect. Since persons do not have moral rights to more property than they need for a decent life and adequate self-development, the legisla-

ture is free to put into effect economic arrangements that will promote
the public interest without coming into conflict with considerations of
moral right once rights to enough for a decent life have been assured.
This might result in allowing, on grounds of efficiency and for the sake
of providing incentives and promoting effort, considerable rewards for
economic success. Such rewards would not, on such a view, have to con-
form to the requirements of Rawls's "difference principle" that they
benefit the least advantaged in a society. The least advantaged should
be assured a decent life and the economic support this requires as a matter of individual right. But above such a level they would not have
rights against the successful, if considerations of maximizing interests
could justify a scheme in which economic winners were permitted to
achieve substantial rewards, and if the political process and cultural activity were adequately insulated from distortion by those with greater
income. If it serves the interests of human beings to be permitted to
gamble and compete in such domains as that of sporting events, the domain of economic activity should not necessarily be off bounds to such
approaches, once the basic rights of everyone to a decent life and adequate self-development have been assured.

The legislature cannot concern itself solely with the maximization
of interests and appeal solely to teleological justifications. As we saw, it
occupies a position in the overlap between the political and the legal
systems. It does not belong almost entirely to the political domain, as
does, say, a political party or interest group. As the agency of the society most responsibile for making law (although the courts in
reinterpreting the constitution and existing law also can, and in my
view ought to, "make law"), the legislature must concern itself to some
extent with the domain of rights. But the legislature can see the domain
of rights as a limit upon its decisions, not the primary objective of its
decisions.

The most obvious limits are those rights guaranteed by a Constitution. A legislator can often presume that in refraining from passing legislation that is rather clearly unconstitutional, he or she has taken into
account to as great an extent as necessary the considerations of deontological morality. Further consideration of deontological moral principles beyond the Constitution is up to the courts, which can legitimately
appeal to fundamental moral principles underlying law as well as to the
Constitution.

When basic human rights that ought to be recognized in a nation's
constitution or fundamental laws and honored by the courts are not being recognized and honored, legislation should bring this about if the

courts do not do so. To this extent the legislator should employ deontological arguments. But in doing so the legislator is correcting a past deficiency rather than performing a function that ought to be a
continuing one. If we can foresee a time when fundamental human
rights, including rights to basic necessities and the requirements for a
decent life such as education and employment, are assured by the social-
political system, then concern for rights can be thought to be primarily
the function of the courts, and legislators can appropriately concern
themselves primarily with the satisfaction of interests, both collective
and aggregated interests and individual ones. Issues of rights and interpretations of law will always remain to be determined, but the responsibility for these will lie largely with the courts as they impose limits on
the decisions of the legislature to pursue the public interest. In a system
where basic rights are assured and interpretations of law, including the
Constitution, are handled by the courts, legislators may confine themselves more appropriately to utilitarian and teleological arguments.

Political Accountability

The notion of accountability is especially useful in discussing the
grounds on which legislators ought to reach their decisions. To be
accountable is to be prepared or expected or required to offer, at some
future time, a justification, in detail, of one's actions. It is to take or
have responsibility for decisions of which one will or should give an account. A person or group is accountable to some other person or group
for acting in ways prescribed by specifiable standards or reasons.

As noted before, we do not expect judges to "sell" their decisions to
the public, but we do expect legislators not only to pursue the public
interest but to persuade the voters that their decisions have been sound
ones. Legislators are legislators only part of the time; the rest of the
time they are, quite justifiably, politicians, seeking support for their
candidacies and proposals or seeking reelection and vindication of their
choices. The inadequacy of the view of legislators as passive recipients
of the demands of backers and interest groups is clear. So is the inadequacy of the view that they have an obligation to do "what the voters
want," or wanted at the time they were elected. Voters choose persons
to make decisions that will be in their interests and in the public interest. They properly expect legislators to be accountable to them, but
ought not to expect legislators merely to accede to the wishes of those
who chose them. If doing the latter were all that legislators should do, a
mechanical or electronic device could do it better.

On some models of democracy, to choose a legislator to make our decisions for us is to surrender our autonomy. If we value our autonomy as we should, we ought not to do this. The outcome of such a view will be direct, not representative democracy. It will indicate that we ought to do without legislators, once we have the means to make and register our own choices directly. A direct democracy in which electronic devices would allow us all to vote on all significant measures would turn the legislator into a minor figure in the political process and elevate the voter to the legislator's place. Various advocates of participatory democracy accept some of these arguments and emphasize the value to the participants of being active agents rather than mere recipients of political decisions. As Peter Bachrach puts it, "A system is democratic to the extent that it recognizes and enforces the right of the individual to participate in making decisions that significantly affect him and his community. Such participation is an essential means for the individual to discover his real needs through the intervening discovery of himself as a social human being."[23]

While there is much to be said for such a view at the local level, there is much to be said against national direct democracy. Not only would it be almost impossible to reach decisions that would not be reversed haphazardly with every swing of popular opinion, but the benefits of participation to the participants might be quite minimal if voting on measures were reduced to pulling a lever and participation were reduced to voting. In summing up the case against participation, M. B. E. Smith says that it "seems reasonable to suppose that widespread participation in government would result either in policy setting and administrative bodies that are too large to move effectively against the problems which beset society, or else would result in a large number of small bodies that are efficient at making decisions but lack power to attack significant problems."[24] While this overstates the case against local participation, it does seem clear that full-scale participatory democracy to solve the national problems of large nations would not be advisable. And we need not conclude that in choosing a representative form of government we are surrendering our autonomy. At a moral level we can decide, autonomously, to adopt this decision procedure for the treatment of political issues.[25]

The notion of accountability allows us to deal with many of the legitimate concerns of the advocates of participatory democracy while avoiding the obvious pitfalls of such schemes at the national level. The legislator is accountable to the voters not in the sense of being obliged to register their preferences or pressures, but in the sense of being responsible for doing what the voters would want if they were fully informed and concerned for one another and for other persons to be affected by a given action or policy. The legislator can foresee that by the time of the next election the voters will surely not be all these things, but the legislator can do her best to enable them to be more so. The legislator ought to calculate whether this can best be done by compromising from what the public interest would, in her view, require, to a degree sufficient to give her a good chance of reelection, or whether it can best be done by a firm stand even if that increases the probability of her electoral defeat. In any case, the decision itself should anticipate and predict what the interests of citizens will be, and the legislator should be held accountable on these grounds. Teleological or consequentialist arguments are especially suitable for determining the justifiability of legislative decisions and for evaluating the performance of legislators.

As part of the process of enabling the voters to understand what their interests really are, and of what coordinating their interests with the interests of others really requires, the legislator may decide that it would be better to thwart rather than serve a given immediate interest of his constituents. In doing this he may act in a way contrary to the expressed wishes of the voters. But the long-range interests of the persons to whom the legislator is accountable should be anticipated, and, as part of these interests, citizens' interests in understanding what realizing these will actually require should be taken into account.

The Case of Energy

A helpful example may perhaps be found in the area of energy legislation. All citizens may have rights—where the resources for this exist without disregarding the rights of those in other countries—to the provision, by society, of enough fuel to keep them from freezing, enough energy for needed cooking and lighting, and perhaps an adequate system of transportation to enable them to reach their places of work. However, a large range of the concerns of citizens with energy availability is surely a matter of interests rather than of rights. It is not the function of the courts to demand that the government supply enough energy to meet all the desires of all citizens for energy, or even that enterprises to produce oil produce at full capacity, assuming that would benefit consumers.

Many of the interests of citizens in ample and available energy supplies have to do with comfort and convenience, not with need. But the political system should certainly concern itself with this important interest of almost all citizens. It should adopt policies that will contribute to the long-term interest satisfaction of its members, within the bounds of the rights of its citizens and within the requirements of international responsibility. At a given time, doing so might require citizens to have actual experience of shortages, in order to begin to take seriously the fact that nonrenewable sources of energy are finite and running out, and in order to begin to think seriously about alternatives to the continual expansion of energy use and the enormous waste of energy that has characterized American life for many decades. A legislator accountable to her constituency might responsibly decide not to act immediately to preclude such shortages, if she thinks they provide a necessary lesson in the need for conservation and reduced consumption. If she or her constituents think that the shortages are contrived by the oil companies to increase profits, the lesson may be a lesson in not trusting corporations, but useful nonetheless.

If a legislator concludes that higher returns on their investments are necessary to induce oil companies to increase domestic exploration and production, he may enact legislation to try to achieve this effect, not because the oil companies have rights to such higher returns, nor because citizens have rights to more exploration and production, but because such increased production may serve the general interest until renewable sources of energy are developed, and allowing higher returns may be thought to be an effective way to increase domestic production. But if the legislator notes that the returns on investment of oil corporations from their domestic exploration activity have already been, for the preceding five years, higher than the return on investment for manufacturers generally,[26] he may be justifiably skeptical of any plan to allow higher returns in order to increase production. He may go on to have serious doubts about the normal arrangements for the production of oil in the United States, arrangements that allow the oil corporations to make decisions on the kinds of investments to make with the sole view of increasing their own profits rather than serving the fundamental needs and interests of the society. He may then consider alternative ways to assure the interests of those to whom he is accountable: the establishment of a federal energy corporation, perhaps, along the lines of TVA to provide a yardstick against which to evaluate whether the oil companies are supplying energy in efficient ways or taking advantage of citizens "hooked" on life-styles that require a large consumption of energy. Or the legislator may consider the nationalization of the entire industry, if this seems to be the best way to serve the genuine, long-term

interests of citizens. And he ought surely to consider measures to promote reductions in the wasteful consumption of energy and to foster the
development of benign and renewable sources of fuel, light, and
heat.[27]

In all of these decisions a legislator should anticipate what the citizens to whom she is accountable would consider the best policy, when
and if they knew as much as she about the behavior of the oil companies
and the needs of the country for future energy and the limited supplies
of petroleum remaining in the world, and when and if they shared her
concern for *all* those to whom she is accountable and could see her reasons to change past values with respect to energy production and use.

The Legislator and Moral Specialization

Why should we presume that legislators are thus "ahead" of those to
whom they are accountable? It would be a serious mistake to suppose
that they are ahead of large numbers of those who vote for them or are
affected by their decisions. Conservationists, antinuclear activitists, advocates of solar energy, and others have been on the issues just discussed
way ahead of most legislators. But since legislators must get elected by
constituencies most of whose members are not greatly interested in,
much less well informed or enlightened about, most of the issues on
which legislators must make decisions, legislators have the ability to be
ahead of the majority of those to whom they are accountable on most issues, though they may often fail to use this ability. The congressional
investigation, as well as the congressional staff available to legislators,
is an important element in making this possible. Such activities could
well be expanded to include more inquiry into the moral issues relevant
to legislators' decisions. With respect to energy, legislators need to
know much more than the facts about oil resources and production and
consumption, though these facts are difficult enough for legislators to
obtain and impossible for most of those to whom they are accountable
to obtain, given the extreme secretiveness in which most corporations,
especially oil corporations, operate. In addition, legislators need to explore a wide range of moral considerations having to do with weighing
preferences and evaluating interests, and even with what constitutes a
good life. In formulating the problems in terms of "interests," we
should not lose sight of what interests are. Although we *have* interests
here and now, we may have great difficulty understanding what our interests really are. Interests are what persons would want in the long run

if they were fully informed and wanted what really will be advantageous to them.[28] Interests cannot be justifiable if they fail to take into account the interests of others, since the generalized pursuit of self-interest is self-defeating for most concerned.

Legislators need not, in my view, turn every problem into a straightforwardly moral problem. As legislators, they have a more specific moral function—to pursue the public interest and to maximize the justifiable interests of those to whom they are accountable. To promote the public interest is not the same as assuring justice or respecting rights. Though legislators should of course respect fundamental human rights such as those discussed earlier, and respect those other rights of which they are aware, it is not their responsibility to try to figure out in detail what further rights there are and how to assure them. Nor is promoting the public interest the same as doing on all occasions that which would be recommended by the most advanced and comprehensive morality possible. The task of legislators is difficult enough without being made impossible. It is reasonable to hold legislators accountable for their contribution to the public interest, but unreasonable to expect them to have the most developed moral understanding of any persons in society.

In his study of *Constitutionalism and the Separation of Powers,* M. J. C. Vile discusses the way traditional separation-of-powers doctrines have become outmoded, but also the way contemporary structural-functional analysis confirms the major features of such doctrines. "The history of Western constitutionalism *is* the history of the emerging specialization of government functions," Vile writes.[29] Although we may now see more clearly than in the past that each governmental structure may perform a number of functions, the notion of a separation of powers balanced in some form of equilibrium and with various segments of government having different *primary* functions is still preserved.

Discussion of these issues has in recent years been almost entirely descriptive. This is unfortunate. For in addition to understanding such functions as "interest articulation" and "rule adjudication," and in addition to considering such ideal normative theories of social justice as Rawls's[30] we need an understanding of the *specialized moral functions* that different structures of government and society perform, of the specialized forms of moral argument they are each best at developing, and of the special norms that ought to guide different roles. I have tried to show in this chapter what the specialized moral function of the legislator is. Comparable arguments can be developed for those who seek to influence legislation and policy in the political system.

The Legislator's Dilemma

In addition to being an assortment of individuals, a legislative body is a collectivity. If it fails, as a body, to take actions that ought to be taken, it is responsible for this failure. As with every collectivity that is capable of acting as an organized group, responsibility for such failure cannot simply be distributed evenly over the entire membership of the group. How it is to be distributed will depend on the internal structure of the group, among other factors. We can perfectly well hold that a statement such as "Congress has failed to do X" is true and that judgments such as "Congress ought to have done Y" and "Congress is deserving of blame for not doing Y" are valid. We cannot conclude from these that Congressman A is to be blamed as much as Congressman B. For judgments establishing the latter we would need to know more, but such judgments are also quite capable of being found to be valid.

There has been much talk in recent years of the inability of the U.S. Congress to act as a body because of the pressure of conflicting groups pulling the members of Congress in divergent directions. Instead of being an organized and cohesive body, Congress is sometimes seen as a random assortment of individuals beholden to warring interests. We read articles on the possible impossibility of governing a United States that is being torn apart by factions; Madison's warning is taken to have been in vain.

Can we then hold this random collection of individuals who occupy seats in a legislature responsible for their failure to act? We can, I think, hold them responsible for failing to form themselves into a more cohesive group, a group with more satisfactory decision procedures, a group that *could* do what it may now be unable to do.[31]

In holding this, however, it might be helpful to consider the problems that arise because of what I shall call the "legislator's dilemma." It parallels the prisoner's dilemma or the free-rider problem, which is an *n*-person prisoner's dilemma. The latter indicates the ways in which the pursuit of self-interest may be self-defeating, but also the ways the pursuit of self-interest may be extremely difficult to overcome. The legislator's dilemma is that if she as an individual tries to act more responsibly than the voters who have elected her or the interest groups that have supported her are ready to approve, while other legislators fail to do so, she will be worse off than if she had not tried to.

Consider a case where a given piece of legislation would be best for the country but would be unpopular with the voters. If all or most legislators vote for the legislation, a given legislator may be let off the hook by the voters, who will come to believe that the position accepted by the body collectively was probably better than the position that was defeated. And if it actually is the better position, the voters will have a chance to experience its advantages, as they could not before, and to realize that the legislator's vote was justified. But if the legislator votes alone or almost alone for the legislation that is best but unpopular, the legislation will be defeated, the voters are more likely to think that she was mistaken, even if she was not, they are less likely to come to believe that the defeated position was the right one, and they are more likely to punish the legislator by defeating her in the next election. So the legislator has strong reasons to choose to avoid voting for unpopular legislation that will be defeated even though it should be enacted, because that would be the worst outcome from the point of view of her own self-interest.

The best strategy for the legislator would be for her to be able to avoid taking any position on the legislation and for it to pass without her. That way the country will get the legislation it needs, the legislator's constituents will benefit, but she will not have angered those who opposed it. Since those who affect a legislator's chances of reelection are more likely to work against her if she votes in a way they disapprove than they are to work for her if she votes a way they approve, the safe course of action for the legislator is to avoid voting on the difficult issues. Hence there are strong reasons for the legislator to think of herself and to avoid the risks that enacting unpopular but justified legislation requires, unless she can be sure that others will vote for it also.

If each legislator tries to avoid the worst outcome for himself, the outcome will be worse for all than if they had overcome their concern for reelection and had the courage to vote for the needed legislation. But the tendencies to avoid the worst outcome for oneself are strong. If enough legislators do so, the needed legislation will not be passed.

Something like this problem seems to afflict legislative bodies at various times. To overcome it requires that a legislator be willing to risk his own interest for the sake of the collective interest, which will not benefit the individual legislator as much as if he had freeloaded on the willingness of others to do so, but which will be better for all or most if enough others are also willing. Although enacting needed legislation may anger various special interest groups, it will certainly be better for the larger group of those to whom the legislator is accountable.

For a legislator to act to promote the public interest requires courage. It often requires courage also of all those who seek to influence the political system to increase the general good.

Chapter 10

Property and Economic Activity

ECONOMIC ACTIVITIES ARE shaped by and take place within the political and legal structures we have already discussed. According to Marxist interpretations, economic realities are more basic than their political and legal manifestations. In a capitalist society, on these views, political arrangements serve the interests of capitalists, not of everyone, and legal institutions reflect economic power, not regard for justice, equality, or freedom.

Without denying that there is much truth in Marxist interpretations, we can still observe that political power and legal decision can shape economic relations as well as the reverse, and other social realities are as fundamental as economic ones. Gender relations, for instance, affect social structures pervasively: women are subordinate in communist and in social-democratic societies as they are in capitalist societies; regardless of the kind of economic system in which they do it, women still do the bulk of the household and child-care work.

How a society produces and distributes economic goods, how it rewards some with and deprives others of material resources, needs to be examined and understood. Theorizing can sometimes conceal more than reveal the realities of a society's economic relations, and much of "economics" has done this with capitalist economies.[1] But in addition

166

to understanding how economic life is conducted, a moral perspective seeks to evaluate both the realities of any actual economy and the possible alternatives to it. Given the economic resources now in place and the existing legal arrangements concerning property and the actual current relations between political and economic structures, what ought we to accept and what ought we to change? And what would morally acceptable arrangements concerning economic activity be like?

Let us begin with the concept of property, to see what property is and consider what it ought to be.

Property Rights

The word "property" usually brings to mind an image of a physical object: an acre of land, say, or a wristwatch. The image is misleading, for as soon as one begins to look into the meaning of the word, it is apparent that property is not a set of things but a set of rights and interests.

Most writers on property have recognized it as a set of rights. John Locke defined "property" so widely as to mean by it rights to "life, liberty, and estate." Most usage since has narrowed the meaning of the term to what Locke meant by "estate." Standard interpretations see property as consisting of rights to possess, use, manage, dispose of, and keep others away from things.[2]

But property is also a set of interests, for if the things we own become worthless, we no longer have property. A person who owns a car has an interest in its resale price. A person who owns a house has an interest in having the value of the property increase through an upgrading of the neighborhood, though he may have no right to have its value increase in this way.

Property rights and interests often give us rights and interests in relation to physical objects. But many property rights and interests, especially in developed societies, are more complicated: we have rights to pay our debts with the balances in our accounts, and interests that the paper they represent not be devalued; we have rights to the dividends that our shares in a corporation accord, and interests in the corporation's paying as high a dividend as possible; we have rights to a pension from the plan we have joined, and interests in the plan's not going bankrupt. We have rights to unemployment insurance when we lose our jobs or rights to a license to practice a profession if we meet the qualifications, and we have interests in increasing our wages or sales and in having the kind of economic system within which we can make economic gains. These rights and interests are aspects of property.

In advanced economies, with governments that seek to curb the deficiencies and abuses of the economic systems with which they are joined, property is increasingly composed of what Charles Reich calls government "largesse,"[3] as government provides public "assistance," health benefits, unemployment insurance, and licenses to practice professions. As others see it, this may be a misnomer, since, as Reich acknowledges, *all* property has always been, in a sense, government largesse. It is law that allows a given physical object to be legally acquired or owned by one person and not another. It is the power of government that prevents those without property from helping themselves to what the law designates as "other people's property." Government often interferes with the freedom of those without adequate property to acquire even enough to satisfy their basic needs. The police and other protection that government provides allows those who have what the law designates as property to hold on to it or get more of it. And the social stability and order that government makes possible allows economic activity to flourish when it does, and economic interests to be served or thwarted. But the misconception persists that new forms of property depend on government while traditional forms do not.

Also misleading is the traditional division between the public and the private, between the political and the economic, between "sovereignty" and "property." The myth beneath the division is that political power coerces us but economic power does not. As Morris Cohen made clear in exploring this contrast, property is power compelling service and obedience, as is political sovereignty.[4] We can be restricted by an employer we cannot defy as by a government official we cannot ignore; we can be forced to do what we do not wish to do by the demands of a landlord as by the nightstick of his protector. And it is partly because we can be compelled by economic necessity, as we can be compelled by threats of legal penalties, that we can demand for the citizens of states with morally justifiable social arrangements that, where the economic development of the society is sufficient to do so, all citizens have assured rights to enough economic sustenance to allow them the liberty we deem such a fundamental right.

For property to achieve what it has traditionally been thought able to achieve—to guard our freedom against the tyranny with which concentrations of power may threaten us—property must include for all citizens guarantees of being able to acquire what they need to live, and not only rights to hold on to what they already have. (See chapters 5 and 8.) And such rights of citizens to a measure of economic self-sufficiency should be secured against governments and the wielders of economic power, just as the rights of citizens to a fair trial or to free speech should be assured against both.

A society that fails to provide ways for persons to acquire food, shelter, and so on through honest employment, or through payments to which they are acknowledged to be entitled, may force them into a surrender of their liberty unworthy of citizens in a free and decent society. If contemporary advocates of economic freedom would recognize the facts of economic coercion in industrial society more adequately than they often do, they could more persuasively represent the tradition of Western liberalism than many now can.

We must distinguish between, on the one hand, rights to have or do something and, on the other, rights to merely try to have or do something. An often used example is that of two persons who see a ten-dollar bill on the street between them. Both have the right to try to be the first to pick it up, that is, they have no obligations not to; neither has the right to *have* the bill (before they win the contest to be first), though they have the right not to be prevented from trying. This situation exemplifies many situations of economic competition. Some writers on rights suggest that rights to try to do or have things should be called liberties rather than rights,[5] but if we keep in mind what rights are rights *to*, we can continue to use "rights" for both kinds. Even the most conservative champions of property rights will agree that the poor and the unemployed should have rights to *try* to obtain what they need to live. The issues in dispute will be whether they should have legal rights not merely to try to have but to actually possess food, shelter, clothing, and employment.

Moral Justification

As soon as we understand that property is a set of rights and interests, we can consider questions about whether the rights and interests into which property has been analyzed are morally justified. What a society decides to make into legal rights, and its policy decisions concerning interests, may or may not reflect what morality requires. As A. M. Honoré makes clear in an excellent recent paper, we could come to a view of what morality would recommend that would specify a set of legal property rights very different from those familiar to us.[6] We might hold, for instance, that people have rights to use property but not to dispose of it as they please; or we might build into our scheme of property rights a moral requirement that people share their surplus property with those in need; we might think people hold property "in trust" for everyone in the society.

A separate but fundamental question is whether property can "exist" without government or law. If there are moral rights to property, we might assert that property claims can be valid even if none of the mechanisms of enforcement that a legal system provides are available. If we could establish what moral rights to property we have, we then could ask that our legal rules reflect and uphold these rights. And if we could establish what property interests of ours are morally justifiable, we could ask for political and economic institutions that would promote these interests.

Some writers assert that in the absence of an enforceable system of law to make moral rights into legal rights, no such rights really exist.[7] In other words, rights that are "merely" moral rights—or, as certain of them may be called, "human rights," or as some of them have been known in a large segment of traditional political philosophy, "natural rights"—are not really *rights* at all.

But if we explore the issues surrounding this controversy, we may come to hold that rights can exist independently of whether they are enforced. To be able to assert claims about rights is often what enables us to argue about what legal systems ought to do even when they are not doing it. It does not seem to be a necessary feature of our concept of "a right" that force *is* used to uphold it, nor, as was seen in chapter 7, does it even seem to be a necessary feature of all rights that force *ought* to be used to uphold them.

Rights, as we have seen already, are central or stringent entitlements yielded by justifiable rules or principles. The rights of a given person impose obligations on other persons, as the right of a given person not to be assaulted imposes obligations on other persons not to assault that person. The obligations that rights impose may be both obligations not to interfere and obligations to enable, as when the right of a child to live imposes obligations on others to provide the child with food and shelter. In some circumstances we respect the rights of persons by leaving them alone, in other circumstances by assisting them.

As we saw in chapter 2, it is part of what we mean by a right that it ought to be respected for its own sake and need not be defended by an estimate of its consequences. This is true both of specific legal rights that reflect moral rights and at the level of deciding whether a moral right of a certain kind exists. The major grounds on which claims to rights can be asserted are those of freedom, justice, equality, and dignity. Moral rights are yielded by moral principles or rules, legal rights by legal rules or principles. (See chapters 7 and 8.)

Rights are not absolute, whether they are moral rights or legal rights. Prime facie rights, or what "at first sight" appear to be rights, may have to yield to other rights with greater stringency. When rights conflict, we need additional principles or rules to determine priorities, as when we might hold that, in a conflict between a person's right to have a promise made to him kept and another person's right not to be killed, the latter would generally have priority. Thus, we would decide that we ought not to cause the certain death of a bedridden occupant of a house, even though we have promised our employer to shut off the electricity by noon. We can adopt principles that will always give some rights high priority: our rights to life and liberty, for instance. But even these are not absolute, and their interpretation will require the working out of meanings and priorities, and the specification of aspects and requirements.

Moral rights should be respected for their own sake, because they are yielded by valid principles; they need no further justification. We ought to respect the rights of persons to be free in specifiable ways, not because of some further use to which we think they will put this freedom, such as to produce more industrial products or to bring about pleasurable feelings, but just because as human beings, they are entitled to freedom within such limits as are required to respect the freedom and rights of others. Again, we have a moral right to have another person tell us the truth just because it is the truth, not because of some further benefit this may bring about, such as that telling the truth will make either or both of us happy. Rights, characteristically, should be respected in themselves, on grounds of the moral principles or rules that yield them, which we can also accept because they are valid in themselves; we need not argue that rights are useful for some further interests. An appeal to consequences, to the effects of such rights, is out of place.

We can understand this as an aspect of what we mean by the concept of "rights," and also as an aspect of the moral theories we find acceptable. A utilitarian moral theory, limited as it is to judging moral issues exclusively in terms of consequences, is thus, in my view as in that of many moral theorists, inherently unable, as we have seen, to provide an adequate interpretation of rights, though it may be quite appropriate for moral decisions concerning interests. Utilitarians characteristically interpret rights as protections of certain central or especially important interests. Reasons to reject this interpretation have been considered, and will be further discussed below.

What could the grounds for moral rights to property be? One answer, developed by Locke, is that we are morally entitled to the products of our labor.[8] Locke and others have argued that as we mix our labor with the natural world, we are entitled to the resulting product, as when we bring in fish belonging to no one from the sea, or when we gather fruit belonging to everyone in common from the forest. But Locke added the important proviso that when a resource is not in unlimited supply, we should take only as much as will leave "enough and as good for others." And he argued that to take more of a limited natural resource than one needs and can put to good use is contrary to the requirements of morality.[9]

The assumptions Locke makes concerning the justifiable acquisition of property are almost never met in the contemporary world. The unowned wilderness waiting to be appropriated, so central to Locke's argument, no longer exists. Rarely do we simply mix our labor with nature. Nearly always we mix our labor with an economic system and an already developed industrial economy, and it makes little sense to think of the result as the outcome of *our* labor. A person cannot distinguish his or her labor from the other labor it is mixed with in producing a product or contributing to production. Furthermore, the service sector of the economy does not fit the depiction, nor does the labor involved in raising the next generation of workers.

Even more serious for this attempt to justify moral rights to property is the difficulty that the Lockean proviso, in the contemporary world of overpopulation and scarce resources, can almost never be met. Instead, more property for some will almost always bring about less for others. And if we allow the loss of a position of equality relative to others to count as a "loss," as some persons move ahead and accumulate more property and some thus fall relatively behind, the problem, as Lawrence Becker indicates, is even more troublesome.[10] The argument from "I made it" to "It's mine" thus loses, in a developed economy, almost all the plausibility it may have had for an image of Lockean man husbanding sheep on the commons or American pioneer putting uninhabited territory to the plow. Such images are defective for more reasons than that they ignore advances in agribusiness and overlook the American Indians.

One can still ask, What am I entitled to as a result of my labor? But the answer should now depend on moral justifications for using, managing, disposing of, keeping others away from, and having access to things. It should not depend on the illusion that a self-sufficient man creates a product from an inexhaustible supply in such a way that a pure gain for him need bring no loss to anyone else, or on the illusion that everyone has an equal chance to be such a creator of products to which he or she is entitled.

Lawrence Becker suggests a complex formulation of what can be justifiably asserted as a moral basis for according those who labor rewards for their labor under certain conditions.[11] Further consideration of the question of what economic rights ought to be recognized by the law will be discussed in the last section of this chapter. In the meantime, it should be remembered that, whatever scheme of property rights a society has, it is a scheme the society has adopted and could decide to change. As John Stuart Mill put this point: "Even what a person has produced by his individual toil, unaided by anyone, he cannot keep, unless by permission of society. Not only can society take it from him, but individuals could and would take it from him, if society only remained passive; if it didn't interfere *en masse*, or employ and pay people for the purpose of preventing him from being disturbed in the possession."[12]

Society thus creates the scheme of property rights that are recognized and upheld. And it should do so for reasons that can be justified on moral grounds. When given provisions within an existing scheme of legal rights to property cannot be justified on moral grounds, they should be changed until they can be.

Property Interests

Let us turn now to a further consideration of property interests, since property includes both rights and interests. Rights and interests are not the same. We may have rights to do things that are contrary to our interests, such as a right to make a bet that we shall probably lose, and we may have interests in things to which we have no right, such as that the market value of the land we own will rise precipitously. We may even have rights to what will never be in our interests, such as to give away all our assets or to endanger ourselves in useless ways.

Not all philosophers share this view, but on my view rights and interests are so significantly different that they belong to different domains of morality and should not be judged on the same grounds.[13] The claim of Charles Fried that "there is an interest behind every right"[14] seems mistaken, since we may have rights to do what will be harmful to our interests, in both the short and the longest run.

Interests, in contrast to rights, need not necessarily be respected for their own sake, but are usually to be judged in terms of the further consequences of pursuing them. Interests are needs or desires or claims for some state of affairs to be brought about, which state of affairs may be good in itself or good for something further. We may have an interest in health for the sake of health, but our interests in all those things we desire for the sake of health will be judged in terms of whether they really are conducive to health and whether their benefits exceed their costs. Justifiable interests are what would be good for us in the long run if we were fully enlightened. They are what we would want if we were fully informed and if we want what is good for us.

Rights are entitlements to something we can either do or have, or not do or not have done to us. Interests, in contrast, are matters of more and less. The relevant questions will concern the degree of a person's interest or how much one interest is greater than another.

When interests conflict, as they so often do, for any given individual, and especially between individuals, between individuals and groups, and between groups, we should seek moral solutions. The solution should be in terms of maximizing something judged to be good: utility, happiness, efficiency, satisfaction. This is different from respecting rights; rights are not subject to maximizing in the way that interests are. When we have a right to vote, it is not a right to vote more for a candidate rather than less, but simply a right to vote. In contrast, our interests in his victory will be greater or less. If we have a right to equal education, we do not have a right to an education that is "more equal" but to an education that is equal, though what this implies requires interpretation. We may have interests, on the other hand, in more and more education. We often have interests in having moral rights—to nondiscriminatory treatment, say—recognized as legal rights when this is not yet the case. Or, if we are unfairly privileged, we may have interests in preventing this from happening, though these interests are morally unjustifiable.

The most plausible moral grounds on which to base judgments about interests are those which look for the greatest good to be brought about by any given decision or arrangement. In the case of property interests, questions of who made the product or how hard it was to hire the workers or whether a certain risk was taken might be relevant but should not be decisive. What should be decisive are the consequences, in terms of goodness and badness, of any decision. For instance, we should consider whether furthering the property interests of entrepreneurs in a certain way would have better consequences in terms of efficiency, growth, or pollution than not doing so, whether paying workers one wage or another would lead to greater happiness or to greater discontent for more persons, whether changing from a labor-intensive to a more mechanized form of production would increase general satisfaction through increased productivity or decrease general satisfaction by increasing unemployment, and so on.

Various interests can be protected as legal rights in any given legal system. Legal rights of this kind are then *merely* legal rights, not moral rights reflected in law. They can, where moral rights cannot, appropriately be changed to promote maximizations of interest. *Moral* rights should be upheld even *against* considerations of the general interest—in Ronald Dworkin's phrase, rights "trump" such interests. But rights that are merely legal rather than both legal and moral need not do so. Still, we ought to judge interests on moral grounds to decide which interests should be protected in which ways and to what extent by such legal rights. And where existing legal rights to property do not reflect moral rights and do not bring about the best consequences for all those affected, they should be changed.

Self-Interest and the Common Interest

In discussing property interests, some of the most important questions have to do with accumulating property. What should we say about using property to create more property? What should we think about the role and justifiability of holding capital and making profits? Is it morally legitimate for an individual or a firm to try to maximize profits?

Adam Smith, of course, argued that in the area of economic activity, each person pursuing his own individual interest would, without even intending it, produce the greatest good for all.[15] To Adam Smith, acquisitiveness can have a better outcome than generosity. Thus the farmer, acting in his own interest, will work harder and produce more than if the economy expected of him the motive of benevolence, a motive that, though not absent, is weak. Similarly for "the butcher, the brewer, or the baker," who, through the natural human propensity for trading, develop economies in which, according to Smith, all can work for themselves in ways useful to all others.

In this framework, the person who sells his labor to someone else for a wage is not doing anything very different from the person who sells his extra wheat or loaves of bread. And the accumulated stock of machines and buildings and products and money that is capital is thought to play a role that is not notably different from the one played by the person who uses his labor to produce things and sells his surplus.

All such transactions are assumed to be made voluntarily, as in the case of an even exchange or barter between equals where both parties gain and no one loses. Labor is assumed to be an item to be bought and sold like any other, and capital is assumed to be a collection of some such items or their equivalents in terms of money. And everyone is applauded for making as large a profit as he can.

Thus Adam Smith can be thought to have offered a moral justification for what has been taken to be capitalism. The moral theory appealed to in this attempted justification is utilitarian. (See chapters 2 and 9.) It is still often claimed by those defending various current economic practices that capitalism operates along the lines supposed by Adam Smith and can be justified on utilitarian grounds. But very different assessments have been made. According to Ricardo, and then Marx, the results of all pursuing their own economic interests in a system allowing capital accumulation and unlimited profits are not at all the results imagined by Adam Smith. Ricardo thought that it is landowners, not everyone, who gain under such a scheme.[16] And Marx thought that it is the capitalist class that gains at the expense of the working class.

One way of interpreting Marx's claims is to see him as holding that the capitalist extracts for himself a part of what the work done by the worker would be worth in an exchange that really was what Adam Smith assumed such exchanges to be. It is only by paying the worker less than his work would be worth in a genuinely even exchange that the entrepreneur makes a profit and acquires capital.[17] Then the entrepreneur can use this capital to make more profits and to acquire more capital. Though capitalist economists scoff at this conception of what labor is "worth," the conception makes perfectly good sense from the point of view of what it would be morally justifiable to accord someone who would freely sell his or her capacity to work from a position of equality.

Marx's vision of the socialism that can be expected to replace capitalism sees human beings as having progressed beyond the self-interested pursuit of individual satisfactions that conflict with the satisfactions of others. But socialism as defended by British socialist thinkers and those they influence has often been defended on utilitarian grounds, in terms of its ability to satisfy individual interests; socialism is then seen as an economic system that can, while capitalism cannot, bring about the greatest happiness of all the individuals affected.

It has been recognized that the power of workers to organize and to assert their interests through political as well as economic channels can modify the disaster for capitalism that might otherwise result if the lot of workers progressively worsened until revolution became inevitable. Workers can press for increasing wages, and even though the rich may get richer at a faster rate, or the relative gap between rich and poor may remain about the same, the lot of workers under capitalism can improve. Much of their opposition can thus be bought off, to the dismay of those who have hoped that the discontent of the working class would lead to a transformation of bourgeois society into more humanly admirable and decent forms of social interactions than the generalized scramble after economic self-advancement.

Still, it can easily be shown—as Joan Robinson made clear[18] and as John Kenneth Galbraith,[19] Robert Heilbroner,[20] and Michael Harrington[21] have recently made plain, in their different ways, to large numbers of Americans—that for many economic activities capitalist mechanisms are highly deficient ways to reach the best outcome. Much that is useful to society is not profitable, and much that is profitable is not useful to society. Thus capitalism may fail to supply adequate public transportation and parks and child-care facilities and may dreadfully overproduce advertising and pollution.

When many try to use various resources to maximize their own interests, the result may be a depletion of the resource and an outcome exactly the opposite of the one predicted by Adam Smith. A striking example is that of the American buffalo. It is estimated that there were between thirty and sixty million of them roaming the West in the mid-nineteenth century. Whereas the Indians had killed only enough to meet their needs for meat and hides, white hunters slaughtered them indiscriminately for all the hides they could sell and even for sport. By 1903 there were only thirty-four buffalo left.

More recently, the pursuit of profits by oil corporations, auto manufacturers, and power companies has led to an enormously wasteful expansion of energy use. The political system has reflected these interests rather than restrained them—as in its vast subsidies to highway construction and mortgage financing for wastefully inefficient homes. Now, as realization dawns that the world's oil may run out before very long and will, despite temporary gluts, become more and more costly to produce long before then, we confront the effects of following capitalism's advice.

The problem is a general one. It may be that it is only within a very restricted area of activity that each pursuing his or her own economic interests, and a market determining the outcome, can possibly produce the greatest good for all those affected. And the problems are greatly magnified when seen on a global scale, with impoverished countries struggling for survival in a world dominated by economic Leviathans.

Economic Democracy

It is clear to many persons who raise moral questions about economic activity that at least a significant proportion of the major economic choices a society can make are moral choices. Questions about what investments should be made, what employment should be provided, and how the gains of economic activity should be allocated are moral questions. Decisions on them ought to be made in terms of what will best serve society, not most increase the profits of corporations. The point is so obvious it is truly remarkable that it remains obscure to so many. But even if we agree with the judgment, it is not clear how it ought to be carried out. The joining of political and economic power in the same hands that has occurred in Communist states has not served the interests of most citizens and has often led to a disregard of political and civil rights. Where some socialist economic and social programs have been joined with strong democratic government, as in many countries of Western Europe and Scandinavia, the result has been an enhancement of respect for rights along with a clear increase in the satisfaction of people's interests, such as in national health insurance, family support payments, and generous unemployment insurance. But whether the United States, which remains so much more commitedly capitalistic, will develop along similar lines remains to be seen. Even Sweden, despite its advanced social programs, has an economy that remains capitalist: 94 percent of it is still privately owned.[22]

Robert Dahl notes the lack of a socialist tradition in America.[23] Perhaps subjecting the giant corporation to some measure of democratic control and developing more responsible forms of economic activity along highly individualistic lines, as in the local development of appropriate technology, will be a more promising route toward economic decency in the United States than trying to import the social-democratic tendencies Americans lack. The tradition of small business, augmented by greater social responsibility than in the past, may provide a stronger base to build on than the hope that if socialism were to come to the

United States it could avoid the bureaucratic abuses that have tarnished its record elsewhere.

It is apparent that the modern corporation bears not the faintest resemblance to Adam Smith's self-sufficient farmer or tradesman. The modern corporation is an almost feudal institution in its hierarchical structure and lack of democratic organization. Some of the same arguments that led to the development of democratic political institutions to replace feudal ones can be applied to economic institutions, once people decide to apply them, though the road from argument to action may be dense with obstructions.[24] Modern corporations are no more "private" in their ability to control people's lives than is a state government. And the fact is, contrary to what most Americans believe, that the United States is *not* becoming more egalitarian. The vast disparities between rich and poor, and between the few in the former category and the many in the latter, have hardly changed at all in many decades.[25] Large corporations often have the power to assure themselves profits in good economic times and in bad, while those persons at the lower end of the economic hierarchy may find no way at all to sell their labor. Minorities, women, children, the sick, and the aged are especially ill-served by American capitalism in its present forms.

Robert Dahl and others suggest that the modern corporation ought to be democratized by having its workers share in the making of its decisions. Another suggestion for making corporations more representative and more responsible is that at least representatives of such groups as consumers and environmentalists as well as of labor be asked to join boards of directors. The reasons for democratic *political* institutions indicate that fundamental developments to make *economic* institutions more democratic are clearly needed, along with more active political concern at a national level with ailing industries and with the direction in which economic development might be encouraged.[26]

Gar Alperovitz is concerned that the workers of large corporations, like their managers, may pursue their own interests at the expense of the wider society.[27] He suggests ways in which certain geographical entities might evolve into communities within which all would act only within a framework of concern and consideration for the interests of others. But residential entities can be as perniciously selfish as corporate entities, as a great deal of suburban zoning regulation as shown.

Women and minorities have been disadvantaged by both big business and big labor. Though equality of opportunity has been the professed standard of even the most reluctant egalitarians, it has been blatantly denied to women and minorities.[28] Feminists, to make an at least temporarily valid point, sometimes apply the individualistic and contractual perspectives of political liberalism to relations within the family and ask how much the work of the unpaid housewife and mother is worth and what her economic rights should be. But feminists also suggest a different approach: that we extend to the wider society some of the traditionally feminine and feminist values of concern, caring, nurturing, and the meeting of needs that are characteristic of the relations that ought to exist within the family. A good place to start would be with the workplace. Why should not organizations for work, whether for service or production, be places where members care about one another, and why should they not try to provide satisfying work and produce useful products, in ways that will reflect concern for the human development and freedom of all members?[29] The corporation might then model itself on the nonprofit service or educational institution or on the economic collective rather than on the profit-greedy industrial firm whose lines of command resemble those of a military unit.

Some critics look at the way work itself might be structured to reflect the objectives of overcoming the domination and control now exercised by some over others in the workplace.[30] These objectives are shared by many young people eager to engage in economic activity but distressed at the authoritarian forms into which almost all of it is now structured.

No basic arrangements for the conduct of economic activity can for long be morally justifiable unless the interests of others are taken into account along with the pursuit of economic self-interest. This does not mean we need to turn into a nation of altruists, sacrificing our interests on some utopian altar. Because the raw pursuit of self-interest is ultimately self-defeating for most people, except in a narrow range of allowable egoistic pursuits, we need to develop forms of cooperation in which all *can* benefit. Under such arrangements, the gain for some individuals will have to be more modest than it would have been if a few lucky winners would continue to triumph over many losers. But the general good will be served. (See chapter 5.)

While we are still groping for the best forms through which to achieve such cooperation, it is clear that the myth of Adam Smith should be overcome. The delusion that all pursuing their own economic interests unrestrained can yield an outcome that will be good for everyone is still prevalent in the ideologies of many, especially among neoconservatives and those who think they have no ideologies but are pragmatic businessmen and value-neutral social sceientists. It is a delusion that should give way to a greater measure of reasonable cooperation between the members of national societies and between the fortunate nations and all the rest.

Economic Justice

Some economic issues concern rights and some concern interests. When we deal with questions of rights, we can recognize that we have rights to justice. We need to ask: What does justice in the domain of economic activity require? What is economic justice? In answering these questions, we will have to consider what the relation between government and economic activity ought to be. We will also have to decide what moral rights persons have to property or to the economic goods needed for a decent life or to a share of the output or to a share in the satisfying work of an economy. Again, how should our rights and interests be reflected in our economic arrangements?

John Stuart Mill, an advocate of a minimum of government control over and intervention into economic activity, recognized that there were valid reasons for some departures from the laissez-faire principle he recommended.[31] He thought the case for governmental provision of services was especially clear in the case of education, which not even those who proclaimed that government should do no more than protect persons and property against force and fraud would really want left to market forces alone to provide. And he thought basic necessities for the poor should be provided by government rather than by private charity, because citizens should be as certain of being able to obtain relief against destitution as of anything society can assure.

Mill also understood the difficulties that have in recent years been discussed under the label of the "free-rider problem."[32] There are many activities that will be advantageous to all if all participate in them, but these are such that it will be still more advantageous to each individual if others bear the burden of supporting the activity while the individual freeloads. For instance, if most *other* motorists install antipollution devices while a given individual does not, the air will get cleaner and the individual will benefit without paying the cost. However, if most people behave this way, devices will for the most part not be installed, and only a few naive citizens will pay the cost of installation without even enjoying any benefit. Government may be needed to ensure that all share fairly in supporting activities that will benefit everyone or many. And the arguments may apply to any number of collective goods, such as parks, libraries, and subways, that are so under-developed by capitalists pursuing high returns on their investments.

The picture presented by writers such as John Hospers and others who call themselves "libertarians" suggests that economic activity takes place quite independently of government and that government, to fund its activities, *takes away* part of the output of useful, independent, economic activity.[33] On this interpretation, government is seen as a kind of impostor or thief, taking from people something to which they would otherwise be entitled and which therefore they ought not to have taken from them.[34]

The picture presumes much of what it tries to show. It begins with an unfounded assumption that people are entitled to what they "earn" or "own" under traditional schemes of property rights. But, as we have seen, the rights of people to have *any* property protected, or to be able to consider anything to be *their* legal holdings—their possessions, products, income, capital, or whatever—depend on government. As we saw earlier, any given scheme of property rights protected by law and assured by the enforcement powers of government is the result of a social decision to enact or maintain *that* scheme rather than some other. And for any such scheme to be justifiable, it must be judged on moral grounds.

The orthodox Western scheme of property rights and interests is by no means the most plausible that could be maintained on moral grounds. Its most obvious deficiency is its lack of a built-in requirement that those with a surfeit share with those unable to obtain what they need. The most acceptable way of achieving such sharing is through taxation and redistribution, but if individuals would satisfy the obligation by voluntary contributions, governmental involvement would only be necessary as a last resort.

That those with greater economic resources than they need have obligations to provide for those who lack what they need was recognized by such forerunners of conservative economic thought as Locke and Mill and is understood by almost all developed schemes of morality. It is as legitimate to use the powers of government to assure that this obligation is met as it is to use the powers of government to assure that obligations of noninterference are met. (See chapter 8.) In denying this, libertarians distort the realities of property and coercion and then draw faulty moral conclusions from their myths. The moral requirement that those with a surplus assist those without enough should certainly find reflection in *any* legal and political arrangements concerning the acquisition and holding of economic goods, if such arrangements lay claim to moral justifiability. But this would be no more than a minimal requirement of decency. Perhaps morality might be more demanding still.

Justifiable Economic Arrangements

By what fundamental principles should we judge any proposed scheme of economic arrangements to be morally justifiable? If we try to make such principles explicit and adequate, what should they provide?

John Rawls has presented one of the most powerful and widely discussed formulations of such principles in many years.[35] In his view, the fundamental principles of justice are ones to which we could all unanimously agree, if we chose them impartially from a standpoint outside any actual society, without knowing which actual positions—rich or poor, male or female, white, tan, or black, untalented or talented—we would ourselves be in. The principles would, Rawls holds, require first of all as extensive a scheme of equal basic liberties for all of us as would be compatible with the similar liberties of others.[36] Once such liberties are assured, we should apply what Rawls calls "the difference principle" to the basic structure of society. The difference principle would require that *all* inequalities of what he calls social primary goods—rights, opportunities, income, wealth, etc.—could be justified only if such inequalities would contribute to improve the position in these respects of the least advantaged groups in the society. Thus high rewards for entrepreneurs could be justified only if their effect was to improve the lot of the least advantaged members of the society, who might benefit from new economic activity that otherwise would not take place. In Rawls's view, then, we have rights to an equal share, thus interpreted, of the whole of what economic activity provides.

Government should, in Rawls's view, continually adjust the rewards allowed to various groups by its scheme of property rights and economic policies so that the results will accord with this principle. Government should tax those whose economic benefits would exceed those allowed by this principle, and government should redistribute these funds, in some form, to those least advantaged in the society. Those who cannot work because of illness (within a normal range) or those unable to find work or those working for the most meager wages should have their situation improved through such redistributions.

In Rawls's view we would certainly choose, from his equivalent of the "state of nature" of traditional social-contract theory, to insure ourselves against the worst outcome that could befall us in organized society: being among the "least advantaged." If we did not know where we ourselves would wind up, we would choose principles of economic justice that would raise us from the bottom, and we would want those at the top to be taxed up to the point at which it would decrease their contribution to our well-being to be taxed further.

C. B. Macpherson also thinks that our economic and social rights extend across the whole range of economic activity and that on moral grounds we all have rights to a share of the total fruits of that activity sufficient for full self-development.[37] He interprets the concept of "property" in as wide a sense as possible, admittedly to bring some of the support now given by society to the protection of property to bear on achieving new rights that ought to be recognized. In his view, every citizen ought to have assured rights of access to the means of labor and the means to live a fully human life. Instead of providing only rights to exclude people from what one owns, property rights should provide persons with rights not to be excluded from employment and from a share in the society's whole material output. And property should include even more: rights to a share of political power and to participation in a satisfying set of social relations. Property, Macpherson holds, with Locke, should provide rights to life and liberty as well as to material revenue, but to an even fuller and freer life than Locke could have imagined.

Economic Rights and Interests

The more moderate view for which I argue would recognize that persons have economic and social rights as well as political and civil rights, but that these economic and social rights are to something like an amount needed for basic necessities, a decent life, adequate self-development, and equal liberty, but not to a certain share in the whole of the economic product of a society. Beyond what is needed for a decent life, adequate self-development, and equal liberty, we have economic interests but not moral rights. Hence we lack the moral rights, which ought otherwise to be reflected in legal assurances, to any proportion of the *entire* product of economic activity.

We can argue on the basis of *any* plausible structure of moral principles that just as citizens are entitled to certain political and civil rights, such as the right to vote, to a fair trial, to be free from assault, or to speak freely, so they ought to be entitled, by law, to enough economic and social goods—food, housing, medical care, etc.—to enable them to live a decent life. "Welfare" payments would then cease to be seen as charity, or benefits, which the fortunate members of an economic system bestow through collective generosity on the unfortunate, expecting the recipients to feel gratitude and shame. And private charity to meet basic needs would be unnecessary. Our rights to adequate well-being would be recognized as *rights*. And rights to employment would be acknowledged.

Article 25 of the Universal Declaration of Human Rights, adopted by the United Nations General Assembly in 1948, states that "everyone has the right to a standard of living adequate for the health and well-being of himself and his family, including food, clothing, housing and medical care and necessary social services. . . ."[38] Although it is a document not free of sexism, it does proclaim a commendable standard for basic political and economic rights to which many countries subscribe, at least in principle. The United States has not ratified *any* of the conventions or covenants designed to implement the declaration, despite its professed commitment to human rights. And no such rights as in Article 25 have been recognized by the U.S. Congress or the U.S. Supreme Court as constitutional rights. What programs Congress has enacted, such as for food stamps, Congress could take away.[39]

In *Wyman* v. *James*,[40] in 1971, a majority of the Supreme Court treated welfare payments as "charity" that persons might be accorded only if they were willing to waive their Fourth Amendment guarantees of the privacy of a person's home. In *Rodriguez*,[41] in 1973, the Supreme Court considered whether basing educational funding on property taxes, which yield seriously disparate budget amounts for rich and poor school districts, was in conflict with the equal protection clause of the Fourteenth Amendment. A majority of the Court decided it was not. They noted that, although education is necessary for the exercise of such other rights as free speech and the intelligent use of the right to vote, this is even more true for "the basics of decent food and shelter." As the Court observed, "empirical examination might well buttress an assumption that the ill-fed, ill-clothed, and ill-housed are among the most ineffective participants in the political process, and that they derive the least enjoyment from the benefits of the First Amentment." But instead of seeing this as the argument for substantive rights to food, shelter, and so on, which, in addition to even better arguments, it is, the Court took it as an argument *against* a right to equal education.

Many advocates of economic and social rights hope for more progressive legislation from Congress or more enlightened Supreme Court decisions to provide, as matters of right, enough economic goods for a decent life for all citizens. But when this may take place in the United States is problematic. Recent decisions have reaffirmed the nonrecognition by the U.S. legal system of any constitutional right to sustenance.

Arthur Okun discusses the way our political and civil rights should be off bounds to market determination.[42] We nearly all agree that rights to a fair trial, to vote, and to hold political office should not be bought and sold, but should be protected alike for those who have and those who lack economic power. Similarly, he argues, rights to those basic economic goods necessary for a modest level of dignity should not be subject to determination by a market that will enrich some while depriving others of these rights. These rights should also be treated as off bounds to the market.

Clearly, there will be some difficulties in drawing a line establishing the level up to which persons are entitled to economic support by a society. One person's necessity is another's luxury, to some extent. And a "decent life" is a vague notion. Still, we would have no difficulty in judging that a person who is seriously malnourished because of poverty is below such a line in a rich society. And if we admit that a line should be drawn, we can get on with questions of where to draw it.

To draw any such line, however, is to take a more limited view of the rights to economic goods to which persons are entitled than does Rawls's difference principle. The rights that the difference principle would provide would be rights to a share of the whole of the production of an economic system. It would subject the *entire* range of property relations to decision on grounds of justice and of the rights it requires. No one would be morally entitled to any property above what would be yielded by arrangements benefiting the least advantaged. Similarly, under Macpherson's conception of the property rights we ought to have, we would not be excluded from *any* of the total production of the economic activity of a society.

Rights to enough for a decent life, adequate self-development, and equal liberty would, in contrast, be rights to economic goods up to a certain level only. Such rights should be respected because they are moral *rights*, whether or not any calculation of utility or efficiency would recommend them. But above the level of the requirements for meeting these rights, economic activity *should*, in my view, then be judged on teleological grounds, rather than on grounds of rights. And it might, on these grounds, be quite appropriate to leave considerable room for egoism in those restricted spheres where Adam Smith's pursuit of individual gain can increase the satisfaction of all. On this view, once the claims of rights have been met, economic activity ought to maximize the satisfaction of the property interests of all those affected, where the interests to be considered are appropriately individual. Many of the interests, however, are collective in the sense that they cannot be broken down into individual gains to be maximized. But this is also an argument against Rawls's conception of economic justice.

Failure and Success

Against Rawls it may be argued that even from an "original position of equality" we might choose to allow some room for gambling on success rather than choosing only to insure against failure. We would want to assure that if we were at the bottom of the society, our rights to a decent life would be guaranteed, and this would surely include rights of access to what we require to meet our basic needs, rather than merely rights to be left alone and not attacked. This much of the argument against the economic conservatives, neoconservatives, and libertarians, with views such as those of Milton Friedman and Robert Nozick, is clear. But we might also want to be able to take a chance on being more fortunate. In doing so we would risk being less well off than otherwise if we did not succeed, but we could look forward to being *better* off than otherwise if we did succeed. If the difference principle were applied, any earnings of movie stars and fast-food moguls that did not contribute to economic activity benefiting the least advantaged would be taxed and redistributed to do so. But on this alternative view, *once* the rights to a decent life to which *all* are entitled had been assured, and politics and culture freed from control or distortion by economic power, winners would be free to retain as much of their earnings as would maximize general happiness while permitting collective gain.

The moral requirements of assuring the economic and social rights of all could be met by only a part of the economic activity that takes place in a society. Claims need not be made on the whole of it. We should not try to encompass every moral question under the rubric of justice or under the purview of the legal and the political. The economic ought to be accorded some measure of independence by our moral theories and by the societies that reflect them. We would then recognize that we could decide on moral grounds to require respect for the economic and social rights as well as of the civil and political rights of all. But we could also on moral grounds allow and encourage economic activity beyond what was needed to fulfill these requirements. And we could adopt a different basis of judgment by which such economic activity should be assessed. Arguments for liberty and for privacy could encompass arguments that persons should be permitted to engage in the economic activities of their choice once their obligations to the society were fulfilled. And which economic activities to encourage or discourage within this range could be decided in terms of how well or badly the activity contributed to the general happiness of society and its members.

The moral considerations by which given property arrangements should be judged and evaluated should be extended in some suitable way to persons elsewhere in the world and to persons in future generations. (See chapters 13 and 14.) Doing so might well involve obligations from government to government rather than from individual to individual. And the requirement from the point of view of actual nations in the actual world, as with the requirements for economic justice between actual classes within a society, would be for progress at a satisfactory rate toward a morally acceptable distribution of wealth. It would not be a demand for the instant dismantling of the privileges of rich nations, but it would preclude a continuation or worsening of present disparities.

Many economists and business leaders depict the sphere of economic activity as a kind of game in which winners and losers compete on friendly terms as if engaged in a sporting event. Their argument, then, is that just as those who win at a fair game of basketball can be accorded trophies without any violation of the rights of the losers, so those who win at a fair game of economic competition can be permitted to enjoy the rewards of doing so. And even losers may prefer having had a chance to play the game, and especially having a chance to play again and win, to being assured all along of an even apportionment of all proceeds.

We might observe that if we consider the rights of human beings throughout the world to what they need for a decent life, such game-playing—as the major life activity of morally serious persons—becomes questionable. Even more so does the squandering of scarce resources involved in the process. But if we could justifiably isolate a given group of persons and consider only the issues of economic justice within that group, then on moral grounds we might agree that *if* all could be assured their rights to a decent life and to adequate self-development, then economic game-playing over and above this level might justifiably be permitted. And it might justifiably result in winners and losers, as players pursue their economic interests. Economic egoism within these bounds would be morally permissible. And while the players would have no *moral* rights to retain any such winnings, society might well decide, on utilitarian grounds, to allow them legal rights to an appropriate proportion of them.

On the view I defend in this book, every person has moral rights. These derive from the moral principles and considerations to which we can subscribe here and now, without presupposing a social contract. They can stand up to the tests to which we should all subject the moral theories to which we commit ourselves. (See chapters 4 and 15.) Among these moral rights are, where it is possible to assure them, rights to the material resources needed for a decent life, rights to adequate self-development as through education, an amount of leisure, and rights to useful employment. Of course, there will be difficulties in deciding how much is adequate and what is decent and useful. But so is there difficulty in deciding how much police protection is adequate and whether a right to free speech must include rights to equal time on the airwaves or not. If we concede that the all-or-nothing views—that persons have no rights to any level of even the most basic necessities or that persons have rights to a share of the total of all economic production and activity—are not persuasive, we must look for ways to draw lines designating levels of adequacy. Such lines will always be subject to discussion and revision, along with all our legal and political decisions. But we will have made progress in deciding that the domain of rights must include rights of access to some level of economic goods, and yet leaving some room for self-interested economic endeavor.

We would then see that, to the extent that property rights are moral rights, they extend only to the satisfaction of needs and of the requirements for adequate self-development. Above that level, property "rights" should be seen *not* as moral rights but as legal fictions resulting from a political decision. Thus, allowing successful entertainers legal property rights to spend lavishly would have to be weighed against the possibly greater interests of others in other forms of spending. If, however, enough persons gain enough enjoyment from being able to watch and aspire to the expensive expressions of the successful, entertainers might be permitted to retain substantial amounts of their winnings.

Whether we call the relevant moral rights "property rights" or "basic economic rights" or "rights to the economic goods necessary for life and adequate self-development" is somewhat arbitrary. The important point is that moral rights to property include rights to what is needed for a decent life and adequate self-development and to what is needed for equal liberty (see chapter 8) and cultural expression (see chapter 12).

Moral rights to property do not include rights beyond this. Beyond this there are no moral rights to property; there are, instead, property interests. Decisions about them should be made responsibly, but not in terms of rights or economic justice. And they should not be allowed to "trump" social progress.

Economic justice is a serious matter. While those with moral rights to decent lives are deprived of these rights, playing games is not only frivolous but immoral. However, if such rights *were* respected along with the political and civil rights we take for granted, and if playing economic games could be justified in terms of the maximization of interests, there might then be nothing morally wrong with egoistic economic pursuits among those who choose to engage in them. These might not be the most admirable activities to which a society's members could devote themselves, and developing alternatives should be an objective of every society with the economic resources to do so. But once those in need have been provided for and the moral rights of all have been assured, the obligations of those engaged in the production and distribution of economic goods have been fulfilled.[43]

Chapter 11

Family and Society

NEARLY EVERYONE BEGINS life and becomes a person within a family. The family has an enormous influence on shaping the kinds of persons we become. People are often overwhelmed by the influences of their childhood as they struggle to lead adolescent and even adult lives. Furthermore, the location of a family in the existing social structure can determine the opportunities or lack of them of a given person for education, personal growth, and occupational success.

Justice and Families

One of the most frequently expressed principles of democratic society is that each child should begin life with equal opportunities to develop and succeed. The realities are nearly everywhere quite different. Even where ideology calls for a classless society, as in communist states, the children of successful party officials have educational and occupational advantages. In countries with social-democratic governments, much class stratification remains. And in capitalist countries, the proclamation of equal opportunity is often a myth by which an unwary working

class and a powerless underclass are deluded. The stratification of
wealth and income in the United States is very great and remarkably
unchanging as it persists from generation to generation in given families. The occasional rise of an entertainer or athlete or business leader
from poverty to great wealth serves to distract people from a class structure that is in reality highly rigid.[1] The children of poor parents suffer
immense disadvantages and lowered opportunities in comparison with
the children of rich parents.[2] And the vast majority of Americans lack
even the semblance of commitment to the classless society that genuine
equality of opportunity would require. Those already in the middle
class expect above all to be able to avoid losing their relative advantage
in the class structure. Those with wealth to pass on to their children expect to be able to favor their own. And most people accept, without
protest, property and tax arrangements that allow some children to be
vastly more privileged than others.

It is often unclear what principles of equality and justice require in
practice, but it is often perfectly clear that they are incompatible with
the kinds of class stratification that exist in many countries.

As we saw in chapter 3, the family at present is greatly misunder-
stood if it is thought to be in a "private" sphere separate from the "public" sphere of politics. In addition to the aspects of class already mentioned, the most personal relations between men and women are based
on power and authority. In this sense, as feminists have made clear,
"the personal is political."[3]

The place of women in the family is shaped by social, economic, legal, and political forces, along with the psychological and biological
forces that contribute to forming families. Women are routinely subordinate within the family, and then subordinate in the "public" sphere,
partly because of their confinement to roles associated with being wives
and mothers and partly because of the greater burdens they bear within
the family.

Women who spend their time raising children and keeping house
work long and hard, and yet their activities are generally not even
identified as "work" or paid anything at all. When women work for
wages outside their households, the jobs open to them are largely in
roles that match their traditional roles in the family: nursing the sick,
teaching children, waiting on tables, and typing and filing for men.

A significant long-range trend has been brought about by the massive movement of women into the labor force since World War II. Most
women in the United States, as in other industrial societies, now work

for wages as well as at child care and housework for a large portion of their lives. As of May 1981, 52.3 percent of women in the United States aged sixteen and over were employed outside of their homes.[4] And women with young children increasingly work outside their homes as well as in them. As of March 1982, 49 percent of married women with preschool children were employed, compared with only 19 percent in 1960, and 45 percent of married women with children under three were employed.[5]

However, women continue to encounter severe barriers to advancement. Most of the jobs available to them are in what has come to be known as the "pink ghetto"'where the work, done almost entirely by women, is painfully routine and poorly paid and where the chances for advancement are extremely low. The typing pool and the clerical work force are examples.

Under the impetus of the women's movement of the 1970s, women are challenging, sometimes successfully, many barriers to better-paying jobs, such as those in the skilled trades. Also, women are moving into many professions, such as law and medicine, formerly all but closed to them. However, they have not yet succeeded in narrowing the gap between the average wages of women and men working full-time and year-round: women in the United States continue to earn less than two-thirds of the wages earned by men.[6] But many more women are working for wages than in the past, and the greater independence and self-esteem that come from being self-supporting are leading to changes in the ways women accept, or refuse to accept, traditional roles within the family. The growth of feminist awareness has contributed to profound rethinking of what families ought to be and how their members ought to relate to one another.

Women continue to do the bulk of the work of raising children and keeping house even when they also work at paid jobs. Some men have begun to share somewhat willingly in these tasks, but there is still an enormous disparity between the roles of mother and father as actually practiced. Women are now burdened, in effect, with two jobs. Some feminists argue that the application of liberal principles of equality will have an inevitably radicalizing effect as women recognize the fundamental structural changes that will be needed in the economy and in the family to make it possible for women to achieve equality.[7] Jobs will have to be organized with more of a view to human satisfaction and less to profit, and men will have to share equally in child care and housework.

Household and Society

There are other reasons for child rearing to be shared by men than that
such sharing is necessary to achieve equality for women. Among the
most interesting and important theoretical work of recent years has
been that which explores the effects on human personality of the fact
that the care of infants is done almost exclusively by women. In the best
statement of the theory, Nancy Chodorow argues that our social practice of making mothers but not fathers the primary caretakers of small
children forms the male personality into one in which the inclination
toward combat is overdeveloped and the capacity to feel for others is
stunted. It forms girls into human beings with a weak sense of self and a
diminished ability to assert their independence, and forms boys into
human beings "whose nurturant capacities . . . have been systematically curtailed and repressed."[8]

The extent to which parenting is *not* tied to biology but is instead a
social construction can be suggested by considering the entirely different meanings we give to the sentences "He fathered the child" and "She
mothered the child." Mothers *need not* be the ones who "mother." And,
on various grounds, women should not be the only ones who mother.
According to Chodorow, "the very fact of being mothered by a woman
generates in men conflicts over masculinity, a psychology of male dominance, and a need to be superior to women."[9]

If theories such as this turn out to be sustained empirically, we have
every reason to turn parenting into an activity performed equally by
men and women. The development of human personalities that have
some chance of enabling humanity to survive the risks of nuclear holocaust, environmental decimation, and global revolution may demand
it. Respect for the rights of children, both girls and boys, to the kind of
care needed to develop healthy personalities may require it.

I shall develop in this chapter, however, much more limited arguments. In the next section, I shall ask: if we accept such principles of
equality as argued for in chapter 8, what would the implications be for
the ways in which women and men should agree to arrange their own
lives as parents? Then, in the section after that, I shall consider what
possibilities for social transformation may lie in a transformed relation
between women and men. Feminists have shown unmistakably how
unacceptable traditional relations between men and women are. There
are overwhelmingly good reasons to transform these relations into ones
based on mutual respect and concern rather than on domination and
subordination.

If relations between women and men do become more acceptable at a personal level, how much hope would this hold out for an improved society? Is the political also personal, as well as the reverse? Before liberal and democratic thinking came to dominate our views of political life, arguments were offered that the political order should be structured like a well-ordered household. For instance, a king, it was said, should have authority over his subjects, the way a benevolent father has authority over his wife and children.

Such arguments underlay the theories of Aristotle, of Aquinas, and of Robert Filmer, whose views were decisively replaced by those of John Locke. The principles of liberty and equality subsequently became the dominant norms in the political realm. But they were almost never applied to relations within the family. In recent years many women have demanded that the principles of liberty and equality on which political democracy rests be applied to relations between men and women. But some feminists are considering whether the analogies drawn by the earlier views should not also be built upon if reversed. They suggest that just as relations between persons within the family should be based on mutual concern and caring, rather than on egoistic contracts, so relations in the wider society should be characterized by more care and concern and humane feeling than are the contractual bargains that have developed so far in political life. Transformed, the household might again provide a model for society, and transformed households might contribute to better societies.

These questions lead us to focus on the family as a social institution of the utmost importance. The family is a set of relations creating human persons. Societies are composed of families. And a family is a small society. The family is undergoing profound change at the present time, and the upheavals in the personal lives of many persons hold out the promise of remarkable social change, quite possibly for the better.

Jane Flax, surveying recent feminist writing on the family, points out that "the family *is* central to the oppression and liberation of women. Therefore, the family must be central to feminist theory as well."[10] The family has not yet received the central attention from feminists it deserves, partly because feminist theory is in exploratory stages, trying to understand all at once the multiplicity of forces—social, economic, political, legal, psychological, sexual, biological, and cultural—that affect women. Multiple causes shape the sex/gender structures within which human females and males develop feminine and masculine characteristics and occupy male and female roles. We need to understand empirically how this happens. We also need a normative theory of the family. To develop alternatives to the oppressive relations that now exist requires, Flax writes, "thinking through what kinds of child care are best for parents and children; what family structures are best for persons at various stages of the life cycle . . . ; how the state and political processes should affect families; and how work and the organization of production should be transformed to support whatever family forms are preferred."[11] It is an enormous task, but recent years have seen more new thought on this subject than many previous decades combined.

Mothering, Fathering, Parenting

It is often supposed that insofar as women are *mothers* they perform a primarily *biological* function. Women have accordingly been thought to be closer than men to nature, to the sorts of activities that make human beings like other animals rather than distinctively human. Like so many other assumptions about women, this is almost entirely a mystification contributing to the domination of women by men.

Human mothering is an entirely different activity from the mothering of other animals. It is as different from the mothering of other animals as the work and speech of human beings is different from the "work" and "speech" of other animals. We should not exaggerate the differences—humans are *also* animals and should be far more responsible than they have been toward other animals. But to whatever extent we recognize a difference between "humans" and other animals, we must recognize a comparable difference between human mothering and animal mothering.

Human mothering transmits language and culture. Human mothering teaches morality, not just techniques of survival. A human parent plants the seeds of aspiration, not merely of repetition. Human mothering teaches consideration for others based on moral concern, not merely instinctive tendency. Human mothering creates persons capable of creating art, not merely of propagating a species. In sum, human mothering is as different from animal mothering as humans are from animals, though this conclusion comes as a surprise to those influenced by aeons of misunderstanding about the "nature" of women and the "natural" function of mothering.

Human mothering is above all an activity that *need not* be performed by women. If we decide to turn it into an activity to which we apply principles of equality, what would this require? What does a commitment to considering female and male parents as persons of equal human worth require as applied to parenting?

Over and over, one encounters the argument: if a woman chooses to become a mother, she must accept a recognized set of responsibilities and obligations that are quite different from the responsibilities and obligations of being a father. But why is this so?

Although recent years have seen much change in perceptions of roles within the family, the view that was almost completely dominant until recently was as follows: A father was expected to contribute some of his income for the expenses his child made necessary. A mother was expected to give up whatever other work might interfere with her availability to care for her child and to take full care of the child, cheerfully and contentedly, to whatever extent and as long as the child needed it. And if it was thought that the child would develop problems due to early separations from a parent, it was the mother who was thought to be responsible for preventing these problems.

The law of domestic relations in the United States dealt with "support" of the child almost entirely in terms of paying the bills for the child's food, clothing, shelter, and so on. This was thought to be the father's obligation; if he was unwilling or unable to fulfill it, it became the mother's. The mother, just by virtue of being a wife, was standardly expected by the law to "render services in the home," as it was often put, and these services included, incidentally, caring for any children who happened to be in it.

As summarized in a widely used legal textbook, "The husband is to provide the family with food, clothing, shelter, and as many of the amenities of life as he can manage. . . . The wife is to be mistress of the household, maintaining the home with the resources furnished by the husband, and caring for the children."[12] And, wrote the author, "a reading of contemporary judicial opinions leaves the impression that these roles have not changed over the last two hundred years."[13]

The author of this textbook recently undertook to revise it and found that he had to rewrite it rather completely. In 1983 he could say that in the previous fifteen years, "very little of family law remains unchanged. There's been a complete revolution."[14] And if the federal Equal Rights Amendment is adopted, it may bring about quite significant further changes in the law. However, the extent of the changes should not be overstated. Courts continue to be dominated by conservative middle-aged men. More important, the law seldom enters into the domestic picture until there is a breakdown of a marriage. While the marriage is intact, the law leaves husband and wife great latitude to work out their domestic arrangements. If the marriage fails, courts decide how to divide up possessions and obligations. The possibilities of dividing parental obligations equally, even at this point, are only beginning to be explored. [15]

Attitudes are changing, but the depth or permanence of the change is still unclear. In the United States in the 1980s, more fathers are involved in the care and upbringing of their children than was the case a decade ago. But traditional arrangements still prevail. Even among couples most influenced by changing attitudes, it is nearly always the wife who will interrupt her career to care for the children while they are very young. And it is still mothers rather than fathers who will restrict their activities the most, to be able, for instance, to stay home when a child is sick or to avoid as much as possible being "away on business."

In the attitudes of society, "motherhood" has often been taken to be an occupation (though unpaid) that women could perform the way men could be autoworkers or bankers or professors. In an article by a social scientist, this typical view was incorporated into the following point:

> Once these successive needs—the physical, the social-affectional, and the equal esteem or dignity needs—are sufficiently gratified, humans are not even then content: they then begin to look for that kind of activity that is particularly suited to them as unique individuals. Whether their competence is to be a ditchdigger, a powershovel operator, a construction foreman, a civil engineer or a building contractor, an architect, a mother, a writer, or a politician—they must do these things when they have become rather sure in the gratification of their even more basic physical, social and esteem needs. [16]

At least the ranking in this list was favorable. In contrast, the skill level thought to be needed by a homemaker, child-care attendant, or nursery school teacher was rated in a U.S. Department of Labor publication at only 878 on a scale from 1, the highest skill level, to 887, the lowest (hotel clerks were at 368). [17]

Just how ludicrous it is from the point of view of equality to see motherhood as an occupation can be seen if one substitutes "father" for "mother" in such lists. As we all know, and yet as even a rudimentary sense of equality must protest, women have routinely been asked to choose between parenthood and having an occupation (or another occupation, if one counts parenthood). Men have routinely been expected to be able to enjoy both parenthood *and* an occupation (or another occupation).

The common view that motherhood is one occupation among others, but virtually the only one open to mothers not driven to factory or farm labor in addition to motherhood, was even shared by John Stuart Mill, despite his awareness, quite unusual among philosophers along with nearly everyone else, that women were entitled to equal rights.[18] It has sometimes been suggested that any different view of the occupational possibilities of women had to await the development of industrialization in the nineteenth century or the development of birth control techniques later. But that this is a lame excuse for millennia of unequal treatment can be seen in the perfectly imaginable alternative view given by Plato, at least in *The Republic*. Plato pointed out to anyone who would notice that whether one bears or begets children is not a relevant basis on which to determine whether one is fit to govern.[19] The same argument could be applied to the whole range of occupations where being or not being a biological mother is unconnected with whether one has the relevant skills. If other occupations are to be open to women, women must not be confined to motherhood. If, on the other hand, mothering *is* an occupation, men may have the skills for it. But instead of recognizing these obvious points, the link between giving birth and caring for children has been and is still widely assumed to be necessary and inevitable.

That so few have been able to imagine, much less support, the notion of both mothers and fathers caring for children and being engaged in other occupations is part of the problem of turning conceptions of equality into practice. But it is unclear, perhaps, what might be required by equality or what parents who acknowledge each other as equals and as having equal obligations toward their children need to do to fulfill these requirements and obligations. It is this question that I shall now try to explore.

Equal Obligations

Must we suppose that equality requires both parents to do approximately the same tasks, taking approximately the same length of time, so that one parent might, for instance, be completely in charge of the children from around 6 A.M. to 2 P.M., and the other parent completely in charge from around 2 P.M. to 10 P.M., while both work at paid jobs to support themselves and their children in the hours they are not engaged in child care, and both take turns at getting up in the night if needed? Are staggered and perhaps shorter work shifts in industry and the professions an obvious objective? Or should we consider the possibility that if the abilities of the two parents are significantly different, the child is entitled to care "from each according to his or her ability" rather than "from each the same kind of activity for the same length of time"?

It is inadequate to consider questions of parental obligation in isolation from the social situation. Societies ought to recognize their obligations to their children. Societies ought to provide adequate levels of part-time and full-time child care, of support for parents who take care of children at home if they choose to, of medical care and education. But measures to do so in the United States are, unfortunately, a long way off. We can still deal with the equal obligations of parents in terms of *given* levels, however inadequate, of social support. Doing so should certainly not be taken to imply that current social arrangements are satisfactory, only that women and men may often try to do the best they can to respect each other as equal persons within existing social structures. And the issues can be seen primarily as moral. One hopes the law and social arrangements will come to reflect moral requirements, but long before they do, morally concerned persons must deal with these issues and can try to arrive at reasonable solutions to the problems involved. What I am asking, then, is: if individual women and men recognize principles of equality, as most would presumably by now profess to do, and if both really do respect each other as persons of equal worth, entitled to equal liberty and justice, with equal rights to choose how to live their lives, what are the implications for their obligations as mothers and fathers?

It would certainly not be adequate to think of the relation between parents and children only or even largely in terms of obligations and rights. Children have rights to care and support, and parents have obligations to supply these when the society does not do so, but it is obviously better for children to receive more from their parents than what the mere fulfillment of the parents' obligations would require. A parent who gives love, concern, and attention to a child because it is a joy to do so is obviously a better parent than one who merely with grim determination meets his or her obligations to feed and safeguard the child. And it is surely of more value to the child that there be a genuine relationship of mutuality, of shared concern and respect between the man and the woman who are the parents, than that such a relationship be absent. But the discussion here will be limited to obligations and their equality. Parents cannot be obligated to feel emotions beyond their control or to give a child everything that would be of value to the child. Parents *can* be expected to meet their equal obligations.

What Does Equality Require?

Children are entitled to support and care. To the extent that, under given social arrangements, the moral obligation to provide these falls on the parents, it falls on them collectively. Before parents consider which of them should do which tasks, they should agree on what the child's rights and needs are and on the necessity and relative importance of the tasks that are to be done. They should try to decide how much the child's preferences will count and in which domains they will count before they discover what the child's preferences are. Then the parents should proceed from such judgments as "The parents have an obligation to provide W, X, Y, and Z" to such judgments as "Parent A has an obligation to provide W and Z" and "Parent B has an obligation to provide X and Y." How people move from the former judgments to the latter has traditionally been a matter not of reasonable argument, but of little more than social prejudice. Much thought and goodwill are needed to reconcile views about the obligations of parents with views about the obligations of mothers and fathers in ways that are morally plausible.

If the parents decide that the needs of the child require them to earn, say, thirty additional monetary units a week, and if, as would be likely in American society at present, the mother would have to work at a paid job almost twice as long as the father to earn the fifteen units that would seem like an equal share, then equality of obligation would not require her to provide half of the thirty units. However, if the mother wishes to work, her contribution should not be discounted just because an equal effort will bring in less money. Again, if the work the mother would have to do, even if equally paid, would be significantly less satisfying than the work the father would have to do, and would thus be more of an effort to perform, then an equal contribution would not require the mother to expend as much time at such work or to provide as much money for the child from it as the father.

In a different aspect of their obligations, if the parents decide that on a typical day the child should be given breakfast, taken on a two-hour outing with close supervision, and given lunch, a rest, a bath, and a story, and that the objects the child has scattered about the house should be put away, then equal obligations would not be fulfilled if the mother, because of greater effort, did (or, when appropriate, got the child to do) all these things on the day it was her turn, while the father, because of a lesser effort, managed to get done only two or three on the days, an equal number, it was his turn. But if it really was, at least temporarily, significantly more difficult for him to do these things than for her, he might be required to do fewer of them.

In making these determinations, we could raise the question of whether it is intention or success that should count in establishing when two persons are making an "equal effort." In child-care work, one person may succeed with modest effort in keeping a baby satisfied and occupied, while the other may try much harder and fail. In trying to improve one's position in outside employment, one person may try and repeatedly suffer defeat, and the other may move steadily forward with little effort. But despite the possibilities it may create for deception and self-deception, in the case of meeting one's obligations, it seems to be intention, not success, that should count.[20] But then we must assume sincerity and that statements such as "But I *am* doing the best I can" will not be used to mask willful inefficiency.

Whenever differences of interpretation arise as to what importance to attach to what, and what guidelines to use to weigh obligations, devices to cut down distortions of perception may be helpful. Parents can try to apply the "roommate test" suggested by Sandra and Daryl Bem and ask how the tasks would be divided if, instead of being a male/female couple, they were roommates of the same sex.[21] Parents can acquaint themselves with all the tasks and devise arrangements and divisions of them before knowing which tasks they themselves will perform. They can, for instance, decide whether feeding the children their evening meal should count for more than doing their laundry or count for less, before deciding which parent will do which task. And they can decide whether a typical hour of outside employment is more burdensome or more rewarding than a typical hour of child care before deciding how the hours will be divided. And so on.

Differences of competence can be brought in at a later stage of discussing these arrangements, but here again, procedures to aid impartiality may be helpful. For instance, the parents might agree to evaluate each other's competence rather than their own and to do so before knowing what arrangements will arise from their discussions. And differences of preference that make some tasks more burdensome to one parent than to the other should be considered only to the extent that the preferences of both parents are considered to an equal degree, including higher-order preferences, as when a woman might say, "I do not now like to give lectures, but I want to get practice at it because I would like to like to."

To the charge that "counting" hours and "calculating" who is doing how much will spoil the spontaneous and harmonious relation between parents and with children, will turn family affection into the pursuit of selfishness, and turn children into products, one can point to centuries of experience. Such charges have always been leveled against workers—factory workers, teachers, secretaries—who have "calculated" how many hours they were working overtime or without pay instead of failing, out of "loyalty," to notice. And such charges have routinely been used against women who have finally begun to recognize that, in addition to working all day like their husbands, whether at home or at paying jobs, they have been doing nearly all the evening housework. Those who have been taken advantage of have always been asked by the beneficiaries to be trusting and altruistic.[22] But the result of acquiescence in arrangements that are unfair is the growth of resentment and mistrust. *The response must be that when respect and equality become habitual, calculation becomes unnecessary.* Mutuality and sharing are to be sought, but on a basis of equality, not exploitation.

Can Work Be Different but Equal?

Equality of obligation would certainly not rule out *all* differences in the tasks performed by mothers and fathers. We now have, I think, no reliable empirical knowledge of any genuinely differing talents and tendencies of mothers and fathers (except the dispensable and brief capacity of mothers to nurse their infants). We should be very wary of accepting any division of labor between mothers and fathers based on their differing talents at the time they become parents, since these may be due to years of sex-stereotyped preparation, in which boys are encouraged to study and work at various jobs and girls are expected to baby-sit and do housework. One significant feature of parenthood is that *neither* parent has much previous training for the work, although this is often overlooked, as it is assumed that the mother will "know what to do" and hence, since it is so much "easier" for her, that she should take care of the children. Anyone who has studied or experienced the anxious and helpless feelings that affect women faced with a first newborn baby to care for, or the feelings of guilt and incompetence of mothers not able to handle "smoothly" the outbursts and demands of small children, has every reason to believe that fathers would be equally capable of preparing themselves for child-care work as best they could, and of learning fast on the job.[23]

Still, we cannot preclude altogether the possibility that differences of parental ability and preferences between men and women may be significant. If, in fact, it suited our empirically given natures better for most of us to be, at different stages of our lives, successively either tenders of children or earners of income, rather than to try to keep the two in balance or to yield to one activity or the other over the whole of our lives, then possibly more mothers than fathers *would* be suited to care for small children and possibly more grandmothers than grandfathers *would* be suited to run the world. And the requirements of equality between parents would not seem to be violated by life cycles that might be significantly different.

Equality of obligation, then, does not require that both parents perform exactly the same tasks, any more than equal opportunities for occupational attainment require that each person spend his or her working life at exactly the same kind of work. But it does require a *starting presumption* that *all* the tasks connected with supporting and bringing up children should *each* be divided equally. Dividing the tasks equally might be done by having both parents engage in the same activities for the same periods of their lives, as when they both split their days equally between child care and outside work. Or dividing the tasks equally might be achieved through taking somewhat longer turns, one parent working away from home for a few years, for instance, while the other stayed at home, and then, for the next few years, reversing the roles. These latter divisions may be especially appropriate for parents who are separated or who must live separately at times for professional or other reasons. But women should be cautious about relying on agreements to have their years of child care "made up for later." The effects of divorce are highly unequal. In a study of divorce in California, the standard of living of men increased by 42 percent in the first year after divorce, while the standard of living of women and children decreased by 73 percent.[24] Another study showed that two-fifths of the divorced, separated, and single mothers legally eligible to receive child-support payments from the fathers of their children "have never received even a single payment" and many of those fathers who do provide support do so irregularly and in trivial amounts.[25] Furthermore, fathers who take little part in raising their children in the early years may not be able to suddenly develop close relations with them later on. And it may be very difficult for children to adjust to a complete shift of care from one parent to the other at different stages of their childhoods.

Equality of obligations *does* require that every departure from each parent performing the same tasks be justified in terms of relevant criteria and appropriate principles. There must be good reasons, and not merely customs and social pressures, for such departures. Simply being male or female is not a relevant ground for such departures and cannot be the basis for justifiable differences in parental roles. And equality of obligation requires that the choices to perform given tasks at given stages of our lives should be no less voluntary for one parent than for another.

For this principle to be recognized, we would have to abandon not only the view that the obligations of mothers and fathers are unequal, but also the view that they are in *any* way different. *Any* differences in tasks performed would have to be the result of voluntary agreement between the parents, arrived at on the basis of initial positions of equality, such agreements to include provisions for any later reversals of roles that equality would require.

Taking care of small children for a few years of one's life is enormously interesting and satisfying work, full of joyful as well as exhausting times. If mothers who choose this kind of work were not expected to pay so heavily for it in terms of their chances for self-development, few would wish to miss out on it.[26] In fact, women would probably, if given the choice, be glad to agree to more than an equal share of childcare work temporarily in exchange for more than an equal share of occupational opportunity and career advancement later on. But fathers should not be expected to agree to let mothers get more than their fair share of the best work of young adulthood, and to let grandmothers get more than their fair share of the best work of late middle age. If fathers *would* agree, they would still be *entitled* to equality, and mothers would have an obligation to help them realize it.

For both parents, the claims of their children should normally be primary. If the empirical claims of Chodorow and others turn out to be as strongly supported by further evidence as they seem on the basis of the evidence so far available,[27] then the case for equal parenting from the very beginning of an infant's encounter with the world and on through the years of childhood and adolescence will be overwhelming.

An encouraging recent study of college students shows a trend in the direction of shared parenting along with more equal career aspirations for men and women. Students at seven leading colleges showed a remarkable similarity of goals: a quarter of the women surveyed want to resume full-time careers by the time their children are two to five years old, and a third of the male students want to stay home or work part-time while their children are preschoolers.[28]

The Personal and the Social

What are the possibilities of remaking society by remaking relations between persons? Societies are composed of persons in relation to one another. "Personal" relations are among the most affective relationships. Western liberal democratic thought has been built on the concept of the "individual," seen as a theoretically isolatable entity. This entity can assert interests, have rights, and enter into contracts with other entities. But this individual is not seen as related to other individuals in inextricable or unseverable ways. This individual is assumed to be motivated primarily by a desire to pursue his or her own interests, though he or she can recognize the need to agree to contractual restraints on the ways all persons may pursue their interests.

As we saw in chapter 5, the difficulties in building trust and cooperation and society itself on the shifting sands of self-interested individuals are extreme. Perhaps we need people to be tied together by relations of mutual concern and caring as well as by contracts that may be in their interests to break. The relation between mothering parent and child, hardly understandable in contractual terms, may be a more fundamental one than the relation between consenting contractors. But what sorts of relations ought to prevail between adults?

To understand what a relation of mutual concern freely entered into would be like, let us examine the relation between man and woman as a possible paradigm for social relations.

Could a transformed relation between man and woman provide a model for a transformed society? Certainly it is not hard to argue that the relation between man and woman is the key social relation, and that if genuine mutuality of concern and respect did characterize this relation, the effects on the rest of the society would be extraordinary. Even though John Stuart Mill could not imagine mothers playing a role in society comparable to fathers, since he saw motherhood but not fatherhood as a kind of full-time occupation, he was able to see that "the example afforded, and the education given to the sentiments, by laying the foundation of domestic existence upon a relation contradictory to the first principles of social justice, must, from the very nature of man, have a perverting influence of such magnitude, that it is hardly possible with our present experience to raise our imaginations to the conception of so great a change for the better as would be made by its removal."[29] An understanding of the relation between man and woman has not yet really begun to be tapped for insights into conceptions of community, though it is probably the most fruitful source of insight for such conceptions and for discovering whatever it is that might tie human beings together in societies.

Mutual Concern and Respect

In one sense, the relation between man and woman, as a conscious relation, is abstract and "ideal." At the same time, as Marx says, it is a *natural* relation, "sensuously manifested, reduced to an observable fact."[30] We should not, however, be deceived about the sense in which it is observable. When we think we experience, sensuously, the feelings of mutuality, sometimes we experience only our side of what we mistakenly take to be a relation of mutuality. To "know" that the relation exists may require some education of the sensibilities, but it is still, in Marx's sense, to experience something human and concrete, not a Hegelian abstraction.

A relation of mutuality is quite different from a relation of power, where two persons, as entities possessing power, simply stand in some factual relation to one another, as when we can empirically describe that one person has greater power than another. A relation of mutual concern and respect is also different, although both are conscious social relations, from a mere mutual recognition by each person of the factual relation of power in which they stand, even when it is one of equal power. Equality is in general a precondition for a relation of mutual concern between man and woman, but it in no way assures the presence of such a relation.

By the relation of mutual concern and respect in its distinctive sense I mean a relation in which neither person uses the other, neither sees the other primarily as a means to the satisfaction of his or her own self-interest. The relation is genuinely mutual; it is only achievable together, and consciously. But the relation of mutuality is different from mere reciprocity, where *both* use the other to increase their own satisfaction, as in a trading relation. If mutual surrender of the primacy of self-interest is absent, or awareness of this surrender not present, there can be no mutual concern and respect, and this relation cannot "exist" as a relation. This does not mean, however, that the relation of mutual concern and respect is *contrary* to self-interest, that it requires altruism or charity toward the other. It is, rather, a relation in which neither the interest of self nor the interest of the other is pitted one against the other, because for both persons, cooperation simultaneously replaces competition. (See chapter 5.) We can, perhaps, understand the relation most easily in a sexual context, where genuine mutual consideration between a man and a woman making love is neither the joint pursuit of self-satisfaction nor the joint bestowing of charity, but the mutual pursuit of and awareness of mutual feelings and values.

The value of mutual concern and respect may be discussed in terms of the conceptual difference between the collective or social value of a relation of mutuality and a sum of the self-interested values of a number of individuals. Applied to the sexual relation between a man and a woman, although the man may gain pleasure from the states of arousal or satisfaction of the woman, if her states are considered primarily as factors contributing to his greater pleasure, the resulting value of his initial pleasure, increased by the pleasure that her pleasure gives him, is still an egoistic value. It may often happen that a certain state of consciousness in her may contribute to his pleasure, but if he is a callous man, it may simply not affect his pleasure. Either way, whether her pleasure affects him or not is a contingent matter of fact; concern for her pleasure is not required by the definition of his pleasure as an egoistic value. If a similar interpretation is applied to her, and a summation made of his total pleasure and her total pleasure, the resulting value is a sum of individually self-interested values. Insofar as the values are seen as values *to* individuals, even though their fullest realization may causally depend on other individuals, we have not yet reached the social value of the relation of mutual concern and respect.

The latter would be a mutual relation between two persons in which the man would recognize the woman's pleasure as primarily good in itself, not primarily good as a means to his greater pleasure, the woman would do the same with respect to his pleasure, and each would be aware that the other did so. For an extended relation of mutual caring then to exist between them, each would have to value the other for the other's sake as well as for his or her own and know that the other did the same. Such a relation of mutuality might in fact be less conducive to individual satisfaction, at least at times, than an egoistic relation. Or it might be more so. Either way, the mutuality might itself be judged to have a value—for the society, for instance, or for the children of a couple—a value distinct from the sum of the egoistic values the relation would provide for the individuals involved.

A relation of mutual concern and respect as an immediate and purely sexual relation is not at present altogether rare. But when the same characteristics of genuine mutual concern are sought in other aspects of the relation between sexual partners, the more other aspects are included, the more rare the relation becomes. Many men are still unaccustomed to regarding the other-than-sexual needs and satisfactions of the women with whom they make love in terms of the interests and goals of the woman herself. And many women, trained to expect that the other-than-sexual satisfactions of their husbands or lovers should satisfy them too, are often still unaccustomed to expressing, and sometimes even to recognizing, their independent interests. In a relation of mutual concern, both would take pleasure in the self-development and wider satisfactions of the other. And they would mutually recognize that both were doing so.

The contrast between mutuality and self-interest is not one between reason and emotion, with reason recommending one thing and emotion the other. There are two traditions of what is rational: the Kantian tradition recommending rational, universal rules of morality valid for all persons, and the egoistic tradition recommending that each person act on the basis of rational—meaning prudent and efficient—self-interest. And at the level of the emotions, there are two conflicting traditions, each with much empirical evidence in its favor: that human beings are essentially selfish, and that human beings are capable of love and self-sacrifice.

A recommendation to promote cooperative social values, or to forget them, can thus not simply be derived from a commitment to either rationality or human feeling, since either can be used on the side of "community" or the side of "egoism." Nor can such a recommendation be decided in a historical vacuum. If attachment to the value of community would become overwhelming and stifling of diversity, the reassertion of individual interest and uniqueness might be appropriate. But in our own time and region, it is clear that individual values have, at the level of both theory and practice, become excessively dominant, with social values distressingly discounted in theory and ignored in practice. For the social changes the assertion of cooperative social values requires—and both are essential to the future of humanity—the relation of mutual concern and respect between man and woman may point the way as no other area of experience so central to human beings can.

A further crucial aspect of the relation between man and woman is that for it to be one of mutual respect, rather than of paternalism or maternalism, each must respect the autonomy of the other, renouncing the right to decide for that other what is best for him or for her. And each must be aware of the other's recognition of such self-denial. Of course, a relation of mutual respect must not involve the imposition of one will upon another, or even the *attempt* to coerce, whether for the benefit of coercer or coerced. In their dealings with each other, man and woman discover not only that man can overpower woman (I am speaking not of physical force or rape, but of the force of sexual attraction) and woman can overpower man—that is, at the level of *sexual* power, as opposed to muscular and other power, they really *are* equal. What human beings also discover is that in this relation, mutual respect is only possible when neither overpowers the other, and coercion of any kind, including the use of sexual power in coercive ways, is transcended.[31]

At present, as with mutual concern, the lesson is too often lost as the relation between man and woman extends into other areas than the purely sexual, and the moment of noncoercive mutuality experienced in bed is often overwhelmed by the strength of male dominance beyond. For the relation of mutual respect to develop, coercion must be renounced at all levels and even more fundamentally than as an aspect of mutual concern where the partners are inclined to resist being overpowered. To respect another person is to renounce the use of coercion against that person even when he or she is powerless or not inclined to resist.

Women and Power

As recent analyses have helped us to realize more acutely than ever before, the relation between man and woman is at present suffused with a vast disparity of power in all but the capacity to affect purely sexual encounters once man has renounced the power to rape. The wider disadvantage that so often undermines the possibility of mutuality for the woman is often effectively masked by her capacity and need to hide her feelings while she accommodates her behavior to her situation. Certainly it is more satisfying for the man if he is wanted, and for himself, rather than sought or stayed with for the economic and social favors he can bestow. But the insensitivity that men have so much more easily than women been able to afford has frequently kept them ignorant of women's dissatisfaction and discontent. And the woman's relative powerlessness in so many other aspects of their relation has frequently assured her need to feign desire, affection, approval, and consent.

Imagine woman now psychologically, socially, economically, and politically as free to ignore man's wishes as he is free to ignore hers. Imagine man having to consider her feelings not only for that brief span of time before he establishes his hold over her, but *continually*. The sensitivities of the male rulers and shapers of our future are bound to be affected, as are the prospects for female participation in the shaping of that future. If, in the relation between man and woman, it is no longer possible for one will to impose itself upon another, and not necessary for that other to yield, certainly this will change habits of behavior and thought at wider and higher levels for the better. Mutual concern and respect between man and woman will develop not only in their sexual activity but throughout the whole of the association between them. Both men and women can then pursue their economic, political, social, professional, and other activities not only as equals but as persons who have become accustomed to mutual concern and respect as a normal condition covering a very extensive part of their lives. Mutuality will then no longer be, as it so often now is, a mere isolated and momentary experience.

To make possible the relation of mutual concern and respect between man and woman, and especially to expand it beyond a fleeting moment in a limited part of their lives to wider and more distantly related aspects of the relations between human beings, most of what advocates of women's rights demand is indisputably necessary: women must have enough economic, social, political, and psychological independence to be able to subsist satisfactorily without this relation of mutuality. Otherwise the actual relation between man and woman becomes subverted into a relation of dominance aand submission. But these economic, social, political, and psychological requirements are *preconditions* for the maintenance of the relation—and in one sense not new, composed as they are of the familiar elements of power. The relation itself, on the other hand, is characterized by a *mutual renunciation of the use of power*. Equality of power may be a precondition for any such satisfactory, voluntary, extended renunciation; otherwise the breakdown of the relation leaves woman, as usual, in a position to be overpowered. But *exploration* of the relation need not await the full achievement of such equality. And if we seek to explore alternative and more satisfactory relations with which to construct society than the relations of power and self-interest that now pertain, women and men must try to build some relations in which they renounce the use of power, although they must do this in addition to and not instead of building the economic, social, political, and psychological foundations with which the power of women can be equal to that of men.

Of course, there is the danger that when the relation depends on mutuality, nothing happens; it is the danger of all cooperative ventures that when cooperation is absent, the cows don't get milked and the crop goes to seed. But the difference in the relation of mutual concern and respect between man and woman is that it is not causally necessary for anything else. If it is absent, man and woman continue to exist as separate persons and continue to copulate. Of course, humanity cannot continue to exist without some relation between man and woman, but it need not be, as it has not been, a relation of mutual concern and respect. In the absence of the relation of mutuality, instinct will ensure that at least we will have as before the relation of sexual and other forms of power, and we will not be worse off than at present. The creation of the relation of mutual concern and respect is thus an open choice, not a requirement forced upon us, and again, for that reason, its exploration creates an island of escape from necessity, an island to be extended into the wider society. Perhaps the survival of humanity requires that men become more capable of cooperation and less inclined toward aggression than at present, and perhaps a transformation of the relations between men and women, and between men and children, would contribute more to this outcome than any other likely development.

The activities feminists recommend often concern the use of power: how can women marshal their strength to attack and win concessions from the structures of entrenched male power and privilege, and how can women develop their own sources of power and their own organizations? Where superior power is being used to exploit and oppress women, women must develop power sufficient to resist and overcome such treatment.

They should also, however, develop the possibilities of alternatives to such encounters of power, as many feminists now recognize. If men and women are to transform society in ways that will not merely distribute power more equally while remaining based as much as before on its use, then both women and men must learn new habits of dealing with one another in different terms, the terms of cooperation, of trust, of openness, and of mutuality.

Women who experience mutual concern and respect—and some do so between each other more substantially and steadily than with men[32]—can try to discover ways of extending this alternative to egoism and competition. In working out the actual behavior and expectations reflecting mutual concern and respect, they will have to abandon most traditional interpretations of how relations between men and women should be constituted.

Mutuality in Society

We should not conclude that cooperative social values are inherently and at all times better than individualistic ones or that an extended relation of mutual concern and respect between man and woman or between friends of either sex is always to be sought. Whether to create such relations is an open question. But in suitable circumstances, and consciously, persons can decide to take a chance on such relations, to discover those ranges of feeling and experience that are impossible without it, and to explore its possibilities. In society, to be enveloped completely in an all-consuming mutuality can be stifling, and so it can be in relations between lovers and friends. At both levels it is essential to establish, to maintain, and sometimes to guard adamantly some regions of privacy. But without mutuality, there can be no felt sense of community, either between intimates or in the wider society.

The argument so far developed depends on drawing an analogy between moral relations among a small number of closely associated persons, such as a family or group of friends, and moral relations between a very much larger number, such as fellow citizens in a state. It is sometimes suggested that such analogies are faulty because the relevant emotions are not transferable. Even if there can be mutuality between lovers and friends, that is no guarantee, certainly, and perhaps not even any indication that there can be mutuality between fellow citizens.

However, in response to the argument that the feelings that would allow for mutuality between lovers and friends are impossible on the scale of whole societies, one has only to look at the sentiment of nationalism to see how powerful such feelings *can* be. Throughout history many persons have willingly subordinated even powerful personal sentiments for "the nation," "*la patrie*," "national independence," or for establishing a "homeland." Such sentiments are often inimicable to more global concerns, but in recent years increasing numbers of people are becoming devoted in what may become a comparable way to saving the world from nuclear destruction, environmental pollution, and the decimation of other species. Even if the sentiments for larger units such as the city, the nation, or the globe are normally far weaker than those for lovers, children, and friends, this is still a matter of degree. As we saw in chapter 5, the willingness to cooperate enough to allow a society to exist rather than to disintegrate need only be a weak sentiment, tipping the balance in favor of cooperation rather than unmitigated self-interest. Once the balance has been tipped, the social relations that cooperation makes possible *are* in the interests of most people. So the kind of deep mutual concern and respect possible between lovers is not at all necessary for global sanity. What is necessary is some low level of mutual concern and respect, rather than pure egoism. To understand what the relation is as a social relation, binding persons and enabling some development of trust, we may do well to look at the relation in the context of lovers or close friends. We can then strive to encourage such relations in our lives. For many persons, the most important actions they can take are to reject relations that are not becoming progressively more cooperative, and to develop the kinds of social relations in which mutual concern and respect can grow.

In the early years of the recent feminist movement, the arguments went largely in the other direction, with the familiar liberal political framework of conflict and competition modified by self-interested contracts being applied to relations between women and men. Such analyses showed how *little* the relations between women and men resembled contracts between the free and equal persons presupposed by liberal theory. And they spelled out the sorts of changes that could make relations within the family more justifiable on grounds of equal rights and the interests of women as well as men.

In recent years, however, feminists have increasingly argued that we should not want to turn the family into a minibusiness or ministate based on contracts and self-interest.[33] We should preserve what is best about the relations of caring and concern that have characterized the relations between, especially, mothers and children, and sometimes women and other women, and occasionally women and nonsexist men, and extend these to the wider society. If mutuality between lovers and friends and genuine caring between parents and children can come to replace the domination and patriarchy of the past, it seems entirely possible that this will eventually affect relations between persons at the levels of nations and continents in beneficial ways. Instead of turning families into little states, we should aim to turn the globe into something resembling at least slightly more than at present a household freed of its patriarchal past.[34]

Chapter 12

Free Expression, Culture, and the Good Life

THOSE OF US who have been highly critical of American society have often found it possible to celebrate what Thomas Emerson calls our "system of freedom of expression."[1] We *do* have a lot of free expression. Critics and crazies of various sorts often get a hearing for their views and works. We do take the kinds of rights protected by our First Amendment extremely seriously. Although we lag grievously behind most other advanced societies in our recognition of rights to basic necessities as genuine rights, we *can* pride ourselves on being in the forefront in our protection of rights to express oneself without interference. During the Falkland Islands crisis, it was gratifying to see the British press learning a few things from the American press about objectivity as a standard for reporters and encountering the flak from home that followed when British reporters were thought to be insufficiently "patriotic."[2] And I have found in conversation that members of the French press look to American reporters with admiration as models of resourcefulness and certain kinds of independence.

There is, however, another view, and here the picture is much more bleak. The culture, which more than anything else shapes the way society sees itself and its future, is so thoroughly beholden to commercial interests in the United States that any views seriously challenging the corporate political economy that surrounds it are perceived as little more than a kind of entertainment. The society seems to enjoy being diverted now and then by what it sees as a furious Marxist, a morose black, a bellicose feminist. But having enjoyed the show, it continues with business as usual. And business as usual, in its cultural life as in its economic activity, is overwhelmingly in the interests of business.[3] Whatever political party is in office, no serious alternative to the dominant corporate culture obtains a serious hearing. And according to some predictions, the successors of those with power during the Reagan years may offer a climate even less hospitable to challenges to traditional interests than do those with power in the Reagan years.[4]

We often hear it lamented that communist societies *cannot* reform themselves because as soon as there is a serious challenge to the power of the state, repression will crush the challenge.[5] Events in Poland do not yet offer counterevidence to this thesis. But we should consider the way a comparable argument may apply to ourselves. As soon as any serious challenge to the American political economy begins to become visible on a substantial scale, economic power engulfs it. Corporate power and its agents absorb those willing to be absorbed for a decent salary or lucrative contract. This business society is remarkably adept at turning critics into just another product or service to be sold or used. And corporate power and its agents undercut those who resist absorption, depriving them of ways to earn a living or to be heard. The way our cultural forms of expression, especially but not only television, contribute to turning opposition into forms that can be bought up by the prevailing economic powers is a model of efficiency.

The outcome of this "price war," however, like the outcomes of most social conflicts, is still very much in doubt. What we choose to defend as rights to free expression will affect the way the contest is conducted and thus the shape of the eventual truce.

Freedom of Expression

Our concerns for free expression may be divided, I think, into five segments. In each, there are the following clusters of rights:

1. The rights of persons to know what their government is doing
2. The rights of the press to inform such persons
3. The rights of persons to express themselves through speech, print, broadcasting media, and symbolic action
4. The rights of persons to form and join associations
5. The rights of persons to assemble and protest

To see these rights merely in terms of an absence of governmental censorship is a highly inadequate way of seeing them. Even to see them in terms of an absence of *any* kind of censorship, such as that of a TV station's management in firing a newscaster or canceling a series for political reasons,[6] is still an unsatisfactory way of seeing these rights. That we so often tend to see them this way is *explainable* in terms of our traditionally distorted view of freedom as merely negative—the liberty to be left alone—but it should, I think, be corrected. An absence of censorship except in very special cases is very important, and especially where even overt censorship of first-rate literature takes place, its importance needs to be emphasized. But many are speaking up on this subject. I shall deal here with some issues that are hardly discussed at all—the enablements that are needed along with an absence of censorship. An absence of censorship is a necessary but by no means sufficient condition for freedom of expression.

I shall try in this chapter to deal with two aspects of our rights to free expression: the rights of reporters to gather news and the rights of citizens to have the means to express themselves. These will be aspects of the rights I have clustered above under numbers 2 and 3. They are central to the workings of democratic society and to the pursuit of better lives and cultures.

The Rights of Reporters

It is characteristic for persons in academic life to disparage the press, to use "journalistic" as synonymous with "shoddy" and "shallow." It is not surprising that even conscientious and clever members of the working press often return the sentiment by thinking of "academic" as synonymous with "pedantic" and "out of date." There is some truth on both sides, and much falsehood.[7]

Many of the issues of press responsibility should be approached, I think, through the development of professional norms for those who work in journalism and broadcasting. It will be difficult to make headway along these lines without considerable economic restructuring of the society. But this is true for most of the other professions, such as medicine and the law, and if the norms of professional journalism would be as well developed and explicit as the norms of these other professions, that would be progress in the meantime. Some encouraging developments along these lines are taking place, and an overriding regard for the truth occasionally manifests itself as a standard to be paid attention to by professional journalists and newscasters in ways not to be sneered at. The commitment of the legal profession to justice or of the medical profession to health is perhaps not much more notable than the commitment of the journalistic profession to truth, and the differential regard that academic observers have for these professions may have more to do with prejudice than with evidence. In any case, we can agree that of course reporters have responsibilities. They also have rights.

On some interpretations, the rights of citizens to *know* and to *hear* are more fundamental than the rights of other citizens to speak.[8] It does not seem necessary to establish such an order of priority except in terms of procedure: if everyone speaks at once, no one can hear anything. Hence, yes, we need procedural rules, and these may take priority. These limits on speech have traditionally been considered legitimate. They have in the past been applied in rather special contexts of governmental bodies and group meetings. We might *consider* applying them in some different form to the traditional "marketplace of ideas" if the cacophony of innumerable outlets of expression would prevent the hearing of any distinct messages, but this is hardly an issue in the era of giant networks and shrinking numbers of newspapers. We clearly need more, not fewer, voices able to speak up.

We need not say that the rights of citizens to hear are more fundamental than the rights of reporters to speak. Reporters would have rights to speak even if no one wanted to hear. But the rights of reporters to have access to information in such ways as the U.S. Freedom of Information Act provides derive from citizens' rights to know. The press has a responsibility to inform and enlighten because of the rights of citizens to be informed and enlightened by a responsible press. Then, in doing their jobs, reporters have certain rights that need to be respected. The rights of reporters as reporters rather than citizens are connected with the rights of citizens to know what their government is doing.

In two influential articles in the *New York Review of Books*,[9] Ronald Dworkin has asserted that there is no such thing as a citizen's right to know. And he has denied that reporters have rights to report. He has seen the issues entirely in the traditional terms of absence of censorship, defending the view that the First Amendment guarantees of free speech precluding censorship are sufficient to assure our rights in this general domain.

In Dworkin's view, individual citizens have no *right* to know what their government is doing. In his view, the public as a whole has a *general interest* in information and can decide as a matter of policy which governmental actions will be open to scrutiny and which closed. But individuals have no *rights* to this information and reporters have no *rights* to supply it.

In Dworkin's political philosophy, rights trump or take priority over considerations of general interest. (I share this view for many contexts.) But given the way Dworkin has set up the problem, what this means for the context of freedom of the press is that the public's interest in information is overridable *whenever* it conflicts with *any* individual right or with any greater general interest in suppressing information. These implications of Dworkin's position make that position, in my view, unacceptable. They indicate that the premises on which Dworkin's conclusions rest fail to reflect an adequate understanding of the role the press ought to play in a democratic society.

For Dworkin, the issue is not that one right has to be weighed against another, as when one citizen's right to know might have to yield to another citizen's right to privacy. For Dworkin there is *no* right to know, there is *only*—sometimes—an overridable general interest in information. So the right to know can *never* take priority over a majority's interest in restricting information. If, at any time, a majority's interest in restricting information is greater than its interest in obtaining information, a restriction would be justifiable, on this view. It seems clear to me that to have an individual citizen's access to information thus completely at the mercy of what a majority happens to consider advantageous is to misunderstand the bases of free government.

James Madison observed that "a popular Government, without popular information, or the means of acquiring it, is but a prologue to a farce or a tragedy; or perhaps both. . . . A people who mean to be their own governors must arm themselves with the power knowledge gives."[10]

Traditionally, the rights of the press to find out what it can have been thought to provide adequately for the citizen's right to information. The U.S. Congress, in passing the Freedom of Information Act (FOIA) in 1966, established a new standard. The act asserted that "for the great . . . majority of . . . records, the public as a whole has a right to know what its government is doing."[11] This established a presumption in favor of disclosure on the part of the government. Subsequent amendments to the act have reaffirmed and strengthened this position. The right to know does not cover everything that government does; the FOIA specifies a number of exemptions, to protect trade secrets, national security, and personal privacy. Additional exemptions have been considered. But the Freedom of Information Act has strengthened the ability of reporters and citizens to see behind the steel doors of bureaucracy. It has contributed to open government. In her book on secrecy, Sissela Bok vigorously defends the Freedom of Information Act. She applauds its much older Swedish forerunner, the Freedom of the Press Act of 1766, which gives Swedish citizens the right to inspect and to reproduce government documents. "Guarantee of public access to government information is indispensable in the long run for any democratic society," Bok writes. "Otherwise, if officials make public only what they want citizens to know, then publicity becomes a sham and accountability meaningless."[12]

The Freedom of Information Act and open government have been under sustained attack during the Reagan administration. The Senate Judiciary Committee voted unanimously in 1982 not to accept the Reagan administration's proposal to gut the act,[13] but the future of open government is very much in doubt.[14] It is important for defenders of the FOIA to have a clear sense of the theoretical arguments that can be made in behalf of open government, and it is unfortunate that the formulations of the issues by Dworkin and others who see the issues as he does provide such weak support for defenders of open government.[15]

The Right to Know

Almost all of us can easily agree that citizens have a right to participate in self-government and that this is a right of individuals, not just a general interest we have collectively. But then it seems clear, against Dworkin, that of course citizens *do* have a right to know what their government is doing. For one cannot participate in self-government unless one can know what one is participating in.

Dworkin writes that "it is wrong to suppose that individual members of the community have . . . a right to learn what reporters might wish to discover."[16] This is a strange way, indeed, to characterize the responsibilities and goals of citizens and the press. A more plausible view would assert that citizens have an individual right (and even an obligation) to inform themselves about the actions taken in their name by those they choose as their governors, and that reporters have an obligation (and also a right) to enable them to do so. *Even if* it would have been in the general interest for the war in Vietnam, say, to have been prolonged, individual citizens would have had a right to know enough about what their government was doing to have been able to say, *"Ohne mich."*[17] And reporters would have had a right to tell them. They would have had this right even if a majority considered it in its interest to keep such information from potential dissenters.

In the view of Dworkin and many others, the First Amendment rights of the press should be limited to protection against censorship. However, if reporters have no right to know more than a misguided majority deems it in its interest to let them know, the right may reduce to a right to say nothing. Editorials can continue to be written, but the factual information that they should take into account may be totally restricted without this being recognized as an infringement of any rights. Such a position cannot, I think, be taken seriously.

Dworkin worries that the right to speak without censorship may erode if issues of censorship are decided on grounds of policy, and censorship is thus invited "in those cases in which the general welfare, on balance, would benefit from it, or rather when the public thinks that it would."[18] We can all share this worry. However, the same concern should be extended to the right to know. It, too, needs to be protected against policies that would undermine it. This does not mean the right to know has no limits; it means the limits need to be determined by judicious argument.

The Freedom of Information Act, enabling ordinary citizens and reporters to have access to governmental documents unless there are allowable reasons against such access, should be maintained with no more than minor adjustments. This may help to prevent a recurrence of such horrors as the FBI's machinations in the late 1960s when, according to the *New York Times*, the FBI "produced a flurry of anonymous letters and spurious 'publications' . . . that it hoped would cost political activists their jobs, disrupt their personal lives and temper their opposition to the Vietnam war. . . ."[19]

In addition, the right to know requires that reporters have rights to their own journalistic notes and diaries and that these and editorial offices not be subject to searches by government. Reporters must be accountable to editors, and editors must be accountable to readers.[20] Reporters should be protected by responsible "shield laws" from prosecuting attorneys and should be legally entitled to offer confidentiality to those who provide them with news. This does not mean there should be no limits to the confidentiality reporters can offer. It does mean that a presumption in favor of confidentiality should be spelled out in appropriate practices to enable the press to carry out its function in a decent society. A free press in a free society must have reporters able to discover and report the truth. The rights of persons to privacy must also be spelled out, and when the press invades the privacy of persons for the sake of economic gain, claiming to be acting in behalf of citizens' rights to know, the fraudulence of such claims should be exposed and the rights of persons to privacy assured. But so should the fraudulence of innumerable other claims by other persons and enterprises to be serving the public while merely pursuing economic self-interest. Sometimes open discussion of the fraudulent motives of individuals and corporations, including those in the media, is the best antidote to their influence. At other times, rights may be involved: rights not to be the victim of fraud and not to have one's privacy invaded. In such cases, the courts should protect such rights. However, after all these limits on journalistic enterprise have been acknowledged, the genuine rights of citizens to know what their government is doing, and the genuine rights of reporters to make this possible, remain.

Access to Freedom of Expression

The second major aspect of freedom of expression to be discussed in this chapter concerns the interpretation that should be given to the rights of persons to express themselves.

Initially, let me say that I take seriously the distinction between speech and action, and I think it does provide some basis for dealing with the difficult question of whether we can, without inconsistency, protect the freedom of those who would abolish freedom. The answer may be that we *can* allow those who would abolish freedom to *speak* in favor of doing so; we should have no legal requirement that *speech* be consistent and we can permit speakers the freedom to speak against such freedom (and I include publication and broadcasting along with speech). However, we can demand that the action of the *law* be consistent and that the law not protect *actions* that would destroy its *protections*. So it is rights to expression, not action, with which I shall be concerned.[21]

Rights, as we have seen, are central or stringent entitlements yielded by justifiable rules or principles. (See chapters 2, 7, and 10.) Traditionally, in Western liberal political theory, especially in America, rights have been thought of primarily as rights to be left alone by government, rights to have negative liberty, or freedom *from* governmental or other interference. (See chapter 8.) But many persons are beginning to recognize the need for a more satisfactory conception of rights and of rights to freedom. (See chapters 8 and 10.) The arguments are overwhelmingly clear that rights to basic necessities must be assured as enabling rights. Citizens must have *access* to food and shelter, and rights to such access must be assured along with the traditional civil and political rights.[22] It is absurd to think that persons would freely consent to obey a government that refuses to let them acquire what they need to live while it assists those who have more than they need to hang on to their surplus.

Little by little many of us are becoming aware of how distorted have been our perceptions and interpretations of autonomy. Traditionally, we have developed philosophical conceptions and legal interpretations and institutional supports that enlarge and uphold autonomy for those with the economic resources to enjoy it, and we have overlooked the lack of autonomy of those without comparable economic resources. Various discussions are beginning to correct these misperceptions.[23]

If we then apply considerations such as these to the issues surrounding freedom of expression, we can recognize that our conceptions of rights to free expression need to be significantly expanded. Freedom *from* governmental interference or the interference of others is clearly *not* enough. This kind of freedom only begins *when and if* we have the economic and cultural means to express ourselves. This is not an adequate notion of freedom of expression. Those who can finance the publication of a newspaper or produce a television program or afford expensive training may enjoy this right, while all others have a right that is analogous to the freedom to go hungry.

We need a more satisfactory conception of *freedom* in this domain as in the others. We need a new set of enabling rights to expression, rights that include the economic and social and cultural *means* to express oneself. And these rights must not yield to what are imagined to be the rights of property holders to hang on to their excess wealth without interference.

A person develops within a culture and, in complex societies, often within more than one. One of the most fundamental values that a culture ought to encourage in its members is self-development. Persons realize their potentialities when they can flourish autonomously, freely expressing their beliefs, concerns, dreams, and hopes. To do so, they must have the resources that make this possible. These resources ought to be assured to all members of a society. And society ought to support the free development of the individual and collective imagination that creates culture.

Another value that a culture should provide is a sense of community, of belonging to a grouping larger than the self and persisting and developing over a longer time than any individual life. Tensions between autonomy and community ought to be understood and imaginatively resolved as persons develop within cultures and are free to leave or reject given cultural communities and join others. For these developments to proceed in ways that are not coerced and manipulated, persons must have the economic and social resources enabling them to contribute to the flourishing of those cultures of which they choose to be a part and to move away from those cultures they reject. No one should be dependent on any given culture for survival or for aesthetic self-development. The suggestion often made by conservatives that if we are hungry or homeless we should appeal to our local church shows a blatant disregard both for the rights to basic necessities that ought to be assured by society, and for the rights to cultural choice that ought to be respected. Persons should be assured the means to avoid having to accept the teachings or aid of given religious or cultural institutions. Their choices to join cultural groupings should be voluntary.

Rights to Cultural Resources

Instead of considering enabling rights to free expression to be aspects of freedom, as I have advocated, some persons may think it better to understand some such rights as more nearly aspects of well-being than of freedom.[24] We could still agree that an ability to express oneself is an important component of well-being and that rights to well-being should be assured by society. And we could still agree that rights to free expression should be thought to include rights to have *access* to the means to express oneself, not only rights to express oneself if one *already* has the economic and cultural means.

Finally, rights to self-expression are certainly aspects of rights to self-government, which must be seen to include *active* participation and the active articulation and argumentation of ideas and goals. To be the passive recipient of someone else's calculation of our welfare is not a satisfactory outcome of a scheme of democratic rights. Central to active participation in government is the free expression of the individuals and groups governed.

On any of these arguments, we can conclude that persons have rights to the means to express themselves, that is, to the economic and cultural resources with which to develop the expression of self and community. The difficulties involved in interpreting such rights are very great, especially because the idea that freedom of expression must go beyond an absence of censorship is so new to us. But we can explore issues of what they might include.

One cannot dream of being a painter without having some experience of the aesthetic and cultural possibilities of visual art. One cannot work at developing one's skill as a musician without instruments and a place to practice. And in that vast domain of the video shaping of cultural images and thoughts, one cannot take part in expression as opposed to mere reception without access to television studios and air time. And yet we cannot supply all who want one with a piano of their own, and we should not ask that the walls of a given museum be open to all who want to hang their paintings there. It does not follow that we should provide nothing and demand nothing.

How should access be understood in a contemporary context? Jerome Barron has explored some of the issues in a book called *Freedom of the Press for Whom? The Right of Access to Mass Media.*[25] He begins with the position that "freedom of the press must be something more than a guarantee of the property rights of media owners."[26] He shows how our approach to freedom of the press so far "has operated in the service of a romantic illusion: the illusion that the market place of ideas is freely accessible."[27]

Barron acknowledges how easy it is to ridicule the idea that anyone should be able to commandeer magazine pages or network TV time to make whatever crackpot, dangerous, or self-serving pitch he or she pleases. But he shows how the idea of reasonable access could be taken seriously. Barron, a lawyer, argues persuasively that in the letters columns of newspapers, for instance, "a legal obligation for newspapers to publish a letter on a vital community public issue, would be an entirely suitable and salutary remedy."[28] Many cities have only one newspaper. If the newspaper deliberately refuses to offer readers an alternative view for political reasons, rather than because of genuine limitations of space, citizens could have recourse to the courts. "Access," he proposes, "will open up only those parts of the newspaper which maintain the pretense of openness"[29] (the letters-to-the-editor section and the advertising pages for those who can afford to buy space). The problems of deciding when a newspaper is or isn't fulfilling this responsibility to the public would in Barron's view be quite manageable, though courts and publishers have solidly opposed these arguments. Publishers argue that freedom of the press must give them complete control over whatever they publish. But for the issue of freedom of the press to be used to protect monopoly publishers keeping dissenting views from being heard seems a distortion of the intent of the First Amendment.

In the case of broadcasting, the courts have established that those with the economic resources to buy advertising time for political messages have that right of access. But the problem of access for those who cannot afford to buy time is acute. The "fairness doctrine" has evolved, requiring broadcasters to provide some opportunity for conflicting viewpoints on controversial issues to be presented.[30] But an occasional three- or five-minute statement by a disgruntled citizen or group representative is often little more than decoration on the bulk of TV programming. The fairness doctrine comes into play only after a station has made an issue of something or given time to a major candidate. It gives a person or group a right of reply, but it does not give anyone a right to raise an issue ignored by the station in the first place. As Barron puts it, "in the United States the media are organized to sell products . . . the only way the media can combine making money and talking about ideas is to talk about only those ideas that are not too controversial."[31]

It will surely not be easy to interpret and implement a right of access—either to the mass media or to the educational and cultural resources to express oneself in other ways than through the media. And access to more than the chance to make a brief political statement about an issue already in the news—such as a union's reason for a strike or a group's reasons for opposing the construction of an expensive highway—will raise even more difficult problems than these minimal aspects of what access might require.

The important point at this stage might be to recognize, as hardly anyone who writes about culture or the First Amendment yet does, that some such rights should be acknowledged at the level of social theory. And then we can get on with the discussion of what rights of access to cultural expression should include and how they can best be understood and respected.

Culture shapes political and social life. It has been described as "a system of moralizing demands," as the "organization of permissions and restraints upon action."[32] Our culture shapes the way we see ourselves and our world; it molds the efforts we engage in to reach what it holds out to us as a better future. It holds up to the light the images by which we judge our plans and prospects. There is no more important domain than the cultural in which to be concerned that what is morally valid be given a hearing. And for alternative voices to be heard, they must be loud enough for those who wish to hear to do so.

Culture and Commerce

Rights ought not to be subject to being lost or drowned out in the marketplace.[33] Yet in the United States, rights to free expression are often completely overwhelmed by commercial interests and almost invariably depend on possessing, already, the economic means of expression. One of the most disturbing aspects of our cultural scene is that we so rarely even *imagine* what it would be like to have the media serve human values other than the commercial gain of the economically powerful.

American television, the most powerful cultural force in the society, is itself just another industry pursuing—very successfully—its own economic gain. And the messages that are at present expressed almost without relief on American television are the messages chosen by those with great economic power. Regulation by the Federal Communications Commission is utterly minimal. Licenses are virtually never found unworthy of renewal because of unsatisfactory programming. Programs are chosen to provide as large an audience as possible to industry's commercials.

Other forms of cultural expression are similarly the captives of market forces.[34] Publishers must sell books that are appealing enough to compete with television.[35] Producers of movies and plays gamble for large returns on their investments. And more and more entertainment is produced and offered directly by corporations without even the semblance of independence on the part of the producers.

Why is it that we *accept* the economic determination of the bulk of our cultural life? We expect major art museums and symphony orchestras to be independent entities. Though museums accept contributions from corporations, we would frown on one that allowed commercial messages from, say, Exxon to bombard visitors as they looked at the Van Goghs. And we would find it laughably inappropriate if a professor in a classroom began and ended a lecture with a commercial for, say, IBM, because IBM had "bought the time." In more subtle ways, artistic and educational institutions convey the messages approved by a "business society," and dependence on corporate support may mute fundamental criticism more effectively than overt control. Still, academic institutions have a tradition of "academic freedom," and a few other institutions have less well established but not negligible versions of such independence. The news departments of major networks aspire to someting comparable; although they fall far short of it, at least it is an aspiration. But what about the bulk of TV programming? The mere aspiration to independence is often absent. And the aim to break free of the influence of advertisers is often not even a distant goal.

It seems high time that we begin to extricate various segments of popular culture from the corporate political economy that now owns and controls so overwhelming a share of it.[36] In most of our popular culture, we can hardly imagine what it would be like to have cultural rather than self-interested economic objectives predominate, and this is what we might try to change first.

To help us in imagining what our popular culture might be like if it were not the captive of commercial interests, I would like to sketch out a few possible analogies that might be drawn, instead of the ones that are now in place.

Suppose, first, that one thought of culture as comparable to the knowledge imparted by education instead of as comparable to property to be bought and sold. Although there are still highly unfortunate inequalities in the educational opportunities offered to children and although higher education is often the privilege of the rich, and professional education a way of preserving rather than narrowing class privilege, still, at least we understand conceptually that a right to education cannot be merely a right to *buy* an education, without governmental interference, *if* one's parents can afford it. We do recognize the latter sort of rights, allowing rich parents to buy expensive educations, but we recognize, in addition, that nonrich children must be *enabled* to be educated, that society must *provide* education or the resources with which to buy it for people who cannot already afford to buy it. And so we spend huge sums on public education.

Why, we may well ask, should not television and other forms of expression be understood in terms closer to education and further from those of the marketplace? Why should there not be more socially provided opportunities for expression that are not conditional on the prior possession of the economic means to pay for such expression?

Developments in cable television would have made it easier than before to start thinking along these lines, but the current burgeoning of cable TV purely for profit may undercut rather than encourage what few gains for professionalism had begun to occur among those working for the major networks, and it may do nothing to lessen the commercial greed that has characterized the development of TV so far. Yes, local groups will have access to local audiences at far lower costs than for TV programming in the past. But an adequate view of a right to free expression should go much further. It is not enough for groups to be able to buy time, or benefit from the so far trivial amounts of free time allowed under the fairness doctrine or from the free access offered by some cable outlets. There should be social provision on a *much* larger scale of opportunities for expression for those who cannot now afford it or afford more of it. Producing interesting and professional programs costs money. The costs of production as well as of distribution should not limit expression to those with either wealth or wealthy backers.

In an interim period, until the society became willing to fund cultural activities on a substantial scale the way it funds education, we might encourage or demand TV stations that would operate without profit as their *primary* objective. Enough advertising might still be accepted to enable the costs of production to be met and modest salaries paid, but the wars between networks to win ever-larger shares of the consuming audience would lose their point. And whole segments of the day could be free of advertising. As an absolute immediate minimum, television stations could be required to sell advertising only for nonspecific time slots, the way magazines and newspapers sell ads that are not specifically connected with particular segments of editorial content. Then at least advertisers could not withdraw advertising from specific programs and shows just because they feared adverse commercial effects from that particular program.

Or consider theater and dance. We ought to have *generous* public subsidies for such activities. Perhaps we could have drama stamps and dance vouchers, instead of vouchers for segregated schools, as some propose, and the tax deductions for business entertainment we now have. We the taxpayers now pay for business entertainment through the deductions that business executives can take for attending various events with their "clients." Every such tax deduction is a subsidy that the society now gives to business for the purpose of increasing its economic gains. A more equitable as well as culturally liberating social expenditure would make similar sums available to anyone, either through tax deductions for some level of cultural expenditures or through the public subsidy of artistic production. Similarly, we the consumers pay for the ads that assault our senses from TV screen and roadside billboard: we pay through the inflated prices for products that heavy promotional expenses require and through the tax deductions for advertising that any business can claim.[37] Imagine that businesses could no longer deduct advertising and entertainment as tax-exempt expenditures, and imagine that an equivalent sum were devoted directly to culture and entertainment, either by subsidies to the sources of these or by "culture vouchers" to citizens to spend as they pleased. The sums now bestowed on corporations through tax advantages, and spent on the "culture" of their choice, could instead go more directly into the cultural forms of citizens' choice. We might then not have to be grateful when, occasionally, an advertisement is imaginative and well designed, in the service of sales and economic gain. We could have the images and objects of our choice directly, in the service of human autonomy and aesthetic well-being.

Or consider books and records. Why do we not think of authors and musicians as important to our cultural life the way other subsidized and protected groups are thought important to our economic life? Might we not offer subsidies to bookstores in locations that might otherwise not have a bookstore, and to those who participate in such activities as poetry readings and band performances? Why is it that the closest equivalent to a cultural center that can be found in many American communities is a brand-new shopping center?

We could hope that the TV networks might evolve into institutions more like universities and museums and less like irresponsible business corporations, or that they might at least come to resemble responsible newspapers whose goal is *something* more than economic gain. The development of a professional sense among broadcasters is leading at least some persons in the industry to recognize some responsibilities for the quality of program content. Such developments, however, would be to a considerable extent beyond the reach of rights to free expression. A right to education does not amount to a right to go to Harvard, and a right to free expression, even as an enabling right, would not be a right to express oneself on NBC. But just as assuring rights to education has led to some quite adequate public alternatives to Harvard, one can suppose that public avenues of expression could come to rival the giants. Public broadcasting needs to be *vastly* expanded, both that which would be integrated with existing networks and that which would rely on independent outlets.

Instead, the Reagan administration has made clear its opposition to public broadcasting and has cut back drastically on this competition to the profit-making media. At a time when public radio was capturing attention for such professionally competent and interesting programs as "All Things Considered" and increasing listeners by 40 percent in one year, government support was cut almost in half.[38] In the resulting upheaval, national public radio was almost destroyed.[39] Because of the public outcry, funding for the National Endowment for the Arts was not cut as heavily as the new administration wanted, but its independence in awarding grants to artists and scholars who may be critical of prevailing American values and existing political economic institutions was put in question.[40] When the Chairman of the National Endowment for the Humanities (NEH) asserts that a public television documentary at odds with U.S. policy in Central America should not have been funded by NEH, those who apply for endowment funding in the future may be more cautious; "censorship" may not be necessary.

The argument is often made that government funding will lead to government control of the media. It is a legitimate concern. But when the alternative is corporate control, government funding may provide far more independence for broadcasters. Public funding for universities is compatible with academic freedom. The independence of broadcasting could be fostered by such devices as those which provide for the independence of the Federal Reserve System in the United States or for the independence of broadcasting in other countries where the heads of public media outlets are not removable by political officials. The principles of "academic" freedom could well be developed for other cultural institutions. The most important element for encouraging independence would be that independence become a standard and an aspect of the criteria by which everyone concerned with cultural expression judges everyone else. Independence from commercial control is fully as important as independence from government control. And commercial control is the current reality, whereas governmental control is a distant threat against which to be on guard.

In answering the question "Where will the money for all these cultural subsidies come from?" we need constantly to remind ourselves that the money is now already being spent by a society that expends gigantic sums on the production and promotion and distribution of entertainment. What is required is a redirection of some of what is already being spent. The question is not "How can the society afford it?" but "Who shall do the spending and for what?" The most helpful model to keep in mind may be education. A society in which education was once limited to the rich has developed a massive system of public education. A society that still limits access to expression to the corporate rich, and to those who can win their backing, could evolve a scheme of public provision of access to culture. In that way our images of the goods we wish to pursue and the lives we wish to lead could be vastly enriched.

The arguments for access that we have considered can be extended to all forms of expression, so that we could, as a society, devote greatly increased sums for painters to paint, writers to write, and entertainers to entertain, all as they and their audiences wish rather than as the business interests to whom they now must sell their services demand. Instead of being manipulated for commercial gain, our dreams of the sorts of lives we might consider good would have the chance to flourish freely and to delight us.

We can immediately spend more time *imagining* what such a cultural environment might be like and what it could offer. Fortunately, the production costs of such speculations are low. And if we can ever sell such dreams, of a culture that is not for sale, to as commercial a society as this one, perhaps *we* will have bought up rather than sold out to our competitors.

Chapter 13

The Environment
and the Future

The Wider Context

WE CANNOT MAKE sense of the idea of a state, a nation, or a given society apart from the environment in which it is located. Nor can we comprehend it apart from the future generations that will give or deny it existence or apart from the world to which it is related. Yet the realization of these obvious truths is a remarkably recent development, and moral thinking is only beginning to deal seriously and substantively with them.

A fairly widespread intuitive understanding of both the connectedness of systems and their environments and of the global nature of many problems has begun to develop among activists, journalists, and students. Many people, however, remain attached to highly unrealistic assumptions of which they are often unaware—assumptions about limitless resources that will enable them to enjoy ever-increasing material benefits.[1]

Some choices that societies make are too large to be described as legal, political, or economic. These are the sorts of choices on which historians often focus in chronicling the rise and decline of nations. They have to do with very large-scale trends or events. Often enough, they are fallen into, rather than intentionally chosen by societies. Such choices are those which a society makes with respect to its environment. If a society improves its environment by bringing some hazard under control, or ruins it through despoiling the land, this altering of the physical underpinning of the society may radically change the society's course.

Some groping attention to the empirical aspects of environmental issues is becoming apparent in various academic social science disciplines, although resistance to the kinds of conceptual change that are needed to deal with them is heavy. Hazel Henderson excoriates the discipline of economics for its slowness to recognize the inadequacy of its traditional assumptions.[2] This slowness is characteristic of most of the other social sciences as well. Henderson acknowledges that the post-Keynesians do recognize the absurdity of the traditional "invisible hand" and "free market" assumptions applied to the economies of late capitalism, dominated as these economies are by massive institutions—corporations and governmental agencies that often merely reflect corporate interests in controlling the market. But these post-Keynesians still

> obscure the need to shift direction from quantitative to qualitative growth . . . [and] fall into the same trap of defining "productivity" as only "labor productivity" . . . which is really an "automation index." . . . Only a redefinition of "productivity" that recognizes that energy and raw materials have been taken for granted and undervalued can help us see that what economists deplore as "declining labor productivity" is balanced by *other gains* we have made: in *energy* productivity (via conservation) . . . in *bio*productivity (i.e. investments in restoration of agricultural fertility, reforestation . . . and all forms of recycling).[3]

Even within the notion of *quantity* of production, the standard measures of economists are highly questionable. As Harry Magdoff, long-time critic of capitalist economics, asks, "Does an investment banker who earns $1.5 million a year floating bonds and promoting mergers produce 100 times more services than a $15,000-a-year supermarket cashier and 75 times more than a $20,000-a-year nurse?"[4] The assumption that money value—the price in the marketplace of services and goods (corrected for inflation)—is an accurate measure of even quantity produced is highly flawed. That it is a measure of quality is absurd. Yet the assumption that it measures "growth" runs through almost all existing thinking in economics, even among many who are highly critical of the way economic activity is standardly conducted.

Among politicians and their publics the needed changes of approach are only occasionally beginning to dawn. Environmental protection, however, is an issue that gathers very widespread support, and this development is encouraging. Although corporate groups often succeed in promoting their interests over those of the electorate and in dominating governmental policy or the decisions of governmental agencies, the long-range concern with environmental sanity can be expected to grow. The shift away from nuclear energy may be an example of how an aroused citizenry can cause changes for which corporations and governmental bureaucracies are not yet ready. Nuclear power was celebrated only a few years ago as the hope of the future: cheap, safe, clean. Today, with an awareness of the high risk of accident, of the disastrous possibilities of technical failures, of the problems of disposing of nuclear wastes that will remain radioactive for thousands of years, virtually no new nuclear plants are being planned and many of even those now under construction may never open.[5] Nuclear power is no longer thought of as a solution, but at best as a way of coping with shortages in a transitional period during which widespread conversion to the use of renewable sources of energy ought to take place.[6]

Corporate interests and their supporters in government continue to dismiss renewable sources of energy as marginal. The development of various forms of renewable energy will require large-scale social support.[7] But the development of other fuels that we are depleting and that, once used up, will be gone, has cost massive sums in governmental support. Hazel Henderson writes:

> Since 1918, the federal government has expended between $123 billion and $133 billion to stimulate coal, oil, gas, hydro, and nuclear production. Yet we are asked to believe that new forms of energy such as solar, wind, bioconversion, and others must "compete in the free market" with all the historically subsidized energy supplies.

As Ronald Doctor, commissioner of the California State Energy Commission, stated, "If solar energy is to compete with conventional forms of energy it will have to be subsidized. These subsidies should not be viewed as handouts; but rather as equalization mechanisms."[9] He thinks the subsidies made to other forms of energy has already been closer to $300 billion.

How an industrial society supplies itself with and uses energy is an example of a choice a society must make, whether consciously or accidentally. Consider the question of how resources are to be developed. Are private, profit-seeking enterprises to be accorded the right to find oil, exploit it, and sell it for as much private gain as possible? Or should the institutions that deplete the irreplaceable natural resources of a nation be accountable to the public and subject to public control? The choice in the United States has been for private ownership of oil companies; in various other countries it has been for government control. In practice, the results of both approaches have often been surprisingly similar. [10]

The relevant issues are apt to be whether the interest of the oil-producing enterprise—whether state-owned or privately owned—should be given free rein or whether the interests of the society as a whole should have priority at every stage. It will be in the interest of an oil producer to encourage consumption, for instance, no matter how wasteful, but it will not be in the interest of a society, over the long run, to have its scarce resources exhausted more quickly than necessary. It may also not be in the long-run interest of a corporation or governmental agency, but short-run views are likely to predominate. Thus a society may have to prevail upon the enterprises within it to act on even their own longer-range rather than more immediate interests.

The Moral Framework

How should such issues be considered? It would seem reasonable to begin with the framework developed in this book, the framework of rights and obligations on the one hand and of interest maximization on the other. We can ask whether citizens have rights to energy in any given amount. They would seem to have rights to a supply of moderate amounts to satisfy basic needs in a society able to provide this. They would not seem to have rights beyond this, though they certainly might have interests in ample and inexpensive supplies. The rights and interests of citizens should be considered within the constraints imposed by their obligations to the natural environment itself and in conjunction with a recognition of the rights and interests of other persons in the world.

It is sometimes claimed that allowing large profits for successful exploration is the best, because the most effective, way to assure the new discoveries that are needed for a continuing supply. The evidence suggests that state-owned and state-run enterprises are capable of having incentives to drill and discover. Officials of state-owned industries enjoy success as do those of privately owned industries. But if either approach is adequate to produce enough to fulfill the claims of rights, and if the society assures by its other decisions that these rights are to be honored, then what about the satisfaction of interests? The approach that best maximizes the long-range interests of all those affected may be the most justifiable. Adopting such an approach will require very profound changes in the ways most countries have so far developed and managed their production and distribution of energy. The changes needed in the ways the United States has produced and consumed energy are radical and profound.[11]

In these and many other ways, mature industrial societies will have to change from ones in which resources are squandered, people are displaced thoughtlessly from jobs by technological innovations, and the environment is despoiled for short-term convenience. Societies need to be guided in the decisions of their businesses, governmental units, and citizens by a complex, adequate, and appropriately structured range of values, and not primarily by narrowly economic ones. The choices to be made are through and through normative.

Philosophers in recent years have begun to pay attention to such questions as : what are our obligations, if any, to nature? to other species? to future generations of human beings? They have explored some aspects of the problems of depleting nonrenewable resources such as oil, of producing pollutants that will poison the environment for many centuries into the future, and of causing vast numbers of natural species to become extinct. Although the best-known philosophic works of recent years have hardly touched on these issues, other philosophers have made efforts to deal with some of them, and with the issues of war and peace, our relations to other states and societies, and the imperatives of a more fair and beneficial international economic order.

The moral theory appealed to in these discussions has often been somewhat arbitrarily enlisted, depending on the proclivities of the philosopher who happened to be dealing with whatever problem was under discussion. What such problems themselves seem to indicate is that we need in these newer, more interrelated contexts, even more than in the worked-out contexts of, say, the law of a given state, more interrelated moral theories. A focus on rights will not be adequate for many environmental issues, but a utilitarian calculation of benefits will be inappropriate for many others. We need growing respect for and implementation of an adequate set of basic human rights for each individual. We also need ways of weighing the costs and benefits of alternative programs to control pollution, decrease disease and discomfort, and improve the quality of life and the satisfactions of life for all people. And we need to understand our responsibilities toward the rest of the natural universe, instead of thinking only of "man." The ways in which these various inquiries should be connected to one another is itself another important question.

How the moral approaches we have looked at so far should be developed for these contexts can only be suggested in broad outline at this point. I will focus in this chapter on one question among the range mentioned: on what grounds can we assert, against those who dispute it, that we do indeed have obligations to generations of persons not yet born? And what are some of these obligations?

Future Persons

Why, it may be asked, should we concern ourselves with the problems of persons who may be born hundreds of years from now rather than considering only our own satisfactions? If it suits us to squander resources, produce massive pollution, and destroy other species, why should we care how this will affect persons who do not even exist?

There are analogues here to the problems of egoism, but serious differences make it more difficult to argue for responsibilities to future generations than for responsibilities to other existing human beings. With regard to our contemporaries, we can see that if we do not restrain our egoism, we may *suffer* unfortunate consequences as well as cause them. In the case of distant future generations, however, we need fear no harm from them. And yet we ought to have regard for the persons who will exist in such generations.

As Mary Anne Warren, a philosopher dealing with the problem of our regard for future generations, writes, "It seems only reasonable to believe that we have a moral obligation not to leave our successors a severely impoverished world, one with exhausted resources, poisoned lands and waters, and no escape from poverty for huge numbers of people."[12] But the question remains: *why* would it be unreasonable to disregard future generations?

Let us consider whether our standard moral thinking about rights and obligations—thinking widely shared by many responsible persons—can be applied to issues of environmental concern and future populations. If such thinking can be applied, it will be a fortunate accident, since we certainly need all the help we can get from moral arguments—standard and otherwise—and these theories were not developed with an adequate awareness of the problems of future generations and their environment, problems to which the theories may now be applied by some persons.

In a paper on these issues, Douglas MacLean draws a line around a rather narrow group of what he calls "standard moral theories" and shows how they cannot do what he thinks we can all agree needs to be done in thinking about future generations and our environment. [13] As I have shown in this book, I share some of his dissatisfaction with standard moral theories, but I think that some of them, with modest revisions, are more helpful than he suggests in enabling us to deal with these issues.

MacLean considers as standard moral theories those he can cover by the phrase "utilitarianism and its critics." The deficiencies of utilitarianism for dealing with a whole range of moral issues I have already affirmed, though I have also pointed out the suitability of utilitarian arguments for dealing with another range of issues, those of some public, political decisions *once* rights have been respected for other reasons. But what about the theories of the critics of utilitarianism? Not all of them, I think, share the limitations ascribed to them by MacLean. He dismisses the entire framework of rights and obligations because, he says, rights must be the rights of individuals, and "justice" is not an issue between us and future generations.

"A possible person," he writes, "is not wronged or treated unfairly if left unconceived; no lack of respect is shown. . . . Nonexistence does not give rise to claims of injustice."[14] And so, in MacLean's view, we would not violate any rights if we chose not to bring *any* future persons into existence, or if we poison the environment or deplete the resources of those who may exist, because persons cannot have rights until they exist, and only persons have rights. This is a view shared by many, though I think it is mistaken.

Because of this argument, MacLean finds deontological interpretations of rights and obligations to be incapable of dealing with the issues of future generations. He tries to find, within an alternative framework, the arguments he seeks.

I agree with MacLean that the fact that we may enjoy having a concern for our descendants in the way that we may enjoy acquiring a new car or eating a gourmet meal is an entirely unsatisfactory basis on which to rest our concern for the future of humanity. I don't agree that cost-benefit analyses *must* be limited to calculations of these sorts of values; that they have been is a reflection of the uses and misuses to which such techniques can be put rather than of the faultiness of the techniques themselves.

I would, however, go further than MacLean: not only should the future of humanity not rest on such "phenomenal" values, as he calls them; it should not rest on what he calls "extra-phenomenal" values either. "Extra-phenomenal" values, in MacLean's terminology, are interests that cannot be reduced to what we consume and get satisfaction from. "Our friends, our reputations, and our cultural heritage," he writes, "are examples of extra-phenomenal values. . . . We value our extra-phenomenal interests for the way they make our lives meaningful, not for the way they make us happy."[15] Our interest in posterity is, in MacLean's view, this kind of interest.

In my view, however, we ought to be concerned about future generations not for our sake but for theirs. We might recall at this point an earlier dispute over why we ought to avoid causing gratuitous pain to animals. One school of thought held that the reason we should not be cruel to animals was that it would damage us—our sensitivities, our relations among ourselves, and so on. On this view, cruelty to animals is bad for people, and hence we should not be cruel to animals. MacLean's argument seems to be analogous. Being oblivious to future generations, he says, in effect, is bad for *us*, "it diminishes the meaningfulness of our lives,"[16] as he puts it, and hence we should not be oblivious to future generations. But critics of the former view concerning animals have asserted that the reason we should not be cruel to animals is not that it is bad for *us*, but that it is bad for the animals. And I think almost everyone now agrees. Even if, they might add, some strange psychological mechanism brought it about that causing gratuitous pain to animals would make *us* into better persons, there would still be an at least prima facie reason *not* to be cruel to animals. Similarly, the reason we should concern ourselves with the future of humanity is not that failing to do so will be bad for us, but that it may be disastrous for those future generations. And the case is much more clear for future *persons* than for present animals.

Our concerns for other persons seem to be at present in a highly discouraging state. There is great stinginess, for instance, toward the poor in other countries. A great many Americans begrudge the trifling sums expended on foreign economic aid—less than one-fifth of 1 percent of our output.[17] And they even begrudge social programs for the less fortunate among their fellow citizens. But MacLean's argument does not depend on the values most of us *in fact* recognize, any more than the argument I shall try to develop will rest on the *obligations* most of us, *in fact*, recognize. Still, I think we should hesitate to postulate what extra-phenomenal values future generations will have. We should be cautious in trying to guess the preferences for goods that are good in themselves of different groups of human beings several hundred years from now. The visions of the good life they develop may well be unimaginable to us. I would hope and expect that these visions of the good life would have a great deal more affinity with the values of nurturing and tenderness than have the public values now dominant in *any* existing society. Even within our own generation we should rarely choose visions of the good life for others, but should primarily respect their rights to be in a position to choose for themselves.

The distinction between obligations and rights on the one hand and preferences, interests, and values (of whatever kind) on the other is, I think, as useful for thinking about future generations as it is for thinking about our own moral problems. We can respect the rights of future generations to basic necessities and to an environment that will not cause them significant harm. But we should hesitate to choose for them the values (MacLean would call them extra-phenomenal values) that will compose for them the good life over and above the requirements of human rights, including rights to sustenance.

If we do not accept an argument in terms of values, does that mean that we are left with *no* basis for moral arguments that we ought to provide for the continued existence of humanity, that this existence ought to be a humanly decent existence, with adequate minimums of energy and food, and that we ought to avoid causing major harm to those who will inherit our polluted planet? I do not think so.

Many writers on future generations emphasize the rights side of the deontological framework of rights and obligations. We can agree, I think, that it is part of the logic of rights and obligations that (with perhaps a few exceptions) if one person has a right, others have corresponding obligations and that these can both be understood—if either can—quite apart from any utilitarian considerations.

To look at the alternatives to utilitarianism or to MacLean's approach with regard to issues of future generations, we might do better to look first to our ideas about *our obligations*, rather than to our ideas about the *rights* of the members of future generations. Can we perhaps have obligations without others having corresponding rights?

Obligations to Humanity

Let's consider first to whom or to what sorts of entities we have obligations and whether obligations are always *to* someone or something. We can recognize that we have obligations not to blow up the pyramids and not to despoil the Grand Canyon. How can this be? It is not because pyramids and canyons have rights, nor because the rights of other human beings include our not depriving them of the enjoyment of the pyramids and the Grand Canyon. It seems to be because the obligations of human beings are wider than the rights of those entities to whom these obligations are owed, if they are "owed" to anyone. It may be more satisfactory to suppose that these obligations are not owed *to* any person or things, and yet that they are obligations.

Jan Narveson asserts that "duties which are not owed to anybody stick in the conceptual throat."[18] They do not seem conceptually unpalatable to me. Perhaps the resistance some may feel toward them results from the excessive connections past notions of duty (and obligation) have had with notions of property. For Hume, justice was almost exclusively concerned with property. For many others, duties are duties to pay money, honor debts, and leave other people's property alone. These kinds of duties are always seen as duties *to* someone. Obligations are "owed" to someone. And duties other than economic ones are construed on the economic model or by analogy with a monetary kind of "owing." But this does not mean duties and obligations ought to be so construed.

Recognizing our duties to future generations may lead us to the conclusion that duties are not always *to* someone. This may be a better view than the view that, because in our familiar conceptual scheme duties must be *to* someone, we have no duties to future generations.

That we have obligations not to blow up the pyramids or the Grand Canyon and that we have obligations to future generations can be asserted without any appeal to utilitarianism or preferences or average (or any other kind of) utility or even to what MacLean calls extra-phenomenal teleological values. Obligations, like rights, ought to be respected for their own sakes, quite apart from any *consequences* respecting them may have. We can understand this in understanding the relevant moral principles from which obligations and rights can be derived.

We can begin with the presumption that of course we have obligations to humanity, and we can reject any moral theory that makes it impossible for us to maintain this. Much of the confusion and worry about this issue arises, I think, because we are reluctant to recognize that if this is an obligation *to* anyone, it is to humanity as a *collective* entity, not to *individual* possible persons. Many of the conceptual puzzles that have developed around the notion of our obligations to future generations may be due to the excessive nominalism with which our arguments have usually been developed.[19] We may have to admit that utilitarianism can only deal with the utilities of individual persons and will inevitably be saddled with problems of possible people. But that the principles of freedom, equality, and justice yielding rights and obligations must presuppose that only *individual actual persons* can have rights and obligations need not at all be accepted. And if we grow up from the excessive nominalism of our youthful understanding of such principles, we can, I think, understand our obligations to future generations in a much more satisfactory way.

We have obligations to the collective entity that is humanity not to bring about the termination of its existence. Killing everyone, or letting humanity die by failing to reproduce, would bring an end to humanity. We have obligations as individuals to bring about social institutions that will prevent nuclear war, the murder of everyone, and the death of everyone by starvation. We have obligations to bring about the existence of future generations.

Jonathan Bennett argues that our attitude of holding that there ought to be future generations is based on the strong preference many of us have to see the human adventure continued. In his view, it cannot be based on the happiness of nonexistent people since the notion of "amounts of possibly unowned happiness"[20] makes no sense. Trying to assure that there will be future generations is thus, according to Bennett, not a moral obligation, but the expression of our preference. This interpretation is unsatisfactory. We can easily imagine, if we do not already know several cases of such attitudes, that existing persons will cease to prefer to see the human adventure continued. They might like to see the story end. They might prefer that humanity adopt a maximin policy and "quit while it is ahead" or end its existence for some such reason as to avoid the increased pain they consider probable. We could still argue against such persons that they have obligations to let future generations make the decision of how to live or end their lives for themselves. Any generation might, justifiably I think, decide to permit the suicide of individual members among it but to restrict this permission if it threatened to engulf the whole of humanity. Because such an argument would have to be recognized by anyone as at least plausible, it indicates that our obligations to future generations as collective entities are different from our obligation, or lack of obligation, to individual possible members of such generations and that the lack of the latter sort of obligation does not amount to the lack of the former sort.

The best way to bring about future generations is to create conditions in which persons will want to have an appropriate number of children. Given individuals do not have obligations to have a given number of children, but ought to contribute to those conditions in which those who want to have children can have them and in which people will not want too many children. If not enough people want children to assure the existence of future generations, we may have specific obligations to have children. We should not create more people than we can respect the rights of; if too many people want too many children, we may have specific obligations to refrain from having children, and to bring about conditions in which too many children will not be born. Among the best ways to limit population are to raise the standard of living of the poor and improve the status of women.[21]

Our obligations concerning original existence are to humanity collectively, rather than to specific individuals. No *specific potential person* has a right to be brought into existence. To suppose such a nonexistent entity has a right to become actual makes no sense, even to a utilitarian. As Jan Narveson has said, "non-existence . . . is not a property of individuals."[22] Individual rights to exist *presuppose* the existence of persons. They do not give specific persons rights to come into existence, though they do give already existing persons rights to continue to exist and other kinds of basic human rights.

The Rights of Collectivities

If we have obligations to humanity collectively, to bring about its continued existence, and perhaps also to such lesser groups within it as our fellow nationals or conceivably the ethnic group to which we belong or the family or clan of which we are a member, can such groups then have *rights*? Does humanity have a *right* to continue to exist? Does France? Do the Jews? Does the Kennedy family? We are understandably suspicious of answering yes to some or all of these questions. We value individuals, we are fearful of anything that might require flesh-and-blood individuals to be sacrificed to the good of the collectivity. Our history makes these fears understandable, and many persons may therefore agree too hastily with the view that rights are always the rights of individuals. And they may fail to object when philosophers assert that there is no need to posit the existence of collective entities such as the state, the corporation, the church, because they are all composed of actual individual persons.

In Joel Feinberg's view, when we speak loosely of the rights and obligations of such collective entities, we are speaking of what can always be analyzed into the rights and obligations of actual persons acting in some official capacity.[23]

I have argued against this view. That it is particularly unsuitable in the case of future generations lends further support to the position I have defended. It seems quite appropriate and perhaps morally necessary to say that collective entities have rights and obligations in ways not reducible to the rights and obligations of actual individuals. (See chapter 14.) If we are ever to imagine that nation-states are *anything* other than the products of pure coercive power, we must be able to make some sense of the claim that various peoples as collective entities have rights to self-determination. Of course, it may be extremely difficult to specify what may be meant by this right and which groups have it, but the right presupposes the existence of a collectivity not reducible to its actual individual members at any given time. And if we are going to deal at all adequately with the problems of future generations, we are going to have to be able to say such things as that the United States as a collective entity has the prima facie obligation not to dispose of nuclear wastes in such a way as to cause dangerous levels of radiation that will significantly shorten the lives of persons living in the twenty-second century. And we are going to have to say that those persons will have a collective right not to have this happen. If such persons have rights to exist in the first place, this is a collective right. *Once* they exist, they have moral rights of a kind *any* existing person has. These include rights to have their basic needs met.[24] And among these moral rights will be individual rights and also collective rights.

In recognizing that collectivities can have rights and obligations, it may be helpful to recognize that *individuals*, as they figure in our moral theories, are often as much abstractions as are collectivities. The *person* equal before the law is a legal fiction. Rawls's individuals in the original position are theoretical fictions. Many moral theorists would hold that in these contexts we can see the good reasons for abstraction. But recognizing the reality of such collective entities as corporations and nations may not be more difficult or problematic than recognizing the relevance of unreal individuals.

We may already have doubts about the fantastical aspects of the original position. The argument from what we would do in an original position to what we ought to do here and now is highly tenuous. (See chapter 4.) We could suppose that the beings in the original position are all persons throughout time rather than only all those up to a given time in history.[25] But the further complications of thinking of the hypothetical persons in the original position as including persons who will be the members of future generations give us even stronger reasons than before to choose as our starting point the situation where we are here and now, *rather than* the original position. If we can construct prin-

ciples of liberty, equality, justice, and mutual concern from the starting point of where we are (see chapters 7–11), as I think we can, we will
have much more powerful reasons for acting in accordance with these
principles than if they are valid only for persons from a hypothetical position amended to be even more fully hypothetical by including everyone who will ever exist. In any case, what we will get will be a proposed
scheme of rights and obligations specifying basic moral requirements
and human rights for any person at any time, although how these rights
should be interpreted will depend on where in history their implementation can be located.[26]

Morality and Contracts

Consideration of the issues surrounding future generations has important implications for the grounds of morality. A long tradition, from
Hobbes and Hume to various contemporary philosophers, has seen the
foundation of morality, and especially the foundation of rights and obligations, to be a contract between individuals. Without such a contract, the individuals are thought likely to exercise their power to harm
one another. As Brian Barry notes, it is "surprising to realize that a variety of commonly held views about the basis of morality seem to entail
that the absence of reciprocal power relations eliminates the possibility
of our having moral obligations (or at any rate obligations of justice) to
our successors."[27]

If we notice that the members of distant future generations have no
power to hurt us, we can see—if we hold that we have obligations toward them—that morality must not rest on this capacity to cause reciprocal harm. In my view, morality cannot adequately be based on any
compact, no matter how fundamental, if this implies we have no obligations to those outside it. As Gregory Vlastos has put it,

> My obligations to others are independent of their moral merit. To be sin-
> cere, reliable, fair, kind, tolerant, unintrusive, modest in my relations
> with my fellows is not due them because they have made brilliant or even
> passing moral grades, but simply because they happen to be fellow-
> members of the moral community. It is not necessary to add, "members
> in good standing." The moral community is not a club from which mem-
> bers may be dropped for delinquency. . . . One has no right to be cruel to
> a cruel person.[28]

We can recognize that all human beings have rights to be treated
with the respect due human beings, even if they do not yet agree and

even if we have no social contract between us. That we do recognize obligations to future generations is yet another reason to reject the view that morality, and our rights and obligations, rests on contractual relations.

Brian Barry thinks that in the end we must fall back on notions such as "cosmic impertinence"[29] to explain why we should not choose to put an end to humanity. I would hope that we could see the point of honoring our obligations toward future generations for many of the same reasons that we should respect the rights of present persons. The gross disparity of power that exists, such that we can affect the lives of future generations but they cannot affect ours, does indeed make trouble for those theories which try to ground rights and obligations on no more than a contractual relation between self-interested seekers of advantage. But such theories are already in trouble as grounds for the rights of present people, as some of us have been pointing out for some time. Disparities of power already exist on a massive scale between the rich nations and the poor, between powerful classes and the exploited, between men and women, between adults and children. We ought to honor our obligations toward persons and respect their human rights even though they *lack* the power to make us uncomfortable. It is not much more difficult to argue that we ought to respect the human rights of those persons who will exist in generations to come.

We are still left, after all this, with the problem of weighing the *utilities* of future generations, *after* we have respected their rights, against the utilities of currently existing people, *after* we have respected their rights, but this question is of secondary importance compared with the question on which I have tried to focus. At least it is of secondary importance if one is not a thoroughgoing utilitarian, which is yet another reason not to be one. To sum up: we have obligations to bring about the continuing existence of humanity, and we ought to create the conditions in which the rights of the human beings who will exist can have been respected by us.

Chapter 14

The International
Context

UNLESS WE SUCCEED in preserving a substantial level of world order and global tranquility, there will be no future generations to whom we have obligations. The threat of nuclear holocaust hangs over us all. The dangers inherent in all breakdowns of peace are enormous. Threats to peace from existing conflicts between major powers can easily lead to conflagration. And disaster may come when advanced societies try to preserve their privileged positions against pressures throughout the globe from those whose survival depends on a changed economic order. The position of the majority of the members of mature industrial societies in relation to most of the world's inhabitants is somewhat analogous to that of the French aristocracy before the French Revolution. Unless ways are found to transform the existing distribution of economic power into more just and equitable forms, upheavals can be expected. The fallout of such upheavals, as well as of armed conflict between advanced industrial nations, may leave no one even to debate the justifiability of the destruction caused by such conflicts or to defend the principles supposedly at stake in them. We have responsibilities now to debate how we ought to pursue the achievement of a new and more fair global order and how we ought to uphold such principles as those which condemn armed aggression and the slaughter of the innocent.

Morality and International Affairs

In considering the ways in which it may or may not be justifiable to apply moral arguments to relations between nations, we need to examine the special aspects of this context. It has sometimes been claimed that there can be no moral principles or values that transcend given cultures or nations and that morality is simply inappropriate in the context of international relations.[1] Such a view is based on a misunderstanding of morality, seeing it as no more than an inapplicable ideal or set of ideals. As I have argued in this book, a moral theory that fails to be applicable to such problems as those arising in relations between states is unsatisfactory. The moral theories we ought to be developing will have to be able to address such actual problems.

To be an outstanding moral philosopher, however, may not be of great help in dealing with the dilemmas of international affairs. One must also have a more immediate sense of the realities than most philosophers have. That is, one needs both a wide knowledge of actual cases and a sound grasp of empirical generalizations concerning the effects of different behavior on the conduct of international affairs. In addition, one must have the kind of "good judgment" that no amount of purely academic and theoretical work is likely to produce. One should have had, if not firsthand experience, at least close contact with those engaged in the practical activity of guiding nations away from mutual destruction and toward the ties that, however feebly, cross national boundaries.

Stanley Hoffmann has explored the moral issues involved in relations between nations in an important book, *Duties Beyond Borders*.[2] The book is full of the sort of sound and sensible observations and relatively low-level generalizations that are needed to deal with questions concerning the morality of states. He has at his command an impressive array of examples about which many readers will trust his judgment on the basis of articles of his they have already read.[3] He provides valuable suggestions and reasons for the sorts of middle-level principles one should consider. However, Hoffmann does not suggest how one might put the various elements he considers together into a theoretical system that would enable us to be well guided in other and in future cases. Yet this is clearly what we need. We require some assumptions about moral theory at a high level of generality, and in addition a coherent scheme of intermediate-level principles about international affairs together with guidelines for handling conflicts between principles.[4] These intermediate principles should be concerned with human rights, the justifiability (or nonjustifiability) of the nation-state, and the morally acceptable behavior of states both at a domestic level and in their relationships with one another. In addition, we need a large number of cases with which to draw out and test these principles. Finally, we need a methodology for determining when such a theory of international morality is adequate and how and when it ought to be revised.

Hoffmann correctly senses that neither a thoroughgoing deontological ethics nor a thoroughgoing consequentialism will be adequate for dealing with the moral problems of foreign affairs.[5] To his credit, he trusts his own moral intuitions rather than misguided but more consistent theories at either of these philosophical poles. However, he offers little beyond the suggestion that one should approach the problems with some insights from an "ethics of conviction" and some from an "ethics of consequences."[6]

What we need are some guidelines suggesting to us in convincing ways when a particular approach should be used and which approach should have priority for given kinds of contexts. The possibility that one should, for instance, take a more deontological approach toward issues of human rights, and a more consequentialist approach toward commercial issues, should be considered. The positions for which I have argued in chapters 7 and 10 suggest that there are good reasons to do so. The question of how one should think about, if not calculate, one's interests in such consequences as establishing a scheme of rights in which one could think deontologically about the human worth of each individual should also be considered. This is the sort of framework of progress toward a morally acceptable world that must be appealed to in place of the ideal theories that do not connect with the world as it is (see chapters 4 and 5) and instead of the dismissal of morality as inapplicable. It is the kind of framework I have tried to develop in this book.

Hoffmann recognizes that theories such as John Rawls's theory of justice are too hypothetical to offer much guidance to foreign policymakers.[7] Other commentators have made similar arguments.[8] But the conclusion should not be that philosophy and moral theory are dispensable, as some suppose. Rather, it should be that we must develop philosophical and moral theories more relevant than ideal theories to the actual problems encountered by real people.

Can Nations Be Moral?

Can one demand that states consider the interests of other states along with their own "national interest"? Can one expect them to take seriously international rules of behavior, such as those in the U.N. Charter? Hoffmann rightly opposes the position that morality simply does not apply in international relations. But he himself falls into some of the misrepresentations that led many others to the position he attacks.

He rejects a dichotomy between the appropriateness of morally judging the domestic behavior of a government toward its citizens and the complete inappropriateness of morally judging relations between states. But he exaggerates the contrast between domestic issues and international ones. In his view, states at the domestic level can enjoy a consensus of values, while there is nothing remotely comparable at the international level. He depicts states (at least liberal ones) as not using force against their citizens because their existence rests on their citizens' willing accord, whereas states in relation to other states must see force as continuously at issue. "International order," Hoffmann writes, "has to be established or defended every minute, whereas domestic order is given, and already reflects a conception of justice."[9]

In truth, the contrast is not as sharp as many believe. Some states have a revolutionary or prerevolutionary domestic situation analogous to the fractious and hostile international scene. The stable domestic order of other nations might be compared to stable interstate relations such as those between the United States and Canada.[10] Moreover, we should not underestimate the extent to which the "stability" of domestic societies, even those we admire, is the product of the forcible imposition of class and other interests on those with little power. We should not confuse the state's monopoly on the use of force at home with the absence of force in the relations between the rulers and the ruled. In addition, we should not forget the extent to which privileged nations employ force in the international arena to avoid having to share their wealth with other nations. The problem is not so much an absence of shared values—all agree that human life has worth and that adequate food is needed for life—but an absence of willingness to do what these values would require. Refusal to apply international principles of justice rests far more on brute force than on any more legitimate foundations.[11] The parallels between the moral arguments for greater justice at an interstate and at a domestic level are often more enlightening than are any insights gained from emphasizing the differences.

Another contrast that is sometimes exaggerated is that between the relative assurance and better knowledge of the facts with which we can make moral judgments at the domestic level, on the one hand, and the obscurity in which the representatives of nations must act, on the other. "Far more than domestic statecraft, international statecraft is statecraft in the dark," Hoffmann asserts.[12] But, for example, both the short-term and long-term environmental consequences from what might be considered routine operations of domestic business are often obscure and incalculable. In contrast, all agree that the consequences of nuclear war would be appalling.

An individual who must decide whether to join a revolution or to oppose it is faced with many of the same conflicts of values and rights than complicate moral judgments in an international context. Yet judgments concerning the moral justifiability of revolutions, and the weighing of their costs against their potential benefits, can and must be made. [13]

The Moral Foundations of Government

The fundamental arguments of social and political philosophy are more applicable to international affairs than many of those writing on international affairs acknowledge. If one asks what would justify the renunciation by persons of their capacity to use force to preserve their own lives, some will offer traditional Hobbesian responses concerning the obligations of governments to their citizens. Even with no more appeal to morality or to the grounds for social trust than this, one can argue for certain positions. The citizen agrees to renounce the use of force against fellow citizens; at the same time, the government is bound to "keep the peace" and to protect the lives of citizens. [14] In the eighteenth century, as such arguments entered the common background of democratic theory, such protection was understood largely in terms of protecting the citizen from attack. The citizen (thought of as a male head of household) was presumed to be able to acquire what he needed to feed, clothe, and shelter himself. [15] Twentieth-century interpretations, almost everywhere except in U.S. constitutional law and among some conservatives, include among the obligations of governments the requirement that government assure its citizens that they will be able to obtain the basic necessities without which they cannot live. [16] This modern view suggests that the citizen ought to renounce the use of force against other citizens if the government effectively provides respect for basic rights, including economic and social rights.

At the domestic level, the application of this argument, especially in the United States, is not as widely recognized as one might imagine. However, it is still a consequence of this view that if the government does not provide its citizens with the means to obtain what is needed to live, the citizens have no obligation to treat those who benefit from this denial with the respect that would otherwise be owed one group of citizens by another.

Comparable arguments can well be made at an international level, where a Hobbesian "state of nature" may be less hypothetical construct than model of much of reality. Members of the world domain—whether it is seen as a kind of "state of nature" or as a kind of incipient "community"—would be under a similar obligation to refrain from the use of force if there were some comparable grounds for this obligation. To be sure, this does not require a world government to provide the assurances that a national government provides its citizens. Yet, if the rules of international behavior do assure persons the means to live, this might very well lead to an obligation to refrain from the use of force. The rules, however, would have to assure much more than "peace" in the sense of security from attack. They would also have to assure *access* to the means to live.[17] The argument that the poor of the world morally ought to refrain from the use of force against the rich will only be valid if the rich do make it possible for the poor to acquire what they need. Peace is thus intimately tied to social justice.

Moral theories applied to this and other international issues suggest guidelines for determining when the use of force may or may not be justifiable and what limitations on its use are required by morality.[18] Although violence should be avoided under almost all conditions, it is primarily the responsibility of those in positions of power to bring it about that the conditions under which the use of violence might be justified do not arise. Unfortunately, of many existing international conditions, it cannot be said that there are no excuses for violence. It should be possible to say that there are always more effective and morally better ways than the use of violence to make progress toward the respect for human rights, including the right to peace, which ought to prevail.[19]

Recent years have made clear that human rights, when adequately understood to include economic and social rights along with civil and political ones, are by no means merely a "Western" concern.[20] Progress in respecting them will require a greatly increased willingness on the part of powerful nations to refrain from the use of force. And it will require adherence to international standards that can stand above sovereign self-interest.

The record of the United States in both regards must disturb conscientious persons. Its use of force and intervention in Southeast Asia and elsewhere has been morally abhorrent.[21] It has ratified neither the Universal Declaration of Human Rights nor its covenants nor even the convention banning genocide.[22]

This is not to say that the record of many other nations is superior or to deny that the record of many is worse. For instance, the United Nations has been "unable to persuade rich countries to contribute even three-quarters of one percent of their gross products to international development efforts."[23] But we must all have special concern for the irresponsibilities of the nations of which we are part.[24]

Surveying the appropriate place of attention to human rights in the conduct of foreign policy, Richard Falk suggests that "dealing with the dangers and contradictions of the state system ultimately involves moving toward some kind of more integrated form of world order. . . . The most critical foundation for such an evolution is the growth of sentiments and attitudes of human solidarity. . . . Such a prospect seems intimately connected with deepening the sensitivity of peoples everywhere to human rights issues."[25]

The United States made some progress in the early years of the Carter administration in incorporating a concern for human rights into its foreign policy. But the Reagan administration has reverted to the more established U.S. tendency to use the human rights issue selectively, denouncing Communist repression while ignoring the issues of economic and social rights altogether and overlooking violations of civil and political rights among countries "friendly" to the United States.[26] A sincere and determined respect for human rights is one of the clearest demands of morality in the context of international affairs.

The Rights of Individuals and States

A large and difficult question is whether our moral responsibilities are to others as individuals or to other states. In considering these questions, we need a sound understanding of the realities of national sentiment and the degree to which the nation-state is a morally important entity. To argue that our obligations are to individuals only, and that the principles of justice must be universally applied regardless of whether national governments agree, is to overlook the implications that follow from certain strong moral assumptions applicable to questions of nationhood.

To provide a moral foundation for arguments concerning international morality, one might have to acknowledge that among the individual rights that one must recognize is the right to form collective entities such as nations. Then, our obligations are obligations, in part, to other states, and not only to the individuals within them. The right to form a collectivity can lead to the creation of an entity that is then not reducible to the particular persons composing it at any given time. And there may be a sense, only hinted at by those who write on international affairs and much in need of further exploration, in which a state need not "justify" its existence any more than a human being need "justify" his or her existence. Once a human being is born, that human being is a bearer of rights, among which is the right to live. Similarly, once a nation-state exists, it bears rights at the international level. Among these rights is, perhaps, the right to continue to exist unless the members who form the collectivity decide otherwise. Thus, although a state may legitimately be restrained from without to assure respect for the rights of other states, and destroyed from within by the choice of its own members, others have no right to deprive it of existence—either by attack or by depriving its citizens of their basic human rights such as their rights to subsistence.

We should not be misled by philosophical analyses into thinking that only individuals can have rights.[27] Ordinary discourse in which nations are described as acting and reacting as they invade, or bomb or negotiate or propose or sign treaties, is not mere metaphor. Nations exist and can act and decide in ways not reducible to the actions of their individual members.[28] And discourse about the rights of such entities makes perfectly good sense. Solid philosophical defenses of the capacities of collective entities to act and to have rights and to be responsible can well be given.[29]

Consider the notion of a group right. I have argued that rights to basic necessities should be seen as individual rights rather than merely as rights that persons have because of their membership in such a group as that of the least advantaged (see chapter 8). But consider now some benefit that government provides to which persons as individuals do not have a right, but the provision of which is justifiable on the grounds that it does increase general utility. For instance, governmental decisions concerning tax deductions often benefit people above a level that could be described as providing for basic necessities and for what is needed for a decent life. Some publicly assisted housing could clearly be a benefit above a level to which citizens have rights. But now consider what we would conclude if almost all of those benefiting from the provision were white and if, although blacks would gain as much utility from the provision as whites, blacks were almost never the beneficiaries of it because of the locations of the benefits provided. We could at this point say that the rights of blacks to be treated fairly as a group were being denied. We can ask that governmental programs treat groups fairly even when individuals are not entitled by right to the benefit provided by the program, and even when we should not try to specify which individuals in those groups could or should benefit.

It is far easier to argue that a nation, organized as it is into a collectivity capable of decision and action, has rights. Nations can respect one another's rights or violate and disregard them. Nations can assert their rights and strive to have them respected. These are not misleading ways of speaking but reasonable ways of representing the moral issues.

Nations can also be deemed responsible for their actions and failures to act.[30] If we were not able to make such claims our discourse about the immorality and moral responsibility of nations would be unnecessarily impoverished. Nations would be able to escape judgment more easily than otherwise, although it is the very desire to "hold someone responsible" that often leads people to suppose that only persons and not collective entities can act and be responsible. Of course, we can and should *also* judge the individuals who act in behalf of nations. From judgments about the rights and responsibilities of collective entities we cannot deduce judgments about the rights and responsibilities of their individual members because the structures of roles within such entities provide some members with very different positions than others in which to act and decide and affect what a nation does. We cannot say that because the United States bombed Hanoi at Christmas in 1972, every individual American citizen did so. We can hold individual citizens responsible for electing and supporting the governments they do. And we can hold governmental officials responsible for the actions they take "in behalf of" those they purportedly act for. We need moral judgments about and moral guidelines for both individuals and collective entities even though such judgments cannot be inferred from one another.

To deal adequately with the issues of morality in international affairs, we must deal with the morality of nations as collective entities. But we must also pay close attention to the moral responsibility of individuals in allowing their nations to be what they are and to act as they do. Civil disobedience is often morally justifiable for a citizen protesting the foreign policy decisions of a government claiming to act in that citizen's behalf. As individuals in the world as it is, we may often have the "duty to disobey" our government.[31] The decisions and actions of governments in their dealings with other nations and in their preparations for "defense" against them are among the most difficult but also the most serious occasions for citizens to examine their moral responsibilities. Progress toward morality in international affairs depends heavily on the extent to which individuals not in government recognize their responsibilities for the foreign policy mistakes of their governments.[32] Though it makes good sense to speak of collective entities as "more than" the members composing them, it is also the case that individuals make their nations into what they are and can make their nations do what they decide.

The Autonomy of States

We can often recognize that the governments of various states are not respecting the rights of their own citizens. Should we then intervene? In considering this issue, let us look at the arguments offered by Charles Beitz in his helpful and interesting discussion.

Beitz considers the argument that interference in another state's affairs can be justified "when the state's institutions are unjust . . . and the interference would promote the development of a just domestic constitution within the state."[33]

Beitz does not believe that we ought to respect the autonomy of states the way we ought to respect the autonomy of persons. He thinks this argument depends on a faulty view that states have some independent claim to existence and autonomy when in his view it is only individual persons who have valid claims that they ought to be permitted to exist and to be autonomous. After examining a number of arguments in favor of the principle of nonintervention, he concludes that the forms of intervention that may be permissible vary

> according to the justice of the institutions of the state that is the target of external action. When the target state is just, or is likely to become just if left free from external interference, the prohibition of intervention is based on respect for the rights of persons to associate in the pursuit of common ends, or to live in just regimes. The nonintervention principle prohibits any use of power that interferes with the normal decision-making procedures of a state that is a member of this class. . . . On the other hand, if the target state is neither just nor likely to become just if left to its own devices . . . interference would be permissible on three conditions.[34]

These conditions are that the intervention must promote justice, not "run afoul of other relevant moral restraints on political action" and not be "too costly in terms of the other goals of international politics."[35] Beitz would thus permit intervention far more often and on much wider grounds than would most interpretations of the principle of nonintervention. His position would, in my view, make intervention far too easy to justify.

Michael Walzer calls the principle of nonintervention, a version of which was defended by John Stuart Mill,[36] "the stern doctrine of self-help."[37] He thinks it "not very attractive" because "against the enslavement or massacre of political opponents, national minorities, and religious sects, there may well be no help unless help comes from outside."[38]

But the issues have to do with whether allowing intervention will or will not contribute to the regard of nations for justice and human rights, and there are reasons to believe that intervention is extremely difficult rather than fairly easy to justify.

Stanley Hoffmann, with reasons well founded in experience and moral concern, argues the case for nonintervention. He maintains that "in principle military nonintervention should be the rule not only in cases of people struggling for self-government . . ." to transform their societies into democratic ones, "but also in cases of self-determination,"[39] when people are trying to create a state or rid themselves of foreign domination.

After developing his argument, he concludes: "Given the small number of democracies, and the fog that surrounds the claims to an application of the principle of self-determination, to allow military interventions on behalf of either is a formula for generalized war and hypocrisy."[40]

In considering the arguments for the principle of nonintervention, Beitz begins by asking what it is that might make governments "morally legitimate." He writes as if the existence of a state had to be justified but its nonexistence would not have to be justified. This is, in my view, a questionable starting point in approaching the principle of nonintervention. Given the world that now exists, structured as it is into nation-states, one can plausibly ask what would justify doing away with nations and what would justify creating new ones. Clearly there might be good reasons to get rid of nation-states and to replace them with regional or global governing mechanisms, and there might be good reasons to create or not create certain new nations. There are certainly good reasons to create international mechanisms or strengthen existing ones, to judge violations of the basic human rights of individuals in any state, and to enforce a decent regard for these rights. But discussing these questions would presume the reality of the states that already exist. It would not rest, as Beitz's discussion does now, on the completely hypothetical assumption that no states exist and that creating them is what requires justification. To rest one's argument for or against the principle of nonintervention on what we might choose to do in a totally different world in which there were no states does not indicate much about what we ought to do now that the world *is* divided into nation-states.

Let us agree with Beitz that intervention can include threats to use military force, as well as its actual use, and can include economic pressure. We must also note that intervention presupposes that we can make sense of what it means to say that the intervention is "against the will" of the state or people against whom the intervention occurs. Beitz's own definition of intervention acknowledges this.[41] If we cannot make sense of this, there can be no such activity as intervention. At a moral level, intervention, like rape, can only be understood in terms of a resisting will, though legal conceptions have seen the issues differently.[42]

That intervention is impossible is a patently inadequate position, since intervention is one of the major actual problems for which we need guiding principles. To deal at all adequately with the issues, we must start with a recognition that intervention can and does take place. We need assumptions that allow us to say this rather than ones that preclude our doing so.

But consider also that no state that now exists is just or even close to just. And yet it is clear that states exist and can have something close to national positions that enable us to say that an intervention is or is not "against the will" of the state. But this having of a national position is not something that can be broken down into an expression of individual willings. It is a collective position.

If there is *much* dissention within a state, or if there is civil war, there may not be any national position, and then the issues would have to do with whether it would or would not be morally justifiable to provide the outside assistance sought by one side or another in a dispute between segments of a state. This is not the same issue as intervention that is "against the will" of the state. Restraints on seeking outside aid may be strengthened by each side knowing that if it seeks outside aid, the other side may do so also, and this may lead both sides to favor attempts to settle the dispute internally.

If a state does have a position beyond the multiple positions of its segments, then it has the capacity to have a national will, and intervention is possible. Certainly the national will is not equivalent to the will of the government or of the state's ruling class or of its military. But there seems to be much evidence from history and from the reporting of current realities that it is far more plausible to suppose there can be something describable as a national will than that there cannot.

Beitz and others would have us believe that for a state to have a national will, this must reflect the individual wills of its citizens or it must be the position of a fully legitimate government. But then we would have to conclude that no actual, existing state can have a national will. For no existing state is just, and hence no existing government is fully legitimate. And no existing state can hold positions that fully reflect what the individuals in these states will, *as individuals*, with respect to any national position. Yet the view that existing states cannot have national positions is highly implausible.

If we concede that it makes sense to talk about what a nation wants or wills, we are talking about a collective, not an individual, willing. We can then ask what would justify intervention by outside powers against this collective will. One of the issues on which there seems to be the most general agreement among the most divergent of nations is that people do not want outside intervention in their affairs. They want to deal with their problems within their own national entity rather than have a solution imposed by any outside power. It may well be, then, that arguments for national freedom from outside domination are analogous in important ways to arguments for the freedom of persons from domination by others. The argument is not that states have rights *in the same way* that persons have rights, but that when a nation exists and collectively wills not to be interfered with, others can decide to respect this position and would want it respected in their own cases. The case for the self-determination of a nation should not be thought reducible, as Beitz supposes,[43] to an argument that self-determination will be instrumental to the achievement of justice. Nations are much more than instruments of justice. They tie persons together with cultural and other affinities that have nothing to do with justice.

Intervention and Social Change

Whether or not it would be permissible to respond to a request for assistance by one side or another of an internal dispute is, as I have said, another matter. Here one might only be justified in assisting the side that would be likely to increase rather than decrease the extent to which the society was not only just but conducive to well-being. Some considerations ought to be kept in mind as relevant. An organized governmental structure may more easily be accountable for progress than an unorganized collection of opponents or guerrillas. On the other hand, unorganized groups are often much more dependent than entrenched governments on popular support, and usually could not exist or grow without at least more approval of the people they claim to represent than the government has. There can be more confidence that a dissident force dependent on the public does have popular support than that the government or the armed forces trying to suppress such a dissident group have popular support.

Responding to requests for assistance by dissident groups will be labeled intervention by a government in fear of such groups. But then, requests by a government for assistance in protecting itself from its own citizens must also count as intervention. A principle of nonintervention may help to limit requests for military assistance as well as to limit favorable responses to such requests.

Beitz considers the principle of nonintervention a conservative principle, tending to freeze the status quo by preventing outside interference to dislodge existing, unjust regimes. But the claim seems questionable on empirical grounds. If unjust regimes could no more justifiably request outside military assistance than could their opponents, they would seem to be far more vulnerable to overthrow from within than they often have been in recent years. It has been the aid given by outsiders that has often kept repressive regimes in power and has caused their opponents to seek outside help. Without assistance from the United States, the regime of the Shah of Iran would not have lasted as long as it did, nor would the opposition to him have become as repressive. The Sandinistas in Nicaragua might have rid the country of Somoza earlier and with less bloodshed and less dependence on outside assistance if the United States had not supplied large amounts of aid to a classically unjust regime. And so on.

For the United States to put conditions on its aid to an oppressive regime, demanding improvements in its human rights record, is to make what may already be an intervention into a less morally objectionable one. Aid through an international agency for a populace oppressed by such a regime might be the policy that would best avoid intervention while furthering human rights.

Intervention does not necessarily take place when an outside power merely grants assistance, when requested to either by a government or by its opponents. But it may take place when granting this assistance is against the will of the people whom this government or these opponents purport to represent. And it does take place when an outside power intervenes clandestinely, and assists in overthrowing a government which represents the will of the nation, as the United States did in earlier toppling Mossadegh in Iran and later contributing to the overthrow of Allende in Chile. It takes place also when an outside power sends in troops to impose its will, as Eisenhower did for the United States in Guatemala in 1954[44] and as Israel did in invading Lebanon in 1982 to expel Palestinians from that country and impose a government more in its interests. Such intervention is far more likely to be for the purposes of maintaining the status quo or promoting the interests of the powerful than it is for the purpose of promoting the cause of justice or bringing about a more beneficial world order. Nations that wish to intervene can usually find *some* group within the weaker nation to "request assistance." In trying to make sound moral judgments about intervention, we cannot escape having to ascertain whether the group in question does or does not reflect the national will.

Given that we already live in a world of nation-states, adherence to the principle of nonintervention seems more likely to provide a framework within which progress toward justice can take place than would the easy acceptance of exceptions to this principle. The evidence suggests that a world in which intervention for the sake of justice could take place regardless of whether the nation which was the object of the intervention agreed, would be an even more dangerous world than the one in which we live. The likelihood of conflagration would be seriously increased. The immorality of the resulting destruction might dwarf the immorality of the injustices intervention was designed to remedy.

Applied Ethics and International Affairs

Hoffmann concludes his book with a plea for "despecialization."[45] It is a questionable recommendation, for no lack of specialization will assure increased attention to the moral aspects of these issues. Furthermore, a satisfactory treatment of any very special problem, such as that of national boundaries and illegal immigration,[46] will require appeal to very general moral principles, to a body of theory at an intermediate level of generality (such as that concerning the obligations of states toward the poor of neighboring countries and the rights and obligations of employers and employees across national boundaries), and will require detailed knowledge of very specialized areas of empirical inquiry.

Persons interested in morality and international affairs should pay close attention to the work of institutions and philosophers concerned with applied ethics, where moral philosophers work *with* individuals who themselves have experience with the actual problems of international affairs.[47] The results of such efforts may be far more promising in addressing questions such as these than are either the ideal theories of the best-known philosophers or the nonphilosophical works of social scientists and practitioners.

The specialization that ought to develop would combine real understanding of the relevant philosophical and moral issues, knowledgeable consideration of intermediate-level theories about ethics in international affairs, and detailed familiarity with the more particular domains within which the moral questions are being asked. Dealing adequately with such questions as the morality of nuclear deterrence, or when a state may be justified in going to war or bombing a city, or whether one state should ever withhold aid from a starving population misgoverned by a selfish elite, requires both a good understanding of the most general principles of morality and political theory and a vast amount of specialization.

We cannot escape the problems for which we need adequate and applicable moral theories. That the work of developing them is staggeringly difficult is no excuse for not doing at least what we can to provide them for the most immediately dangerous of all the domains.

Chapter 15

The Practice
of Moral Inquiry

AT TIMES the arguments presented in this book may have appeared suspect: we have sometimes looked at what the moral positions considered would require us to conclude, and then, instead of being willing to accept what morality would seem to demand, we have rejected those moral positions. To do so, however, is an entirely legitimate way to conduct our inquiries. *Modus tollens* (from the Latin *tollere*, to deny) is recognized as a valid form of reasoning: if statement P implies statement Q, and if Q is false, we can know that P is false. This is a form of reasoning by which much fruitful inquiry, including scientific inquiry, proceeds. It does not represent in the moral domain an unwillingness to live up to our moral principles, but demonstrates a necessary openness to what experience and moral awareness can show us about what those principles ought to be and how we can best develop, interpret, and apply them in the contexts of actual moral practice.

I have frequently proceeded in this book as if we could draw an analogy between inquiry in the natural and social sciences, on the one hand, and in ethics on the other. This analogy was suggested in chapter 4 and then worked with as the arguments in the various domains that we considered were developed. The analogy allows us to see that some moral theories can be thought to be valid, that moral theories are applicable to particular situations, that we can subject moral theories to the "tests" of experience, and that we can make progress in developing our moral understanding. Nevertheless, we should preserve distinctive features of ethics that we would not attribute to science: moral theories are normative rather than descriptive, the tests of moral theories are not empirical tests, and moral theories do not require us to assume that human actions are determined in accordance with causal laws.

The major difficulty in trying to develop the analogy between ethics and science concerns the issue of "testability." It is often claimed that there can be no testing of moral theories comparable to the observational testing to which we routinely subject scientific theories.[1] But there are reasons, I think, to hold that moral theories can indeed be "tested" in experience and that the analogy holds.[2]

What would it mean to test a moral theory? First, consider what it means to test anything. To test something is to examine how it stands up under critical scrutiny, to see how it lasts against the erosions of time and opposition, and to watch how it overcomes the trials and obstacles to which it is subjected. One tests a car for speed and endurance. A person's character is tested in adversity, danger, and temptation. We test a hunch when we see what actually happens in contrast to what we expected, and we test a set of directions—for making a dress or fixing an engine—by trying them out.

We have more precise conceptions of testing a scientific hypothesis, but still we test for essentially the same purpose: to see if it and the theory to which it is connected can withstand the criticisms, trials, and disappointments of experience. One way to do this is to predict very particular observation statements that we can derive from the hypothesis. If the hypothesis is true, the predictions will be accurate (if they are the kind that are potentially refutable by evidence). If we predict that we will observe a certain result in a particular set of circumstances, and if we do not observe this, and if this happens several times, or only very few times in a test set up as crucial, then we discard the hypothesis as soon as we can find a better one with which to replace it. Such testing allows for inquiry in which progress is acknowledged. We really do know more than we used to about the causes of diseases, the uses and dangers of chemicals, the characteristics of outer space and of minute particles. And we think we know more about the questions addressed by the social sciences, though hardly any theories in, for instance, sociology or economics or psychology can be considered "true" or conclusively established.

To consider whether anything comparable in the way of progress has been made or might be possible in the domain of ethics, it may be helpful to examine whether we can draw a more explicit analogy between the method by which we might look for progress in moral inquiry and the method by which scientific inquiry is thought to proceed. Can we in any way test the recommendations of ethics as we test the laws of science or the generalizations of the social sciences?

Coherence and Experience

A moral recommendation is in some ways analogous to a scientific prediction of what we can expect to observe. A moral recommendation, like a moral theory, is normative. Hence it does not provide a prediction in the descriptive, scientific sense, but it does predict in some sense: it prescribes for the future. It predicts what we ought to do, and instead of just telling us what we ought to do in general, it predicts what a particular person ought to do in particular circumstances. We often can arrive at this particular judgment or imperative from a general judgment or imperative in a moral theory in the same deductive way we can derive a predicted observation statement from a general statement in a scientific theory. In both cases we may need principles or interpretations to connect the general claims with particular empirical or moral situations, but in both cases they can be constructed.

Though many philosophers of science would not agree with Karl Popper's account of the conduct of scientific inquiry, let us begin with his view of how we arrive at a singular prediction of a scientific event and how observation will decide the fate of scientific theories. It is from universal statements of "hypotheses of the character of natural laws in conjunction with initial conditions that we deduce . . . basic statements . . . that an observable event is occurring in a certain individual region of space and time," Popper writes.[3] We then observe whether our prediction is borne out; if not (and if we continue to hold our statement of the initial conditions to be accurate), we have reason to reject the hypothesis from which it was derived.

If, alternatively, we hold that a "network model" of science is a more accurate representation of the structure of science than the "traditional deductivist account,"[4] we will still share the view that the logical relations between the theoretical and observational claims of science—to the extent that they can be distinguished at all—require coherence and that the process of scientific inquiry requires us to work out this coherence between laws and observation statements and to subject the network to the test of experience.

We might well hold that, analogously, it is from general moral imperatives or universal moral judgments in conjunction with statements about particular circumstances that we can derive a particular imperative or moral judgment about what we ought to do or to hold in these particular circumstances.[5] For instance, from the general moral imperative "do not torture human beings," one can derive the particular imperative "Do not torture this person in this prison." And from the general moral judgment "It is better (in the moral sense) to be healthy than ill," one can derive the particular judgment "It is better for this person in these circumstances to be healthy than ill."

If we think a network model is a more accurate representation of a moral theory, then, instead of starting with general principles and deducing particular imperatives or judgments, we will start anywhere but will arrive at a theory in which there are a limited number of general moral principles and many particular imperatives or judgments indicating how they are to be applied. Between all we will require logical coherence. But should we also demand that a moral theory, like a scientific theory, then be subjected to the tests of experience? Do we know what this would mean? What more than coherence should we demand, and what more can we expect? If we demand no more, if we do not test the particular moral judgment or imperative against experience, then it will have no more standing than that it is consistent with a moral hypothesis we assume to be valid, and the moral hypothesis will have no more standing than that we have assumed it. In science, a particular observation statement or hypothesis or theory can have, until we subject it to experience, no more standing than that it is consistent with what we take to be other, already established, scientific statements.[6] This is almost never thought to be enough to make substantial headway in scientific inquiry, for we demand that scientific claims be tested against observation. A theory or statement that has no more to rest on than coherence is fundamentally weak as science.[7]

The same can be said, I think, of moral theories and the imperatives and judgments of which they are composed. However, if we can decide, independently of our moral theories, that the particular imperatives or judgments are valid on the basis of experience, then we will have provided ourselves with something lending confirmation to the moral theory in a way analogous to that by which observation provides evidence for a scientific theory. Or, more tellingly perhaps, in ethics as in science, if we must decide in the crucible of actual experience that the particular imperative or judgment is *not* valid, then the theory will be put in doubt by this test. In my view we can do this, and the development of moral inquiry should demonstrate how.

All this is quite different from what is meant by Immanuel Kant, or those writing about him or from a Kantian point of view, about testing our moral positions. Kant advises us to test our maxims by considering whether we would be willing to universalize them.[8] This is no test in my sense, because examining the relation between the particular maxim of an action and the "moral law" with which it would have to accord is still purely a matter of coherence. It does not submit the maxim to the test, as I use the term, of experience.

It is also quite different from the testing, if it is called that, constituted by the "thought experiments" recommended by various utilitarian and ideal-observer theories. These so-called tests are still examinations of coherence; they attempt to see if one part of a moral theory at one level of generality coheres with another part of the theory at another level of generality. They are not tests of the theory against something outside it.

What, then, can a test of a moral theory be? In the case of a scientific theory, we predict a given observable result, and then we make an observation to see if it in fact occurs. In the process of observing, we see whether the prediction about what we would observe is true or not. In the case of a moral theory, the theory predicts that we ought to act in a certain way, or that our particular moral judgment ought to be such and such. To test this, we must act as the theory declares we ought to act and then "see" whether we consider the imperative requiring that action valid. Or we must "realize" in the moment of action that we ought not to perform the action required and thus that the imperative requiring it is not valid. Or we must be able to "tell" when confronted with the actual situation whether the moral judgment that our theory predicted is valid or not.

But what can this mean? *How* can we "see" or "realize" or "tell" in such cases whether we ought to have acted a certain way or whether our moral judgments are valid? At this point the argument that we cannot test moral theories purports to be victorious. It is claimed that the only way we could establish the validity or invalidity of the particular imperative or judgment would be to use the very theories we are trying to test to provide the imperative or judgment, and that would be circular.

Comparative Independence

Why, however, do we assume this to be so much more of a problem in the case of a moral theory than in the case of a scientific theory? In science, we may have to refer back to a given theory or forward to a rival theory to understand a particular observation, if we concede that all observation statements are to some extent "theory-laden."[9] Most philosophers of science still claim, and the progress of science strongly suggests, that we can nevertheless test scientific theories against something independent of them. Our claims about the degree to which such independence is possible have become much more modest and uncertain in recent years, but this has not led to an abandonment of the very idea of an independent test. The disparity in the extent to which we consider particular moral imperatives and judgments theory-laden or not as compared with observation statements in science should accordingly reflect this change. If we continue to hold that in science we require more than mere coherence, we should consider requiring this also in ethics and consider how it may indeed be possible. If, on the other hand, we think that a certain kind of coherence is enough to account for progress in the sciences, we should see that it might be enough to allow for progress in ethics. If science does not need "firm foundations" or "ultimate givens," ethics should not be asked to provide them either. And without them, ethics *need not* collapse into emotivism or subjectivism any more than science *must* collapse into literature.

Without taking sides on these disputed philosophical issues, we can still assert that, whatever the degree of independence observation can have from theory in science, it would at least be unreasonable to ask that the degree of independence of particular moral positions from moral theories be any greater. It might even be quite reasonable to allow a particular moral position's degree of independence to be much less and still to speak of testing moral theories, as long as the position has some degree of independence.

It seems clear that we can make decisions about particular moral imperatives and judgments with some degree of independence from our adherence to the moral theories from which they can be derived. What is comparable to the observation by which we test scientific theories is, in the case of testing moral theories, *choosing to act or approve.* We can choose to act or to refrain from action; we can choose to approve or disapprove the actions of others and the consequences of their acts; and we can do these to some extent independently of our moral theories. Whether such testing can achieve intersubjective agreement comparable to that possible in science, or whether it needs to, will be considered later.

Let us consider action first. A moral theory tells us how we ought to act, but it does not itself produce action. If it tells us "Walk out now," we are still left with the decision between "Walk out" and "Do not walk out" in regard to the performance of the action itself. Or if our

theory recommends "Do not walk out" even under a given set of provo-
cations, we may choose to abide by or to defy the recommendation. Certainly we may decide to try to walk out or to refrain from doing so, and
then lack the will and fail to do what we decided, or we may fail for
some other reason. This, then, will not be a fair test of the theory, because we did not do what we chose to do. But if we choose to act and do
perform the chosen action and if we judge that we did the right thing,
we thereby disconfirm for ourselves a theory recommending we not do
so. If we choose to refrain and do so, when the theory recommended action, and if we judge that in doing so we acted rightly, we disconfirm
for ourselves a theory recommending the action we did not perform.

But how is this? How can we choose without reference to the very
theory we are trying to test? What I am asserting is that in truth we do
choose, and the choice *itself* is not fully determined by the theory; *nor* is
the rightness of the choice so determined. A recommendation to choose
a certain way is derivable from the theory, but this is not itself a choice
to act. *Choose we must, to do or not to do what our theories recommend. Our
choices*, when actually acted on in test situations with awareness that
we are in them, *put moral theories to the test.* If we understand a test as a
way of seeing how a theory stands up to the challenges of actual existence, we in this way test our theories through action. We engage in the
practice of moral inquiry through the use of a method of experimental
morality.

Of course, there is a problem in the previous discussion in the
phrase "and judge that we acted rightly." How could we judge this?
Are we not assuming an alternative theory in judging that the action
recommended against by the first theory was the one we were right to
do? Perhaps, but this again leaves moral theory in no worse a position
than scientific theory, where it is often claimed that to make an observation contrary to the one predicted by the theory we are trying to test,
we must connect the statement of this observation with a competing
theory in which this observation makes sense and on which it could be
true or testable. Then the issue is, in both cases, deciding between rival
theories. In the case of science, we make such decisions at the level of
particular observation statements; in the case of moral theories we can
make them at the level of particular imperatives and judgments about
how we ought to act.

The points made thus far about choosing our actions can be repeated when we choose to approve or disapprove the actions of others or the
consequences of these actions. Our theory will predict what we ought to
approve or disapprove, but the final choice to do so is not completely

determined by the theory. Most of us have experienced some choices that have gone beyond what we imagined we thought about a moral issue: we have expected, on the basis of the moral views we held, to approve or disapprove of some action, but then, witnessing the actual event at close hand or living with the actual situation, we have discovered ourselves to be in disagreement with our theories. If we suggest, then, that we ought to seek with deliberate intention to have such experiences that go beyond our theories for the express purpose of putting our moral theories to the test, it cannot be objected that such experiences are impossible, since many people have had such experiences without looking for them.

Certainly we may decide to dismiss the feelings of disapproval or approval we experience in an immediate situation as unduly colored by nonmoral sensations such as nausea or intoxication, or as suspiciously influenced by such factors as popular opinion, our own habitual distaste for certain objects or events, or some faulty association we may make between some previous (frequently childhood) experience and some aspect of the test. But then we simply have grounds to question whether the test situation really is that and whether the choice we make in it really is our choice. If we choose not to dismiss the judgment of approval or disapproval arrived at in an actual experience, then this judgment may test for us our predictions about what we ought to approve or disapprove.

Of course, there will be serious difficulties in deciding when an action or restraint results from weakness of will and when from deliberate choice. It will be almost impossible to tell for others and often difficult to tell for ourselves. However, we can do our best to decide which it was if we set up test situations, or interpret situations we find ourselves in as tests, in such a way that we make the best effort we can to be honest with ourselves. Then we can sometimes be justified in acting as we do and in making the judgments we come to, individually and with others, and we can progressively increase our understanding of what morality requires in various contexts.

Moral Experience

It is important to understand that a test of a moral theory is not an empirical test, although it is a test based on experience. The experience necessary is *moral* experience, not empirical experience.

What is moral experience? The notion of moral experience seems

especially troublesome to philosophers; I suspect it is less so to
nonphilosophers. As I understand it, moral experience is the experience
of consciously choosing, of voluntarily accepting or rejecting, of willingly approving or disapproving, of living with these choices, and
above all of acting and of living with these actions and their outcomes.
We can describe some aspects of such experience in empirical terms, for
example, "He voluntarily did X," "She disapproves of Y," "Action Z
killed twenty people," and so on. But specifically moral language is
needed to address and to express such experience itself. In moral experience we decide to accept "One ought to do X" or "Y is morally wrong,"
for example, as morally valid or invalid. We do so through acting voluntarily or giving or withholding our approval. This connects the
words to something outside them in our direct experience, in a manner
comparable to the way the sensory experiences of seeing or hearing, for
example, connect the words "The infant is dead" or "The sound is fad-
ing" to something outside them.

There is an important difference, however. In the case of perception, we ought to let the world impose its truth on our observations; we
ought to be passive recipients of the impressions leading us to consider
observation statements as true or false. In the case of action and of approval, we ought to shape the world actively in accordance with our
choices. We ought to be active rather than passive beings. We ought,
in actively and voluntarily choosing how to act and what to approve of,
to impose on the world our choices of the prescriptions and judgments
to consider valid, instead of the reverse. But *action is as much a part of experience as is perception.*

Action contains within itself a choice in favor of the action done and
in support of any moral imperative recommending that action or of any
judgment that the action would be the right action. In his chapter "The
Normative Structure of Action," Alan Gewirth makes a case that an
agent performing an action voluntarily must regard the purposes for
which he acts as in some sense good and thus, in acting, "he implicitly
makes a value judgment."[10] Purposes here can include the performance or nonperformance of an action itself for the reason that it is an action of a certain kind, such as when one keeps a promise because it is a
promise, rather than for some further purpose. But in acting, an agent
"regards the object of his action as having at least sufficient value to
merit his acting to attain it, according to whatever criteria are involved
in his action."[11] We need not decide, for my argument here, whether
the agent acting voluntarily *must in every case* act on a moral imperative
or judgment. It is enough to claim that when agents are engaged in sin-

cere moral inquiry and in the testing of moral theories as here discussed, they must—and can—do so.

A choice to act may be based on deontological grounds, as when we tell the truth out of respect for the moral integrity of our hearer or out of a moral commitment to a deontological imperative to tell the truth. In such a case we may sometimes choose without regard for the consequences or even on grounds that conflict with what a consideration of consequences would recommend. Deontological grounds alone will sometimes suffice to justify an action. Sometimes such grounds ought to be overridden by other deontological considerations or by stronger concern for the consequences where they would recommend a different decision. Or the choice may be based on teleological grounds, as when we perform a certain task because we believe it will contribute to the health of many people, and we judge their health to be a good worth trying to achieve. Sometimes such considerations, combined with moral judgments about how to weigh them, will be sufficient to justify a decision to act. At other times deontological considerations should be given priority over a calculation of benefits and harms produced. Sometimes self-interest will be enough to justify an action, and sometimes we ought to act for the good of specific others or of a community. In acting and approving, we take stands on these issues and on specific recommendations about them.

Moral Theories

We need theories to indicate how these choices ought to be made in various contexts. The choices of methods for arriving at such decisions, choices about which considerations to put ahead of which others, should not be ad hoc and arbitrary. W. D. Ross has offered a compelling account of the prima facie principles we might bring to such moral deliberations.[12] But his suggestion that, when two or more prima facie principles conflict when applied to a given situation, we can get no guidance from morality but must simply take a chance that good fortune will guide us to the right act is unduly pessimistic.[13] Moral theories should provide exactly this kind of working out of the conflicts between very general moral principles when applied to actual situations. This does not mean the moral theories will be adequate for all situations, but they should become more and more adequate for more and more actual situations, and in doing so they must develop rules for handling conflicts between such very general principles as "One ought to refrain from killing people" and "One is permitted to defend oneself," or between "One ought not to let people die from illness when medical care is available" and "One ought to help alleviate pain," and so on. Discussions of justifiable self-defense or of euthanasia, for example, show how theories can be developed to try to deal with these conflicts.

We should aim to find moral theories such that the recommendations yielded by the different approaches we experiment with in different domains are compatible with one another, but this may be a distant goal rather than an immediate need. In the meantime we should consider arguments for handling some types of problems in certain appropriate ways and other types of problems in other appropriate ways. I have tried to spell out in this book how these arguments might be made for selected contexts.

The appeal of monistic moral theories is obviously very great. If we could find one satisfactory moral theory to apply to all our problems, we would not have to decide what approaches are appropriate for what contexts or what problems belong in what domain. As Amartya Sen and Bernard Williams note, "the ambitiousness of utilitarianism has itself served as a source of its appeal. In promising to resolve all moral issues by relying on one uniform ultimate criterion, utilitarianism has appeared to be the 'rational' moral theory *par excellence*."[14] Reality, however, has not lent itself to fulfilling the ambitions of those who have sought to embrace all its problems in a unified moral theory. A division of moral labor offers more promising prospects for the foreseeable future. This book has argued for a particular kind of pluralistic theory, one which combines deontological and consequentialist elements, and individualistic and socially concerned approaches.

Different existing institutional arrangements, and persons in the different roles in them, should accordingly emphasize different moral approaches. No one sort of moral inquiry will be equivalent to a full moral understanding of every aspect of human life. But each can incorporate tentative recommendations that within the given range of problems with which they are concerned, it is morally justifiable to handle those problems in that characteristic way. And each can allow for the development of more specialized or more general recommendations within these contexts, and for improvements in any existing practices.

Consider what goes on in a legal context among those who sincerely approach it with moral concern. There is, for example, a continuing effort to specify the requirements for "equal protection of the laws." This provision of the United States Constitution reflects a moral requirement to treat persons with equal respect. In a legal system without such a constitutional provision, a comparable effort would be made to determine what the moral principles, on which the legal system rests or must be judged, require by way of equal treatment by the law. No one seriously concerned with the law would maintain we are under no moral obligation to have our laws reflect the equal treatment of persons in *any* way, though there may be much disagreement about which particular ways.

Debate will always be possible, and should be a continuing activity, as we develop theories about what equality in law requires and how we ought to act in view of this. Of course, many legal systems fall dismally short of reflecting what any plausible view of morality would require in the way of justice and equal treatment. However, we can find agreement on much more than, as the Universal Declaration of Human Rights puts it, "no one shall be held in slavery . . . ," although we should never forget the progress in moral understanding that this article represents. When writers on jurisprudence argue over what is required by morality, they are trying to put relevant theories to the test of decision in a way comparable if not similar to the way scientists argue over the acceptability of theories.

Or consider the changes that have taken place in the last decade in the views of many women and men concerning what their roles and relations to one another "ought to be." When the persons involved are sincere, they suggest recommendations for leading their lives that seem to them fair and considerate. And they try out these recommendations in the ways they live and act and speak and think. They put alternative suggestions to the test of experience. Many who have inquired into these issues in this period have found various theories they previously accepted invalid. And in exploring the implications for human relations and for family life, they have had to accept or reject the particular moral recommendations of alternative theories. Many have practiced moral inquiry in this area.

Inquiry and Disagreement

It is often claimed that disagreement plagues moral inquiry and perhaps undermines the very possibility of progress in moral understanding. I have tried to show in this book why such claims are mistaken. A comparison between ethics and science may again be instructive. There is no need to compare the agreement possible in the 1980s in some domain of moral inquiry with the agreement possible in some area of hard science in the 1980s. We could compare the agreement possible in ethics in the 1980s with the agreement possible in science in the 1580s or 1680s, or with the agreement possible in some very soft area of science such as anthropology or psychotherapy in the 1930s or 1980s. The point is not that progress or agreement is comparable, but that the methodologies of inquiry in ethics and in science, while different in important respects, are in other ways analogous.[15] Theories can be formulated and put to the test of experience in both domains, and more rapid progress than has occurred in ethics might well be possible with a better understanding of how normative inquiry has a methodology and is capable of cumulative advance.

Some persons will surely continue to hold that we are left, in ethics, with a problem of disagreement too severe to accept the analogies I have drawn and the arguments I have made. It is often claimed that whenever we think we can point to a given moral position as being certain and firm, we will have to admit that there are persons who hold some contrary view, and that the tests I have suggested could not yield results that can be agreed upon in a way comparable to the way agreement can be expected among scientists conducting a test of a scientific theory.

A number of arguments may be offered in response. I shall consider only three. First, when people compare agreement in science with disagreement in ethics, the level of generality of the judgment considered is usually very different in the two domains. A very simple particular scientific observation such as "The sodium chloride has dissolved in the water" is compared with a very complex though particular moral judgment, such as "She ought not to have an abortion in this case." If the level of simplicity were more nearly equivalent, the level of disagreement would be significantly reduced. How much disagreement would there be, for instance, in the following case? Suppose you asked a person in severe pain whether it would be better if he suffer this pain or be out of it, provided everything else were equal, no further effects on his health or his soul were at issue, and no one else would be affected one way or the other. He would not be neutral as between his state of pain or freedom from pain; he certainly would think it a better state of affairs to be out of pain. What is at issue here is not just the empirical fact that people shun pain, but the recognition that normal persons can make simple moral judgments that a state of affairs in which they are free from severe pain is morally better than one in which they suffer severe pain, if everything else is equal. There can be agreement among persons about such simple moral judgments to an extent fully comparable to the agreement possible among them when they make empirical statements about what they perceive.

Some persons hearing this argument may respond that to prefer to be out of pain is not to make a moral judgment. I agree. But suppose our getting out of pain or staying in it would depend on the moral judgment we made about it and would not be affected by a mere empirical statement of our preference. Then we can agree, I think, that *if* we make a moral judgment about the situation, the judgment would be "It would be better for me to be out of pain," other things being equal. And we cannot live our lives responsibly without making moral judgments and acting on them.

Second, when critics of the sort of view I am proposing claim that everyone agrees in the case of scientific observation but not everyone agrees in the case of moral judgments, the reference for "everyone" shifts, sometimes drastically. Consider the following appraisal of scientific observation: "Simple laws of mechanics are not taken to be disconfirmed by the experiments conducted in sophomore lab sections, where experience quickly confirms that few sophomore experimenters ever produce observational data that coincides with what the already accepted theories of physics predict."[16] In the social sciences, disagreement is far more rampant, and not only among those making observations.

We all know people who oppose the approach I am taking by telling us what their grandmothers, or the Trobriand Islanders, approve or disapprove in the way of behavior, suggesting that these moral judgments are as reliable as any others. Yet they would not for a minute let what their grandmothers or the Trobriand Islanders think about the electrical charges of particles or the causes of inflation influence their views on these subjects. If disagreement about scientific matters is not to count for a view that scientific theories are merely matters of opinion, disagreement in moral matters should not count for as much as such critics imagine.

Finally, it is the case that in society as organized at present there is a significant disparity between what it may cost a person to heed the evidence in science and in ethics. In science a person's reputation may be enhanced or harmed by the advance of scientific understanding, so that an inquirer may have some stake in preventing some hypothesis from being accepted or in promoting the acceptance of some other. And especially in the social sciences, inquirers are not well insulated from the effects of bias and interest. Nevertheless, the ethics of scientific inquiry help to protect those who accept what a reasonable view of the arguments in favor of one theory or another would require. Unfortunately, those who conduct moral inquiries are much less well protected. There are no accepted ethics of moral inquiry. Persons who test theories in

ethics are apt to be highly exposed to retaliation by those offended—
and many often are—in ways in which those who inquire into empirical
matters often need not be. This situation could change with a changed
understanding of what moral inquiry requires and of the need to protect
moral inquirers from the anger of provoked interests in some such way
as scientific inquirers are now protected, although they were not always
and are not now in some areas. With such a change in the practice of
moral inquiry, agreement might be much more prevalent.

This is not to say that moral inquirers should be ideal observers removed from their actual situations. Hypothetical ideal observers are
unable to confront moral issues as they arise in actual contexts, and everything I have said about testing moral theories requires that they be
tested in actual, not hypothetical, situations. So the moral inquirers I
have in mind will not be protected observers in this sense. However,
among the moral recommendations that can be expected to be developed will be ones having to do with the ethics of moral inquiry. These
recommendations could be followed long before agreement on other
moral issues could be reached.

The Ethics of Inquiry

Among the recommendations that could be made for an ethics of moral
inquiry are the following. We should know the sources of the support
received by those who purport to engage in such inquiry. We should be
on guard against the tendency of persons to say what they will be rewarded for saying, as when "social critics" receive payments and praise
for telling the powerful how admirable they are, and aspiring professionals are rewarded for following in the footsteps of arrogant elders.
We should question the moral perceptions of those who pronounce on
the morality or immorality of actions and persons of which they have
had no direct experience. We should be skeptical of purely theoretical
constructions that may have little bearing on actual moral problems:
they are no substitute for moral inquiry that confronts experience. We
should demand the independence of mind and stance and support
throughout the culture that "academic freedom" purports to provide in
the university.[17] We should provide a much higher level of public support, insulated from the influence of the powerful, especially the economically powerful, for cultural and intellectual and practical endeav-
ors seeking to explore how we ought to live and act. We should require
of those who investigate claims concerning moral rights and goods a

sincerity of purpose and openness of mind at least as deep as we expect in persons who inquire into the truth or falsity of any other claims. If, in the area of moral inquiry, we expect no more than charlatans and publicists and clever minds for hire, we should not be surprised if we find little else. Finally, we should strive to bring about for everyone the conditions that would make possible a greatly enlarged engagement in the practice of moral inquiry.

In the natural sciences and to a far greater extent in the social sciences, we accept and live with the existence of competing theories. If this does not lead us to conclude that we can make no progress in developing better scientific theories, we should not conclude from the existence of competing moral theories that we can make no progress in developing better moral theories. No doubt human action is not as uniform as nature. It does not follow that the choices human beings should make about how to live their lives should be infinitely various. If the process of conducting moral inquiry leads to the development of a multiplicity of moral theories, each with considerable experience in its support, this will still be progress, even if there continues to be no clear way of choosing among them or of arranging for different problems to be treated in different ways.

It should be noted that the view of moral inquiry for which I have argued does not lead us to the unacceptable conclusion that whatever moral theories do in fact get accepted by human beings are therefore valid. Anyone can dispute, on the basis of his or her own experience, any prevailing theories. As history has shown many times, the moral theories of a few isolated and rebellious inquirers can come to prevail, and anyone can argue, on the basis of his or her own theories and insights, against any other theories in danger of becoming prevalent.

We can fully expect that the practice of moral inquiry as here discussed will result in disagreement and in the existence of rival theories. (See chapter 4.) There will then be legitimate arguments about whether the experience in question really is relevant or crucial, about whether and how it counts for or against the theories, and so on. We already have such arguments in other domains. We should have more of them in ethics. In the end, all of us are responsible for the theories we accept or reject, in ethics as everywhere else, and we must make judgments about acceptance and rejection for ourselves. We will live our lives and practice moral inquiry well, or we will do so badly.

Notes

Chapter 1   Introduction

1. John Rawls, *A Theory of Justice* (Cambridge, Mass.: Harvard University Press, 1971).
2. "Act only according to that maxim by which you can at the same time will that it should become a universal law." See Immanuel Kant, *Foundations of the Metaphysics of Morals,* transl. with introduction by Lewis White Beck (New York: Liberal Arts, 1959).

Chapter 2   The Revival of Ethics

1. Plato, *Euthyphro, Apology, Crito,* ed. R. Cumming (New York: Liberal Arts, 1956).
2. See, e.g., Robert Lekachman, *Economists at Bay: Why the Experts Will Never Solve Your Problems* (New York: McGraw-Hill, 1976); and Lester C. Thurow, *Dangerous Currents: The State of Economics* (New York: Random House, 1983).
3. The major importance of J. L. Mackie's *Inventing Right and Wrong* (New York: Penguin, 1977), with its absolute claim that "there are no objective values," is to show all those readers already committed to what they take to be "subjectivism" how they can, after all, find reasons to invent a

morality that will uphold a very sensible and well-reasoned version of political liberalism.

4. Gilbert Harman defines relativism, which he defends, as the denial of the view that "there are certain basic moral demands that everyone accepts or at least has reasons to accept" ("Relativistic Ethics: Morality as Politics," *Midwest Studies in Philosophy* 3 [1978]: 109). Many nonrelativists would partially share this position if they thought, with Ronald Dworkin, that "acts which cause unnecessary suffering, or break a serious promise with no excuse, are immoral, and yet they could give no reason for these beliefs. They feel that no reason is necessary, because they take it as axiomatic or self-evident that these are immoral acts" ("Lord Devlin and the Enforcement of Morals," *Yale Law Journal* 75, reprinted in Richard A. Wasserstrom, *Morality and the Law* [Belmont, Calif.: Wadsworth Publishing Co., 1971], p. 65). Harman, like Mackie, thinks we ought to work out in practical detail moral principles and their implications for the group of persons who have reasons to share our basic moral demands. "The principles that give you moral reasons to do things are the moral principles that you actually accept," Harman writes ("Relativistic Ethics," p. 120). On such a view, once a relativist accepts the whole of humanity as a group meeting this description, his views coincide with those of a nonrelativist.

5. See pp. 21–22.

6. Morton White has drawn the analogy between ethical inquiry and scientific inquiry in *What Is and What Ought to Be Done* (New York: Oxford University Press, 1981). I disagree, however, with his advocacy of dissolving the difference between descriptive and normative beliefs, and I think his suggestion that we revise our empirical descriptions to serve our normative purposes more dangerous than sound.

7. An article on "Recent Work on the Concept of Rights" by Rex Martin and James W. Nickel, *American Philosophical Quarterly* 17 (July 1980): 165–180, provides a useful report on a large amount of work on this topic. Of course, there have been other issues of importance on which work has proceeded, in addition to the work in "applied ethics" mentioned earlier. Among them have been problems of egoism, of collective and individual rationality, of universalizability; I shall not try to elaborate.

8. For further discussion of the concept of a right, see Ronald Dworkin, *Taking Rights Seriously* (Cambridge, Mass., Harvard University Press, 1977); Rex Martin and James W. Nickel, "Recent Work on the Concept of Rights"; David Lyons, ed., *Rights* (Belmont, Calif.: Wadsworth, 1979); Joel Feinberg, *Social Philosophy* (Englewood Cliffs, N.J.: Prentice-Hall, 1973); and John Plamenatz, "Rights," in Aristotelian Society, *Psychical Research, Ethics, and Logic,* suppl. vol. 24 (London: Harriss & Sons, 1950), pp. 73–82.

9. J. J. C. Smart, "Extreme and Restricted Utilitarianism," reprinted with revisions in Michael D. Bayles, ed., *Contemporary Utilitarianism* (New York: Doubleday Anchor, 1968), p. 107. See also J. J. C. Smart and Bernard Williams, *Utilitarianism: For and Against* (Cambridge: At the University Press, 1973).

10. William Frankena, *Ethics,* 2d ed. (Englewood Cliffs, N.J.: Prentice-Hall, 1973; first ed. 1963), p. 41.

11. Isaiah Berlin, *Four Essays on Liberty* (New York: Oxford University Press, 1969).

12. A few passages in this chapter appeared originally in my article on recent developments in ethics in *Social Research* 47, no. 4 (Winter 1980). They are used here with permission.

Chapter 3   The Division of Moral Labor: Roles

1. Plato, *Republic,* I, 347.

2. In *Professional Ethics* (Belmont, Calif.: Wadsworth Publishing Co., 1981), Michael D. Bayles considers the obligations that fall on professions collectively. "A profession as a whole has an obligation to make services equally available to all," he writes, and he rightly does not mean merely: available to all who have the money to pay for them. "A liberal society," he continues, "should devise a system for delivering health and legal services that both provides them equally to all and preserves as much freedom of choice as possible for clients and professionals." (p. 49). He notes the irresponsible omissions in the codes of ethics of both the medical and legal professions of provisions that would address themselves to these obligations of the professions as a whole.

3. See, e.g., R. S. Downie, *Roles and Values: An Introduction to Social Ethics* (London: Methuen, 1971), especially chap. 6, "Persons and Roles."

4. Dorothy Emmet, *Function, Purpose and Powers: Some Concepts in the Study of Individuals and Societies* (London: Macmillan, 1958), p. 26. In *Rules, Roles and Relations* (Boston: Beacon Press, 1975; first published 1966), Emmet offers one of the most useful discussions available of social roles. She appreciates the existentialists' criticism that to accept a role is to evade responsibility, to be, in Sartre's terms, in "bad faith," as one hides behind one's social function. But she argues that "to live in society means . . . that a certain number of reasonably stable functions and expectations can be depended on" (p. 155). And she notes that we are all faced with conflicts of roles and must choose between them. Hence, little hiding is possible. On the relation between roles and rules, Emmet writes, "as a directive for behavior in certain kinds of relationship, [role morality] is structured by rules; if not by explicit and sanctioned rules, at least by implicit understandings, and maxims, or rules of thumb, as to how such a person would behave in this kind of relationship" (p. 158).

5. This issue has been discussed recently in connection with professional roles especially. Writers on legal ethics, for instance, note that "the lawyer is asked to do 'as a professional' what he or she would not do 'as a person'; to subordinate personal qualms about results in particular cases to the general rule of law and the bar's role within it" (Gary Bellow and Jeanne Kettleson, "The Mirror of Public Interest Ethics: Problems and Paradoxes in Professional Responsibility," *A Guide for Attorneys* 219 (1978): 257–58. This has led critics to wonder: "Can a person appeal to a social institution in which he occupies a role in order to excuse himself from conduct that would be morally culpable were anyone else to do it?" (David Luban, "The Adversary System Excuse," in David Luban, ed., *The Good Lawyer* [Totowa, N.J.: Rowman and Allanheld, 1983]). Many philosophers understandably resist the "institutional excuse." I shall try to show how the norms for different professions and roles ought often to be different and special to them without being excuses. My paper "The Division of Moral Labor and the Role of the Lawyer" in *The Good Lawyer* makes this argument for the role of lawyer. A few passages from that paper are included in this chapter with permission.

6. Niccolo Machiavelli, *The Prince* (1532), XVIII, trans. George Bull (New York: Penguin, 1961), p. 101.

7. Max Weber, "Politics as a Vocation," in H. H. Gerth and C. Wright Mills, eds., *From Max Weber: Essays in Sociology* (New York: Oxford University Press, 1970; first published 1946), p. 120.

8. Stuart Hampshire, "Morality and Pessimism," in Stuart Hampshire, ed., *Public and Private Morality* (Cambridge: At the University Press, 1978). For a somewhat similar view, see also Annette Baier, "Theory and Reflective Practices," unpublished paper.

9. Hampshire, "Morality and Pessimism," p. 21.

10. Stuart Hampshire, "Public and Private Morality," in Hampshire, ed., *Public and Private Morality,* p. 52.

11. Hampshire, "Morality and Pessimism," p. 19.

12. Hampshire, "Public and Private Morality," p. 26.

13. Henry Kamm, from Hong Kong, *New York Times,* August 13, 1981.

14. Five percent of wives in the United States are reported to be severely beaten by their husbands at least once a year. (*New York Times,* July 26, 1981). Violence against children is common.

15. A lack of discussion of various aspects of this point characterizes the entire collection of essays on public and private morality edited by Stuart Hampshire.

16. An especially useful account is Susan Moller Okin's *Women in Western Political Thought* (Princeton, N.J.: Princeton University Press, 1979).

17. Sartre, for instance, thought that to identify oneself with one's social roles is a prime example of bad faith. See Jean-Paul Sartre, *Being and*

Nothingness, trans. Hazel Barnes (New York: Washington Square Press, 1966), part I, chap. 2.

18. Virginia Held, "Justification: Legal and Political," *Ethics* 86, no. 1 (October 1975). ©1975 by the University of Chicago. A few passages in chapters 7 and 9 have been drawn from this paper.

19. Andrew Oldenquist, "Rules and Consequences," *Mind* 75 (April 1966): 180.

20. Other special moral considerations than those mentioned might also be relevant, however. Alan Goldman assumes that the only relevant norm that could provide for those in business occupations being in "role-differentiated" positions would be the norm of profit-maximization. That he can imagine no other special norms for business indicates his own limited view rather than any inherent aspects of economic enterprise. A business manager could well consider producing products that are more rather than less useful, or organizing the workplace to bring about more job satisfaction rather than less or more experience with participatory forms of organization. This might be done in response to special norms applicable to economic activity but not to all activity, and might often conflict with the maximization of profits. See Alan Goldman, "Business Ethics: Profits, Utilities, and Moral Rights," *Philosophy and Public Affairs,* 9, no. 3 (Spring 1980): 260–86.

21. Hazel Henderson disputes the claim of Adam Smith and sees no propensity to trade. See Henderson, *The Politics of the Solar Age: Alternatives to Economics* (Garden City, N.Y.: Doubleday, 1981), especially chap. 7.

22. Dorothy Emmet's characterization of morality is suggestive. We can see it, she says, as "a matter of discovering how it is possible for people to live together in ways which lead to an increasing capacity for mutual trust and moral growth" (*Rules, Roles and Relations,* p. 179). For discussion of mutual trust, see chapters 5 and 11 of the present work.

23. See, e.g., David Braybrooke, *Three Tests for Democracy: Personal Rights, Human Welfare, Collective Preference* (New York: Random House, 1968), especially part II.

Chapter 4   Moral Theory and Moral Experience

1. R. M. Hare, *Freedom and Reason* (New York: Oxford University Press, 1965).

2. Roderick Firth, "Ethical Absolutism and the Ideal Observer," *Philosophy and Phenomenological Research* 12 (1952): 317–45.

3. Hare, *Freedom and Reason,* pp. 92–93.

4. Hare, "Rawls's Theory of Justice: I," *Philosophical Quarterly* 23 (1973): 154.

5. Hare, "Ethical Theory and Utilitarianism," in H. D. Lewis, ed., *Contem-*

porary British Philosophy, 4th series. (London: Allen and Unwin, 1976), p. 119. See also Hare's "Rules of War and Moral Reasoning," *Philosophy and Public Affairs* 1, 1971–72, and his "Principles," *Proceedings of the Aristotelian Society,* 1972–73.

6. Hare, *Freedom and Reason,* p. 183.

7. Ibid.

8. See Richard Henson, "On Being Ideal," *Philosophical Review* 65 (1956): 389–400.

9. For a useful discussion, see Joseph Raz, "The Claims of Reflective Equilibrium," *Inquiry* 25 (1982): 307–30.

10. John Rawls, *A Theory of Justice,* (Cambridge, Mass.: Harvard University Press, 1971), p. 47.

11. Rawls, *A Theory of Justice,* p. 46.

12. John Rawls, "The Independence of Moral Theory," *American Philosophical Association: Proceedings and Addresses,* (1974–75):8.

13. Peter Singer, "Sidgwick and Reflective Equilibrium," *The Monist* 58, no. 3 (July 1974): 494.

14. Hare, *Freedom and Reason,* pp. 87 and 91–93; Rawls, *A Theory of Justice,* p. 579, and especially Rawls's "Outline of a Decision Procedure for Ethics," *Philosophical Review* 60 (1950).

15. Rawls, *A Theory of Justice,* p. 121.

16. Rawls, "The Independence of Moral Theory," p. 9.

17. Hare, *Freedom and Reason,* pp. 88–89.

18. Singer, "Sidgwick and Reflective Equilibrium," p. 516.

19. See Virginia Held, "The Political 'Testing' of Moral Theories," *Midwest Studies in Philosophy* 7 (1982): 343–63, and chapter 15 of the present work.

20. Rawls, "Outline of a Decision Procedure for Ethics," p. 179. Italics added.

21. Ibid., p. 181.

22. Ibid., p. 182.

23. Hare, *The Language of Morals* (Oxford: Claredon Press, 1952).

24. David A. J. Richards has suggested to me that the characteristic refusal of the Supreme Court to deal with hypothetical problems, and to insist that before it agrees to consider an issue there be a case in which actual persons press actual claims in an actual controversy, may reflect a concern similar to the one I am here discussing. The Supreme Court shuns "every form of pronouncement on abstract, contingent, or hypothetical issues" (Robert H. Jackson, *The Supreme Court in the American System of Government* [Cambridge, Mass.: Harvard University Press, 1955], p. 12).

25. Hare, *Freedom and Reason,* p. 197.

26. This point was suggested by Sidney Morgenbesser.

27. See Virginia Held, "Rationality and Reasonable Cooperation," *Social Research* 44, no. 4 (Winter 1977), and chapter 5 of the present work. I have incorporated a few passages from this paper into Chapter 5; they are used with permission.

28. See on this J. O. Urmson, "Saints and Heroes," in *Essays in Moral Philosophy*, ed. A. I. Melden (Seattle: University of Washington Press, 1958), although I do not share Urmson's view that utilitarianism is best suited to deal with this problem. See also Joel Feinberg, *Doing and Deserving* (Princeton, N.J.: Princeton University Press, 1970), chap. 1.

29. Rawls, *A Theory of Justice,* p. 8.

30. Ibid., p. 9.

31. Ibid., p. 8. See also Rawls, "Fairness to Goodness," *Philosophical Review* (October 1975): 548.

32. See Virginia Held, "On Rawls and Self-Interest," *Midwest Studies in Philosophy* 1 (1976).

33. Normal Daniels, "Wide Reflective Equilibrium and Theory Acceptance in Ethics," *Journal of Philosophy* 76 (May 1979): 256–82.

34. See David Lyons, *Forms and Limits of Utilitarianism* (London: Oxford University Press, 1965), especially chap. 3.

35. See Ronald Dworkin, "The DeFunis Case: The Right to Go to Law School," *The New York Review of Books,* February 5, 1976, pp. 29–33. See also James W. Nickel, "Classification by Race in Compensatory Programs," *Ethics* 84, no. 2 (January 1974): 146–50.

36. See A. I. Melden, *Rights and Right Conduct* (Oxford: Blackwell, 1959), pp. 31–35.

37. This would expand and extend to other areas a method resembling somewhat the one suggested by Ronald Dworkin for discovering the moral principles that underlie an existing body of laws. See Dworkin, *Taking Rights Seriously* (Cambridge, Mass.: Harvard University Press, 1977), pp. 66–68.

38. On this issue, see David A. J. Richards, "Equal Opportunity and School Financing: Towards a Moral Theory of Constitutional Adjudication," *University of Chicago Law Review* 41, no. 1 (Fall 1973): 32–71.

39. Dworkin, *Taking Rights Seriously,* p. 227.

40. See also Bruce Ackerman, *Social Justice in the Liberal State* (New Haven: Yale University Press, 1980).

Chapter 5   The Grounds for Social Trust

1. William Butler Yeats, "The Second Coming." *Collected Poems,* 2d ed. (New York: Macmillan, 1956).

2. Peter Rodino, "Scars of the 'Nightmare,' " *New York Times,* Op-Ed Page, August 9, 1979.

3. For a survey of the overwhelming evidence of a lack of trust in American institutions, see Seymour Martin Lipset and William Schneider, *The Confidence Gap: Business, Labor, and Government in the Public Mind* (New York: Free Press, 1983).

4. This is so overwhelmingly the standard view that there is no need to single out proponents. Among the most frequently cited are Hobbes, in the *Leviathan,* and Garrett Hardin in several recent articles. For criticism, see Held, "Rationality and Reasonable Cooperation," pp. 732–33.

5. Sissela Bok, *Lying. Moral Choice in Public and Private Life* (New York: Vintage, 1979), p. 28.

6. See especially Lucian W. Pye and Sidney Verba, *Political Culture and Political Development* (Princeton, N.J.: Princeton University Press, 1965), and Gabriel A. Almond and Sidney Verba, *The Civic Culture* (Boston: Little, Brown, 1965).

7. *The Oxford English Dictionary* (Oxford: Clarendon Press, 1933).

8. *Webster's New International Dictionary of the English Language,* 2d ed. (Springfield, Mass.: G. & C. Merriam Co., 1949), p. 2727.

9. See also Virginia Held, "On the Meaning of Trust," *Ethics* 78, no. 2 (January 1968): 156–59.

10. See especially Erik Erikson, *Childhood and Society* (New York: W. W. Norton & Co., 1950).

11. See Held, "On the Meaning of Trust." See also John Klenig, "Crime and the Concept of Harm," *American Philosophical Quarterly,* 15 (January 1978):35–36.

12. See, e.g., David Gauthier, "Rational Cooperation," *NOUS* 1 (March 1974): 53–65.

13. David Hume, *A Treatise of Human Nature* (New York: Doubleday, 1961; first published 1739), III,II,II; p. 442; and *An Inquiry Concerning the Principles of Morals,* ed. Charles Hendel (New York: Liberal Arts Press, 1957; first published 1752), app. III, p. 123.

14. See Jean-Jacques Rousseau, *The Confessions,* trans. J. M. Cohen (Baltimore: Penguin, 1957; first published 1781), pp. 61–62.

15. For a brief and helpful introduction, see Anatol Rapoport, *Strategy and Conscience* (New York: Schocken, 1969).

16. See especially Mancur Olson, *The Logic of Collective Action* (Cambridge, Mass.: Harvard University Press, 1965).

17. For further discussion, see Held, "Rationality and Reasonable Cooperation."

18. For further discussion, see ibid. and J. Rawls, "The Basic Liberties and Their Priority," *The Tanner Lectures,* University of Michigan, April 10, 1981.

19. Harry C. Bredemeier, "Exchange Theory," in Tom Bottomore and Robert Nisbet, eds., *A History of Sociological Analysis* (New York: Basic Books, 1978), p. 439.

20. See especially Robert Nisbet, *Twilight of Authority* (New York: Oxford University Press, 1975).

21. See Christopher Lasch, *The Culture of Narcissism* (New York: Norton, 1979).

22. A long-term decline in voter participation in midterm elections was reversed in 1982, owing perhaps to dismay about unemployment. In 1978, only 38 percent of eligible voters voted, the lowest percentage since 1942, reflecting a steady downward trend since 1962, when turnout was 49 percent. Hedrick Smith, *New York Times,* November 10, 1982.

23. See Lipset and Schneider, *The Confidence Gap.*

24. Joseph LaPalombara, "Italy: Fragmentation, Isolation, and Alienation," in Pye and Verba, *Political Culture and Political Development.*

25. Sidney Verba, "Conclusion: Comparative Political Culture," in Pye and Verba, p. 556.

26. See U.S. Bureau of the Census, *Current Population Reports.* Figures on consumer income show how remarkably static the distribution of income has been. For instance, the wage and salary earnings of persons in the lowest fifth were 2.6 percent of the total in 1948 and 1.7 percent of the total in 1977, while the earnings of persons in the highest fifth were 49.3 percent in 1948 and 48.1 percent in 1977. Changes for the fifths in between were comparably slight: for the second lowest fifth, from 8.1 percent to 7.7 percent; for the third, from 16.6 percent to 16.1 percent, and for the fourth from 23.4 percent to 26.4 percent.

27. Joseph A. Pechman and Benjamin Okner, *Who Bears the Tax Burden?* (Washington, D.C.: Brookings Institution, 1974), p. 428.

28. See Martin Carnoy and Derek Shearer, *Economic Democracy: The Challenge of the 1980's.* (Armonk, N.Y.: M. E. Sharpe, 1980), p. 86. For a helpful discussion of the implications of the static aspects of economic inequality in the United States, see Paul Blumberg, *Inequality in an Age of Decline* (New York: Oxford University Press, 1980).

29. Richard H. DeLone, *Small Futures* (New York: Harcourt Brace Jovanovich, 1979).

30. See Larry Blum, Marcia Homiak, Judy Housman, and Naomi Scheman, "Altruism and Women's Oppression," in C. Gould and M. Wartofsky, eds., *Women and Philosophy* (New York: Putnam, 1976).

31. U.S. Department of Labor, Bureau of Labor Statistics, *Employment and Earnings,* vol. 30, no. 1 (January 1983).

32. Robert B. Hill, *The Illusion of Black Progress,* Report of National Urban League, 1978.

33. See Lasch, *The Culture of Narcissism.*

34. This is the claim of a whole host of opponents of affirmative action. For opposing arguments, see especially Robert K. Fullinwider, *The Reverse Discrimination Controversy: A Moral and Legal Analysis* (Totowa, N.J.: Rowman & Littlefield, 1980); J. W. Nickel, "Discrimination and Morally Relevant Characteristics," *Analysis* 32 (1972); and Onora O'Neill, "How Do We Know When Opportunities Are Equal?" in Mary Vetterling-Braggin et al., eds., *Feminism and Philosophy* (Totowa, N.J.: Littlefield, Adams, 1977). A member of the U.S. Civil Rights Commission recently wrote: "It is almost ludicrous to assume that society and the courts cannot distinguish between quotas that seek to include rather than to exclude, to overcome inequality rather than to enforce it" (Murray Saltzman, "Affirming Affirmative Action," *New York Times,* June 28, 1983). The point is even stronger for goals rather than quotas.

35. For this and other relevant figures see Lester Thurow, *The Zero-Sum Society* (New York: Penguin, 1981). This is on p. 201.

36. See Louis Henkin, "Rights, American and Human," *Columbia Law Review* 79 (April 1979): 405–25.

37. For an excellent discussion of how even civil liberties depend on having property, see William W. Van Alstyne, "The Recrudescence of Property Rights as the Foremost Principle of Civil Liberties," *Law and Contemporary Problems* 43 (Summer 1980).

38. This is the situation Thurow describes in *The Zero-Sum Society.*

39. A good discussion of self-respect is in Thomas E. Hill, Jr., "Servility and Self-Respect," *The Monist* 57, no. 1 (January 1973).

40. For further discussion, see Virginia Held, "Reasonable Progress and Self-Respect," *The Monist* 57, no. 1 (January 1973). A few paragraphs in this chapter are based on that article. Reprinted from *The Monist* 57, no. 1 (1973) with the permission of the Editor and the Publisher.

41. For further discussion, see Virginia Held, "Can a Random Collection of Individuals Be Morally Responsible?" *Journal of Philosophy* 67 (July 23, 1970): 471–82.

Chapter 6 Acceptance or Rejection of the State

1. See especially C. B. Macpherson, *The Political Theory of Possessive Individualism* (New York: Oxford University Press, 1972).

2. John Rawls, *A Theory of Justice* (Cambridge, Mass.: Harvard University Press, 1981).

3. A philosopher recently told a story about some friends who decided to move to a location in the world where they could be sure of raising their children in a peaceful, healthy environment, far away from the turmoil and torments of modern society. They chose the Falkland Islands! A few years later, Argentina invaded the Falklands and Great Britain recap-

tured them at a total cost of 970 lives. After these events, the inhabitants of the Falklands were afraid to walk around because of land mines.

4. Plato, *Euthyphro, Apology, Crito,* ed. R. Cumming (New York: Liberal Arts Press, 1956).

5. See Martin Luther King, *Stride toward Freedom: The Montgomery Story* (New York: Harper, 1958).

6. John Rawls, "The Justification of Civil Disobedience," in Hugo Adam Bedau, ed., *Civil Disobedience: Theory and Practice* (New York: Pegasus, 1969), p. 246.

7. Richard Wollheim has suggested what might be thought to be a possible solution by drawing a distinction between direct principles, which refer to the morality of actions and policies, designated by general descriptive expressions, such as "murder is wrong," and oblique principles, which refer to the morality of actions and policies designated by means of an artificial property that they have as a result of an act of will, such as "What is commanded by the sovereign is right." Wollheim asserts that "A ought to be the case" and "B ought to be the case" are not incompatible, even where A and B cannot both be effected, "*if* one of these judgments is asserted as a derivation from an oblique principle—provided that the direct and the oblique principle are not themselves incompatible." But again, this argument provides no solution to the problem we have been considering, since it supposes that an individual may simultaneously commit herself to principles which yield conflicting recommendations on what she should accept or reject. See Wollheim, "A Paradox in the Theory of Democracy," in Peter Laslett and W. G. Runciman, eds., *Philosophy, Politics and Society,* 2d Series (Oxford: Basil Blackwell, 1962), p. 85.

8. See W. V. O. Quine, *From a Logical Point of View* (New York: Harper, 1961; first published 1953).

9. The same assumption that law "allows" whatever it does not "forbid" cannot be supposed to suggest that the legal system of a society somehow "includes" or "covers" whatever anyone in it does, although some legal theorists write as if one can legitimately think this way.

10. See Rudolph H. Weingartner, "Justifying Civil Disobedience," *Columbia University Forum* 9 (Spring 1966): 42.

11. See Virginia Held, "Civil Disobedience and Public Policy," in Edward Kent, ed., *Revolution and the Rule of Law* (Englewood Cliffs, N.J.: Prentice-Hall, 1971). For a discussion of the distinction between the legal and the political, see chapters 7 and 9.

12. Thus Stuart M. Brown, Jr., claims as one of the necessary conditions an act of civil disobedience must meet in order to be justified that "the protests, in the course of which the breaches occur, must be directed at constitutional defects exposing either all the people or some class of the peo-

ple to legally avoidable forms of harm and exploitation" ("Civil Disobedience," *Journal of Philosophy* 58 [Oct. 26, 1961]:677). And John Rawls cites as a condition for civil disobedience to be justified that "there has been a serious breakdown" in normal democratic processes such that "not only is there grave injustice in the law but a refusal more or less deliberate to correct it" ("The Justification of Civil Disobedience," p. 249).

13. Hannah Arendt, "Civil Disobedience," *The New Yorker,* September 12, 1970, pp. 7–105.

14. Many writers on civil disobedience have asserted that for an act of lawbreaking to qualify as an act of civil disobedience, it must be done openly and with a willingness to accept the penalties. I have argued against the former requirement in "Consent and Civil Disobedience," *Archives for Philosophy of Law and Social Philosophy,* Beiheft Neue Folge, Nr. 12 (Wiesbaden: Franz Steiner Verlag, 1979). Gordon Schochet has argued against the latter requirement in "The Morality of Resisting the Penalty" in V. Held, K. Nielsen, and C. Parsons, eds., *Philosophy and Political Action* (New York: Oxford University Press, 1972).

15. A comparison between the shaping of power and the production of wealth is suggested by Harold D. Lasswell and Abraham Kaplan in *Power and Society* (New Haven: Yale University Press, 1950): "The *arena* of power is the situation comprised by those who demand power or who are within the domain of power. . . . An *encounter* is an interaction in the power process. . . . An encounter in the arena sets in motion a process of focusing the activities of all concerned to the end of affecting the outcome. The process is equivalent to the *production* of wealth, which is not concluded until the claim to the service is offered for exchange in the market. Power is not completely made available (shaped) until it is involved in fighting, arguing, boycotting, negotiating—all of which may be resorted to in a particular process of power determination" (pp. 78–81). On the meaning and justification of authority, see Richard E. Flathman, *The Practice of Political Authority: Authority and the Authoritative* (Chicago: University of Chicago Press, 1980).

16. For a discussion of the grounds on which such judgments might be made, see Virginia Held, "Coercion and Coercive Offers," in J. Roland Pennock and John W. Chapman, eds., *Coercion: Nomos XIV* (New York: Atherton, 1972).

17. Hugo Adam Bedau has pointed out that "the law has long managed to obviate much civil disobedience by clauses providing exemption for conscientious objectors" and that similar exemptions from prosecution and penalty for violations of law on conscientious grounds could well be provided for laws other than those concerned with military service (Bedau, "On Civil Disobedience," *Journal of Philosophy* 58 [1961]: 655). Long before such legal provisions are enacted, political decisions to refrain from enforcement might become frequent.

18. A few passages in this chapter have been drawn from my paper "On Understanding Political Strikes." From *Philosophy & Political Action: Essays edited for the New York Group of the Society for Philosophy & Public Affairs*, edited by Virginia Held, Kai Nielson, and Charles Parsons. Copyright ©1972 by Oxford University Press, Inc. Reprinted by permission.

19. For further discussion, see Virginia Held, "Violence, Terrorism, and Moral Inquiry," *The Monist* 67 (1983).

Chapter 7   Law and Rights

1. Giovanni Sartori, "What Is 'Politics'?" *Political Theory* 1, no. 1 (February 1973): 17–18.

2. Ibid., p. 18.

3. Alf Ross, *On Law and Justice* (Berkeley: University of California Press, 1959), p. 58. Italics added.

4. Hans Kelsen, "The Pure Theory of Law and Analytic Jurisprudence," *Harvard Law Review* 65 (November 1941): 44–70, reprinted in Kelsen, *What Is Justice?* (Berkeley: University of California Press, 1957), p. 281.

5. James A. Robinson and R. Roger Majak, "The Theory of Decision-Making," in James C. Charlesworth, ed., *Contemporary Political Analysis* (New York: Free Press, 1967), p. 183.

6. Morton Kaplan, *System and Process in International Politics* (New York: John Wiley and Sons, 1957), p. 14; italics added. An example of an interpretation of the court system as itself a political system within a wider political system, using David Easton's model for both, is Sheldon Goldman and Thomas P. Jahnige, *The Federal Courts as a Political System* (New York: Harper & Bros., 1971). See also Glendon Schubert, *Judicial Policy-Making* (Chicago: Scott, Foresman and Co., 1965), and Jay Sigler, *An Introduction to the Legal System* (Homewood, Ill.: Dorsey Press, 1968).

7. H. L. A. Hart, *The Concept of Law* (Oxford: Clarendon Press, 1961), p. 3.

8. Franz Neumann, "Approaches to the Study of Political Power," *Political Science Quarterly* 65, no. 2 (June 1950): 165–66. See also on this Judith N. Shklar, *Legalism* (Cambridge, Mass.: Harvard University Press, 1965), and J. Roland Pennock and John W. Chapman, eds., *The Limits of Law: Nomos XV* (New York: Lieber-Atherton, 1974).

9. This thesis is compatible with Ronald Dworkin's distinction between principles and policies, in *Taking Rights Seriously* (Cambridge, Mass.: Harvard University Press, 1977), pp. 14–45, but it goes further in considering their relations to appropriate argument forms and systems, as does Dworkin himself (pp. 81–130). As will be discussed, I do not fully share his identification of principles with individualistic and policies with collective concerns. See also James F. Doyle, "Principles and Policies in the Justification of Legal Decisions," in H. Hubien, ed., *Le*

Raisonnement juridique, Actes du Congrès mondial de philosophie du droit et de philosophie sociale (Brussels: Emile Bruylant, 1971).

10. See especially Hart (n. 7 above) and Dworkin, *Taking Rights Seriously,* pp. 14–45. See also Graham Hughes, "Rules, Policy and Decision-Making," in Graham Hughes, ed., *Law, Reason and Justice* (New York: New York University Press, 1969).

11. See especially Dworkin, *Taking Rights Seriously,* pp. 14–45, and "Judicial Discretion," *Journal of Philosophy* 60 (October 1963): 624–38; and Gerald MacCallum, "Dworkin on Judicial Discretion," ibid., pp. 638–41. See also the articles by Bruce L. Miller and Thomas R. Kearns in *Social Theory and Practice* 2, no. 2 (Fall 1972): 163–76, 177–87.

12. See especially Herbert Wechsler, "Toward Neutral Principles of Constitutional Law," *Harvard Law Review* 73, no. 1 (1959): 1–35; reprinted in Wechsler, *Principles, Policies and Fundamental Law* (Cambridge, Mass.: Harvard University Press, 1961); and Martin Golding, "Principled Decision-Making and the Supreme Court," *Columbia Law Review* 63, no. 1 (1963): 35–58.

13. See especially Rolf Sartorius, "Social Policy and Judicial Legislation," *American Philosophical Quarterly* 8 (April 1971): 151–60.

14. See especially Dworkin, *Taking Rights Seriously,* chaps. 2, 3, and 4. See also Joseph Raz, "Legal Principles and the Limits of Law," *Yale Law Journal* 81, no. 5 (April 1972): 823–54.

15. Rolf Sartorius, "Justification of the Judicial Decision," *Ethics* 78 (April 1968): 173.

16. Richard Wasserstrom, *The Judicial Decision* (Stanford, Calif.: Stanford University Press, 1961).

17. Ronald Dworkin, "Wasserstrom: The Judicial Decision," *Ethics* 75 (October 1964): 56 n. Although the interpretation of law of Henry M. Hart and Albert M. Sacks is at times in terms of its purposive aspects, their characterization fits more nearly into a deontological framework than they seem to acknowledge. "The central idea of law," they write, is *"the principle of institutional settlement. . . .* The alternative to disintegrating resort to violence is the establishment of regularized and peaceable methods of decision. The principle of institutional settlement expresses the judgment that decisions which are the duly arrived at results of duly established procedures of this kind ought to be accepted as binding upon the whole society unless and until they are duly changed." (Henry M. Hart and Albert M. Sacks, *The Legal Process: Basic Problems in the Making and Application of Law,* tentative ed. [Cambridge, Mass.: 1958], p. 4).

18. Dworkin, "Wasserstrom," p. 51. The Supreme Court has at times made its decisions on grounds that seem to be teleological: the "balancing of interests" test has sometimes treated even constitutional rights such as First Amendment rights as mere interests to be promoted which must be

balanced against other interests to be promoted. But it may be far more adequate to interpret Supreme Court decisions over the years in terms of the "preferred position" that some rights occupy relative to others: constitutionally protected rights are accorded, intrinsically, a higher standing in the legal system. For a discussion see Fred R. Berger, "Some Aspects of Legal Reasoning Concerning Constitutionally Protected Rights," in *Le Raisonnement juridique;* and Dworkin, chap. 4.

19. See especially Dworkin, "What Is Equality?" parts I and II, in *Philosophy and Public Affairs* 10, nos. 3 and 4 (1981).

20. See especially Guido Calabresi, *The Costs of Accidents: A Legal and Economic Analysis.* (New Haven: Yale University Press, 1970).

21. For further discussion of the role of the lawyer, see Virginia Held, "The Division of Moral Labor and the Role of the Lawyer," in David Luban, ed., *The Good Lawyer* (Totowa, N.J.: Rowman and Allanheld, 1983).

22. See, e.g., Hans Kelsen, *General Theory of Law and State,* trans. A. Wedberg (New York: Russell & Russell, 1961; first published 1945).

23. H. L. A. Hart maintains the former view in "Are There Any Natural Rights?" *Philosophical Review* 64 (April 1955): 175–91, though he qualifies it in footnote 6. For a different view, see David Lyons, ed., *Rights,* introduction, p. 3; Hart's paper is reprinted in this volume. Jeremy Bentham maintained the latter view; see especially his *Anarchical Fallacies,* vol. 2 of the *Works,* ed. John Bowring, 1843.

24. John Austin, *The Province of Jurisprudence Determined,* (New York: Noonday Press, 1954; first published 1832), p. 184.

25. David A. J. Richards, "Taking *Taking Rights Seriously* Seriously: Reflections on Dworkin and the Revival of Natural Law," *New York University Law Review* 52, no. 6 (December 1977): 1276.

26. Ibid., p. 1297.

27. Ibid.

Chapter 8 Rights to Equal Liberty

1. Hobbes, *Leviathan,* chap. 21.

2. Milton Friedman, *Capitalism and Freedom* (Chicago: University of Chicago Press, 1962), p. 13.

3. *Statistical Abstract of the United States 1982–83* (Washington, D.C.: U.S. Government Printing Office, 1982), p. 385.

4. See Isaiah Berlin, *Four Essays on Liberty* (London: Oxford University Press, 1969).

5. See Berlin, *Four Essays,* p. 171, but also the note on p. lviii.

6. Gerald MacCallum, "Negative and Positive Freedom," *Philosophical Re-*

view 76 (July 1967): 314. See also Felix Oppenheim, *Dimensions of Freedom* (New York: St. Martin's Press, 1961).

7. C. B. Macpherson, *Democratic Theory* (London: Oxford University Press, 1973), p. 96.

8. John Rawls, *The Basic Liberties and Their Priority,* The Tanner Lectures on Human Values, delivered at the University of Michigan, April 10, 1981.

9. S. I. Benn and W. L. Weinstein, "Being Free to Act and Being a Free Man," *Mind* 80 (April 1971): 197.

10. See Held, "Coercion and Coercive Offers," in Pennock and Chapman, *Coercion: Nomos XIV* (New York: Aldine-Atherton, 1972).

11. See especially Amartya Sen, "Entitlements and Capabilities," James Lecture, New York University, November 15, 1982.

12. See also Henry Shue, *Basic Rights: Subsistence, Affluence, and U.S. Foreign Policy* (Princeton, N.J.: Princeton University Press, 1980).

13. On this see Louis Henkin, "Rights, American and Human," *Columbia Law Review* 79 (April 1979): 405–25. See also Frank I. Michelman, "On Protecting the Poor through the Fourteenth Amendment," *Harvard Law Review* 83 (1969–70): 7–59.

14. Richard Funston, "The Double Standard of Constitutional Protection in the Era of the Welfare State." *Political Science Quarterly* 90 (Summer 1975): 286.

15. Locke, *The First Treatise of Government,* section 42.

16. Ibid.

17. Robert Nozick, *Anarchy, State and Utopia* (New York: Basic Books, 1974), p. 169.

18. Ibid., p. 162 n.

19. For further discussion of Nozick, see Virginia Held, "John Locke on Robert Nozick," *Social Research* 43 (Spring 1976), and "What Is Minimal Government?" *The Personalist* (Fall 1978).

20. See *Wyman v. James,* 400 U.S. 309 (1971).

21. See Peter Steinfels, *The Neoconservatives.* (New York: Simon and Schuster, 1979).

22. This chapter is based in part on my paper "Men, Women, and Equal Liberty," in W. Feinberg, ed., *Equality and Social Policy* (Urbana: University of Illinois Press, 1978). Selected passages are used with permission.

Chapter 9   The Goals of Politics

1. For a list of familiar references, see William C. Mitchell, "Systems Analysis: Political Systems," *International Encyclopedia of the Social Sciences,* ed.

David L. Sills (New York: Macmillan, 1968), vol. 15, pp. 473–78.

2. David Easton, *A Framework for Political Analysis* (Englewood Cliffs, N.J.: Prentice-Hall, 1965), p. 56.

3. David Easton, *The Political System* (New York: Alfred A. Knopf, 1965; first published 1953), p. 132.

4. Gabriel Almond and G. Bingham Powell, *Comparative Politics: A Developmental Approach* (Boston: Little, Brown & Co., 1966), p. 18.

5. Sheldon Goldman and Thomas P. Jahnige, in *The Federal Courts as a Political System* (New York: Harper, 1971), interpret the distinctive aspects of judicial decision-making entirely in terms of the roles that judges are "expected" to play; these now include the meeting of certain standards of impartiality and faithfulness to law, but implied in this analysis is no suggestion that, if expectations were to abandon these standards, the remaining system might no longer be a *legal* system.

6. Otto Kirchheimer, "Politics and Justice," *Social Research* 22 (1955): 377–98; reprinted in Kirchheimer, *Politics, Law and Social Change* (New York: Columbia University Press, 1969).

7. David Braybrooke, *Three Tests for Democracy: Personal Rights, Human Welfare, Collective Preference* (New York: Random House, 1968), p. 88.

8. Ibid., p. 85.

9. Rolf Sartorius, "Justification of the Judicial Decision," *Ethics* 78 (April 1968): 175.

10. Although the present discussion departs from some conceptions there, see Virginia Held, *The Public Interest and Individual Interests* (New York: Basic Books, 1970).

11. On some of these issues, see Alfred F. MacKay, "Interpersonal Comparisons," *Journal of Philosophy* 72, no. 17 (October 2, 1975).

12. See especially Kenneth J. Arrow, *Social Choice and Individual Values* (New York: John Wiley, 1963).

13. The maximin rule recommends that we maximize the minimum, or choose the alternative whose worst outcome is better than the worst outcomes of the other alternatives.

14. See John C. Harsanyi, "Can the Maximin Principle Serve as a Basis for Morality?" *American Political Science Review* 69, no. 2 (June 1975).

15. In "Pluralism Revisited," Michael P. Smith writes that "political pluralism is at once a descriptive theory of politics, a set of normative preferences, and an ideology used to legitimize the role of organized interest groups in shaping American public policy" (p. v). The effects, he says, are as follows: "The very philosophy of pluralism serves to legitimize the resolution of policy issues through direct participation by interest groups. The result is either logrolling between the government and powerful interest groups who have stakes in preserving the status quo, or gen-

erally ineffective compromises between countervailing interest groups. Neither of these outcomes is likely to alleviate such comprehensive national problems as poverty, underemployment, or technical obsolescence" (p. 18). Smith and associates, *Politics in America: Studies in Policy Analysis* (New York: Random House, 1974).

16. See especially Gabriel Almond and Sidney Verba, eds., *The Civic Culture: Political Attitudes and Democracy in Five Nations* (Princeton, N.J.: Princeton University Press, 1963); Lucian Pye and Sidney Verba, eds., *Political Culture and Political Development* (Princeton: Princeton University Press, 1965); and Gabriel Almond and G. Bingham Powell, *Comparative Politics: A Developmental Approach* (Boston: Little, Brown and Co., 1966).

17. See Ronald Rogowski, *Rational Legitimacy: A Theory of Political Support* (Princeton, N.J.: Princeton University Press, 1974); and Brian Barry, *Sociologists, Economists and Democracy* (London: Macmillan, 1970), pp. 86–87.

18. David Easton, *A Systems Analysis of Political Life* (New York: John Wiley, 1955), p. 275.

19. Rogowski, *Rational Legitimacy,* p. 21.

20. Ibid., p. 3.

21. See, e.g., Dan W. Brock, "Recent Work in Utilitarianism," *American Philosophical Quarterly* 10 (October 1973): 241–76; and Amartya Sen and Bernard Williams, eds., *Utilitarianism and Beyond* (Cambridge: At the University Press, 1982).

22. Ronald Dworkin, *Taking Rights Seriously* (Cambridge, Mass.: Harvard University Press, 1977), p. 91.

23. Peter Bachrach, "Interest, Participation, and Democratic Theory," in Pennock and Chapman, *Participation in Politics: Nomos XVI* (New York: Lieber-Atherton, 1975), p. 40.

24. M. B. E. Smith, "The Value of Participation," in *Participation in Politics,* p. 128.

25. See Robert Paul Wolff, *In Defense of Anarchism* (New York: Harper & Row, 1970), for a related though different version of this problem, and Grenville Wall, "Philosophical Anarchism Revisited," in *Anarchism: Nomos XIX,* ed. J. Roland Pennock and John W. Chapman (New York: New York University Press, 1978), for an attempt to solve Wolff's problem by ruling out "ethical individualism." My suggestions for dealing with Wolff's problem would not require us to abandon individualism at the level of morality.

26. In 1979, they were over 20 percent compared to 13 percent (*New York Times,* June 17, 1979, p. 1.)

27. On some of these issues, see Barry Commoner, *The Poverty of Power, Ener-*

gy and the Economic Crisis (New York: Bantam, 1977); and Amory Lovins, *Soft Energy Paths* (Cambridge, Mass.: Ballinger, 1977).

28. For a helpful discussion, see Christine Swanton, "The Concept of Interests," *Political Theory* 8, no. 1 (February 1980): 83–101.

29. M. J. C. Vile, *Constitutionalism and the Separation of Powers* (Oxford: Clarendon Press, 1967), p. 290.

30. John Rawls, *A Theory of Justice* (Cambridge, Mass.: Harvard University Press, 1971).

31. See Virginia Held, "Can a Random Collection of Individuals Be Morally Responsible?" *Journal of Philosophy* 67 (July 23, 1970); and Peter A. French, ed., *Individual and Collective Responsibility* (Cambridge, Mass.: Schenkman, 1972).

Chapter 10   Property and Economic Activity

1. See, e.g., Edward S. Herman, "The Institutionalization of Bias in Economics," *Media, Culture and Society* 4, no. 3 (1982): 275–91. See also Jürgen Habermas, *Knowledge and Human Interests,* trans. J. Shapiro (Boston: Beacon Press, 1968).

2. For an account of these rights, see especially A. M. Honoré, "Ownership," in A. G. Guest, ed., *Oxford Essays in Jurisprudence* (Oxford: Clarendon Press, 1961), pp. 107–47.

3. Charles Reich, "The New Property," *Yale Journal* 73 (April 1964): 733–87.

4. Morris R. Cohen, "Property and Sovereignty," in his *Law and the Social Order* (New York: Harcourt, Brace & Co., 1933).

5. See especially Wesley Hohfeld, *Fundamental Legal Conceptions as Applied to Judicial Reasoning* (New Haven, Conn.: Yale University Press, 1919); and H. L. A. Hart, "Are There Any Natural Rights?" *Philosophical Review* 64 (April 1955): 175–91.

6. A. M. Honoré, "Property, Title and Redistribution," in Carl Wellman, ed., *Equality and Freedom: Past, Present and Future,* Archives for Philosophy of Law and Social Philosophy, Beiheft Neue Folge, Nr. 10 (Wiesbaden: Franz Steiner Verlag, 1977). Reprinted in V. Held, ed., *Property, Profits and Economic Justice* (Belmont, Calif.: Wadsworth, 1980).

7. An outstanding example of this view was pressed by Jeremy Bentham in *Anarchical Fallacies,* thought to have been written about 1791.

8. John Locke, *Two Treatises of Government* (1690), especially The Second Treatise, chap. 5.

9. Locke went on to maneuver around his own suggested principles by holding that the introduction of money changed the applicability of the principles: since money does not "spoil," a person who has more of it than he

needs is not "wasting" it. And Locke argued that the bequeathing of property from fathers to sons could lead to acceptable accumulations far beyond what a person needed or could make good use of. But Locke's principles, would they be applicable, were more persuasive than his evasions of them.

10. Lawrence Becker, *Property Rights* (London: Routledge & Kegan Paul, 1977), chap. 4.

11. The first of four principles states: "When it is beyond what morality requires them to do for others, people deserve some benefit for the value their (morally permissible) labor produces, and conversely, they deserve some penalty for the disvalue their labor produces" (Ibid., pp. 53–54).

12. John Stuart Mill, *Principles of Political Economy* (1871), book 2, chap. 1.

13. This entire book explores the division of moral labor of which this issue is an aspect.

14. Charles Fried, *Right and Wrong* (Cambridge, Mass.: Harvard University Press, 1978), p. 85. (The interests are those of the same person having the right.).

15. Adam Smith, *The Wealth of Nations* (1776).

16. David Ricardo, *The Principles of Political Economy and Taxation* (1817).

17. See especially Karl Marx, *Capital,* vol. 1 (1867).

18. See Joan Robinson, *Economic Philosophy* (London: C. A. Watts, 1962), now, sadly, out of print.

19. See especially *The New Industrial State* (New York: New American Library, 1968) and *Economics and the Public Purpose* (New York: New American Library, 1975).

20. See especially *Between Capitalism and Socialism* (New York: Vintage, 1970) and *Business Civilization in Decline* (New York: Norton, 1976).

21. See especially *The Twilight of Capitalism* (New York: Simon and Schuster, 1976).

22. See Robert L. Heilbroner, "The Swedish Promise," *The New York Review of Books,* December 4, 1980. But see also Heilbroner, "The Coming Invasion," *New York Review of Books,* December 8, 1983.

23. Robert A. Dahl, *After the Revolution? Authority in a Good Society* (New Haven, Conn.: Yale University Press, 1970).

24. See Martin Carnoy and Derek Shearer, *Economic Democracy: The Challenge of the 1980's* (Armonk, N.Y.: M. E. Sharpe, 1980).

25. See Lester Thurow, *The Zero-Sum Society* (New York: Penguin, 1981), especially chap. 7.

26. See, e.g., Sidney Blumenthal, "Drafting a Democratic Industrial Plan," *New York Times Magazine,* August 28, 1983.

27. Gar Alperovitz, "Notes toward a Pluralist Commonwealth," in

Staughton Lynd and Gar Alperovitz, *Strategy and Program* (Boston: Beacon Press, 1973).

28. The gap between women's and men's wages in the United States has not decreased in the last two decades. Women still earn less than sixty cents for every dollar earned by men. For a useful report, see "Paying Women What They're Worth," *QQ, Report from the Center for Philosophy and Public Policy*, University of Maryland, 3, no. 2 (Spring 1983).

29. See, e.g., Charlotte Bunch et al., eds., *Building Feminist Theory: Essays from Quest* (New York: Longman, 1981).

30. See Carnoy and Shearer, *Economic Democracy.*

31. See especially John Stuart Mill, *Principles of Political Economy,* book 5, chap. 12.

32. On this problem, see especially Mancur Olsen, *The Logic of Collective Action* (Cambridge, Mass.: Harvard University Press, 1963).

33. See John Hospers, "The Nature of the State," *The Personalist* 59 (October 1978): 398–404. Also Milton Friedman, *Capitalism and Freedom* (Chicago: University of Chicago Press, 1962).

34. Robert Nozick, in *Anarchy, State and Utopia* (New York: Basic Books, 1974), begins with similar assumptions and reaches, by long and clever routes, similar conclusions.

35. John Rawls, *A Theory of Justice* (Cambridge, Mass.: Harvard University Press, 1971). One of the best short expositions of Rawls's theory is his article "A Kantian Conception of Equality," *Cambridge Review,* February 1975, reprinted in Held, ed., *Property, Profits and Economic Justice* (Belmont, Calif.: Wadsworth, 1980).

36. See pp. 127–28 for Rawls's recent modification of this formulation. The modification does not affect the discussion in this chapter.

37. See C. B. Macpherson, *Democratic Theory: Essays in Retrieval* (Oxford: Clarendon Press, 1973), especially essay VI, "A Political Theory of Property."

38. For the texts, see Ian Brownlie, ed., *Basic Documents on Human Rights* (Oxford: Clarendon Press, 1967); or Louis B. Sohn and Thomas Buergenthal, *Basic Documents on International Protection of Human Rights* (Indianapolis: Bobbs-Merrill, 1973).

39. See Louis Henkin, "Rights: American and Human," *Columbia Law Review* 79 (April 1979). See also chapter 8.

40. *Wyman, Commissioner of New York Department of Social Services et al. v. James.* 400 U.S. 309(1971).

41. *San Antonio Independent School District, et al. v. Rodriguez et al.* 411 U.S. 1 (1973).

42. Arthur M. Okun, *Equality and Efficiency* (Washington, D.C.: Brookings Institute, 1975). But for a disturbing account of the degree to which they

are not off bounds, see William Van Alstyne, "The Recrudescence of Property Rights as the Foremost Principle of Civil Liberties," *Law and Contemporary Problems* (Summer 1980).

43. This chapter is based on my introduction to *Property, Profits, and Economic Justice* (1980). Various passages have been used with the permission of Wadsworth Publishing Co.

Chapter 11   Family and Society

1. See, e.g., Ira Katznelson and Mark Kesselman, *The Politics of Power* (New York: Harcourt Brace Jovanovich, 1975).

2. See Richard de Lone, *Small Futures: Children, Inequality, and the Limits of Liberal Reform* (New York: Harcourt Brace Jovanovich, 1979).

3. A good summary of the arguments and history surrounding this slogan may be found in Linda Nicholson, " 'The Personal Is Political': An Analysis in Retrospect," *Social Theory and Practice* 7, no. 1 (Spring 1981): 85–98.

4. U.S. Government *Statistical Abstract,* 1981.

5. Anita Schreve,,"Careers and the Lure of Motherhood," *New York Times Magazine,* November 21, 1982, p. 39.

6. U.S. Government *Statistical Abstract,* 1981.

7. See especially Zillah Eisenstein, *The Radical Future of Liberal Feminism* (New York: Longman, 1981).

8. Nancy Chodorow, *The Reproduction of Mothering: Psychoanalysis and the Sociology of Gender* (Berkeley, Calif.: University of California Press, 1978), p. 7. See also Dorothy Dinnerstein, *The Mermaid and the Minotaur* (New York: Harper Colophon Books,,1976).

9. Chodorow, p. 214.

10. Jane Flax, "The Family in Contemporary Feminist Thought: A Critical Review," in Jean Bethke Elshtain, ed., *The Family in Political Thought* (Amherst, Mass.: University of Massachusetts Press,,1982), p. 253.

11. Ibid., p. 252.

12. Homer H. Clark, Jr., *The Law of Domestic Relations* (St. Paul, Minn.: West Publishing Co., 1968), p. 181.

13. Ibid.

14. Georgia Dullea, "Wide Changes in Family Life Are Altering Family Law," *New York Times,* February 7, 1983, pp. A1 and A14.

15. See ibid. and Georgia Dullea, "Joint Custody: Is Sharing the Child a Dangerous Idea?" *New York Times,* May 24, 1976, p. 24; see also Charlotte Baum, "The Best of Both Parents," *New York Times Magazine,* October 31, 1976, pp. 44–46.

16. Ironically, or appropriately, the quotation comes from an article called

"The J-Curve of Rising and Declining Satisfaction as a Cause of Some Great Revolutions and a Contained Rebellion," by James C. Davies, in Hugh Davis Graham and Ted Robert Gurr, eds., *History of Violence in America* (New York: New York Times Books, 1969), pp. 693–94.

17. See Ann Crittenden Scott, "The Value of Housework," *Ms.* 1, no. 1 (July 1972): 56–59.

18. See John Stuart Mill and Harriet Taylor, *Essays on Sex Equality,* ed. Alice S. Rossi (Chicago: University of Chicago Press, 1970), especially pp. 74–75 and 179–80.

19. On the distortions of Plato's argument by various interpreters of him, see Christine Pierce, "Equality: Republic V," *The Monist* 57, no. 1 (January 1973): 1–11.

20. For discussion, see Michael A. Slote, "Desert, Consent, and Justice," *Philosophy and Public Affairs* 2 (Summer 1973): 323–47.

21. Sandra L. Bem and Daryl J. Bem, "Homogenizing the American Woman," reprinted in Alison M. Jaggar and Paula Rothenberg Struhl, eds., *Feminist Frameworks* (New York: McGraw-Hill, 1978).

22. See Larry Blum, Marcia Homiak, Judy Housman, and Naomi Scheman, "Altruism and Women's Oppression," in Carol Gould and Marx Wartofsky, eds., *Women and Philosophy* (New York: Putnam, 1976). See also chapter 5 of the present work.

23. For a perceptive discussion, see Angela Barron McBride, *The Growth and Development of Mothers* (New York: Harper, 1973).

24. Dullea, "Wide Changes in Family Life. . . ."

25. *Search* (Washington, D.C.: Urban Institute), Spring 1977.

26. On many of these issues, see Jessie Bernard, *The Future of Motherhood* (New York: Penguin, 1975), and Adrienne Rich, *Of Woman Born* (New York: Bantam, 1977).

27. See Chodorow, *The Reproduction of Mothering,* chap. 3, for discussion.

28. Sharon Johnson, "For Students, a Dramatic Shift in Goals," *New York Times,* February 28, 1983, p. B5.

29. John Stuart Mill and Harriet Taylor Mill, *Essays on Sex Equality,* p. 220.

30. Karl Marx, "Economic and Philosophical Manuscripts of 1844," in *Karl Marx: Selected Writings,* ed. David McLellan (Oxford: Oxford University Press, 1977).

31. Power is not necessarily coercive, but where its use is unsuccessful, the temptation to resort to coercion is ever present. In "Coercion and Coercive Offers," (*Coercion: Nomos XIV,* ed. Pennock and Chapman [N.Y.: Aldine-Atherton, 1972]) I have argued that coercion is the activity of causing someone to do something against his or her will and that it may be brought about through either threats or inducements.

32. See Sara Ann Ketchum and Christine Pierce, "Separatism and Sexual Re-

lationships," in Sharon Bishop and Marjorie Weinzweig, eds., *Philosophy and Women* (Belmont, Calif.: Wadsworth, 1979).

33. On the history of this analogy, see Susan Moller Okin, *Women in Western Political Thought* (Princeton, N.J.: Princeton University Press, 1979); and Jean Bethke Elshtain, *Public Man, Private Woman* (Princeton: Princeton University Press, 1981). See also Barrie Thorne and Marilyn Yalom, eds., *Rethinking the Family* (New York: Longman, 1982).

34. This chapter draws on my two previously published papers, "The Equal Obligations of Mothers and Fathers" and "Marx, Sex, and the Transformation of Society." The first paper appeared in Onora O'Neill and William Ruddick, eds., *Having Children: Philosophical and Legal Reflections on Parenthood*, copyright © 1979 by Oxford University Press, Inc., and selected passages are reprinted by permission. The second was published in *The Philosophical Forum* V, no. 1–2 (Fall–Winter 1973–74): 168–83, and selected passages are used with permission.

Chapter 12   *Free Expression, Culture, and the Good Life*

1. Thomas I. Emerson, *The System of Freedom of Expression* (New York: Vintage, 1970).

2. *New York Times*, May 11, 1982, p. 6.

3. On the extent to which small numbers of large corporations control broadcasting and publishing in the United States, see Ben H. Bagdikian, *The Media Monopoly* (Boston: Beacon Press, 1983).

4. See Kevin Phillips, "Post-Reagan America," *The New York Review of Books*, May 13, 1982, pp. 27–32.

5. A recent version of this thesis is propounded by Jeanne J. Kirkpatrick in *Dictatorships and Double Standards* (New York: American Enterprise Institute/Simon and Schuster, 1982).

6. See Todd Gitlin, "The Screening Out of 'Lou Grant,' " *The Nation*, June 26, 1982.

7. See Virginia Held, "The Error of Misplaced Disparagement," *The New Leader*, March 14, 1966.

8. See Alexander Meiklejohn, *Political Freedom: The Constitutional Powers of the People* (New York: Oxford University Press, 1965), and "The First Amendment Is an Absolute," *Supreme Court Review* (1961): 245.

9. Ronald Dworkin, "The Rights of Myron Farber," *The New York Review of Books*, October 26, 1978, and "Is the Press Losing the First Amendment?" *The New York Review of Books*, December 4, 1980, pp. 49–57. See also Frederick Schauer, Virginia Held, John Hess, and Ronald Dworkin, "The Rights of M. A. Farber: An Exchange," *The New York Review of Books*, December 7, 1978, pp. 39–41.

10. Letter from James Madison to W. T. Barry, August 4, 1822, in *Letters*

and Other Writings of James Madison, vol. 3 (Philadelphia: J. B. Lippincott Co., 1867), p. 276.

11. Senate Report 813, 89th Congress, 1st Session (1965); 5.

12. Sissela Bok, *Secrets: On the Ethics of Concealment and Revelation* (New York: Pantheon, 1982), pp. 178–79.

13. *New York Times,* May 21, 1982, p. 1.

14. See, e.g., Anthony Lewis, "Reagan vs. Madison," *New York Times,* March 17, 1983, p. A23.

15. For a discussion of issues relevant to the FOIA, see Thomas I. Emerson, "The First Amendment and the Right to Know," *Washington University Law Quarterly,* 1 (1976): 1–24.

16. Dworkin, "Is the Press Losing . . .", p. 52.

17. "Without me," the stance of conscientious Germans against Nazi outrages.

18. Dworkin, "Is the Press Losing . . . ," p. 54.

19. "Documents Show FBI Harrassed Foes of War," *New York Times,* June 25, 1975.

20. For a discussion of accountability, see chapter 9.

21. For a discussion of symbolic action and its relation to speech, see Fred R. Berger, "Symbolic Conduct and Freedom of Speech," in Fred Berger, ed., *Freedom of Expression* (Belmont, Calif.: Wadsworth Publishing Co., 1980).

22. See Universal Declaration of Human Rights, Article 25.

23. See James W. Nickel, "Cultural Diversity and Human Rights," in Jack Nelson and Vera Green, eds., *International Human Rights: Contemporary Issues* (Stanfordville, N.Y.: Human Rights Publishing Group, 1980); and Henry Shue, *Basic Rights: Subsistence, Affluence, and U.S. Foreign Policy* (Princeton, N.J.: Princeton University Press, 1980).

24. Alan Gewirth develops a scheme of rights to freedom and well-being in *Reason and Morality* (Chicago: University of Chicago Press, 1978).

25. Jerome A. Barron, *Freedom of the Press for Whom? The Right of Access to Mass Media* (Bloomington: Indiana University Press, 1973).

26. Ibid., p. xiv.

27. Ibid., p. 320.

28. Ibid., p. 52.

29. Ibid., p. 309.

30. An amendment in 1959 to Section 315 of the Federal Communications Act is the basis for the fairness doctrine.

31. Barron, *Freedom of the Press for Whom?,* pp. 311–12.

32. Philip Rieff, *The Triumph of the Therapeutic: Uses of Faith after Freud* (New York: Harper & Row, 1966), pp. 4 and 11. He continues: "To speak of a *moral* culture would be redundant. Every culture has two main functions: (1) to organize the moral demands men make upon themselves into a system of symbols that make men intelligible and trustworthy to each other, thus rendering also the world intelligible and trustworthy; (2) to organize the expressive remissions by which men release themselves, in some degree, from the strain of conforming to the controlling symbolic, internalized variant readings of culture that constitute individual character" (pp. 232–33).

33. See, for example, Arthur M. Okin, "Rights and Dollars," in V. Held, ed., *Property, Profits, and Economic Justice* (Belmont, Calif.: Wadsworth Publishing Co., 1980), and chapter 10 of the present work.

34. For one classic statement of the role of culture in capitalist society, see Max Horkheimer and Theodor Adorno, "The Culture Industry: Enlightenment as Mass Deception," in *Dialectic of Enlightenment*, trans. John Cumming (New York: Herder and Herder, 1972; original edition, 1944). For a useful account of recent work and of work that needs to be done, see Graham Murdock and Peter Golding, "Capitalism, Communication and Society," in James Curran, M. Gurevitch, and J. Woollacott, eds., *Mass Communication and Society* (Beverly Hills, Calif.: Sage, 1979).

35. See L. Coser, C. Kadushin, and W. Powell, *Books: Culture and Commerce* (New York: Basic Books, 1982), and Charles Kadushin, "Intellectuals and Cultural Power," *Media, Culture and Society* 4, no. 3 (1982): 255–62.

36. Ben H. Bagdikian, a Pulitzer prize–winning journalist, writes: "Modern technology and American economics have quietly created a new kind of central authority over information—the national and multinational corporation. By the 1980's, the majority of all major American media— newspapers, magazines, radio, television, books, and movies—were controlled by fifty giant corporations. These corporations were interlocked in common financial interest with other massive industries and with a few dominant international banks. . . . The fifty men and women who head these corporations would fit in a large room. They constitute a new Private Ministry of Information and Culture" (*The Media Monopoly,* pp. xiv–xv).

37. See Bagdikian, chap. 8, "The High Cost of Free Lunches."

38. James Traub, "Making Waves," *First-Class, Worldwide,* June 1982.

39. See "Fate of Public Radio Could Be Decided Today," *New York Times,* June 28, 1983, p. A1.

40. See Richard Goldstein, "The War for America's Mind," *Village Voice* 27, no. 23 (June 8, 1982).

Chapter 13   The Environment and the Future

1. See Jason Epstein, "Going for Broke," *The New York Review of Books,* September 23, 1982, pp. 17–22.

2. Hazel Henderson, *The Politics of the Solar Age: Alternatives to Economics* (Garden City, N.Y.: Doubleday Anchor, 1981).

3. Ibid., pp. 72–73.

4. Harry Magdoff, "A Statistical Fiction," *The Nation,* July 10–17, 1982, p. 47.

5. Irvin C. Bupp, "Nuclear Power: The Promise Melts Away," in Robert Stobaugh and Daniel Yergin, eds., *Energy Future: Report of the Energy Project at the Harvard Business School,* 3d ed. (New York: Vintage, 1983).

6. See Irvin C. Bupp and Jean-Claude Derian, *Light Water: How the Nuclear Dream Dissolved* (New York: Basic Books, 1978), and Amory B. Lovins, *Soft Energy Paths* (San Francisco: Friends of the Earth, 1977).

7. See Modesto A. Maidique, "Solar America," in Stobaugh and Yergin, eds., *Energy Future.*

8. Henderson, *The Politics of the Solar Age,* p. 138.

9. Quoted in ibid.

10. See Anthony Sampson, *The Seven Sisters: The Great Oil Companies and the World They Shaped* (New York: Viking Press, 1975), especially chap. 3.

11. See, e.g., Robert Engler, *The Brotherhood of Oil: Energy Policy and the Public Interest* (Chicago: University of Chicago Press, 1977), and Barry Commoner, *The Poverty of Power: Energy and the Economic Crisis* (New York: Alfred A. Knopf, 1976).

12. Mary Anne Warren, "Future Generations," in Tom Regan and Donald VandeVeer, eds., *And Justice for All: New Introductory Essays in Ethics and Public Policy* (Totowa, N.J.: Rowman and Littlefield, 1982).

13. Douglas MacLean, "Posterity and Liberalism," paper delivered in Rutgers Colloquium on Energy, Oct. 22, 1980. A revised version will appear in *Energy and the Future,* ed. Douglas MacLean and Peter G. Brown, Maryland Series in Public Philosophy (Totowa, N.J.: Rowman & Littlefield, 1983.)

14. Ibid., p. 8.

15. Ibid., p. 19.

16. Ibid.

17. "Bonn U.N. Delegate Chides West on Aid," *New York Times,* September 17, 1980.

18. Jan Narveson, "Future People and Us," in R. I. Sikora and Brian Barry, eds., *Obligations to Future Generations.* (Philadelphia, Pa.: Temple University Press, 1978), p. 45.

19. For further discussion of individual and collective entities, see chapter 14.

20. Jonathan Bennett, "On Maximizing Happiness," in Sikora and Barry, *Obligations to Future Generations,* p. 68.

21. See "U.N. Study Sees Slower Growth in Population," *New York Times,* June 19, 1983.

22. Jan Narveson, in Sikora and Barry, *Obligations to Future Generations,* p. 50.

23. Joel Feinberg, "The Rights of Animals and Unborn Generations," in his *Rights, Justice, and the Bounds of Liberty* (Princeton, N.J.: Princeton University Press, 1980).

24. See James Sterba, "The Welfare Rights of Distant Peoples and Future Generations: Moral Side-Constraints on Social Policy," *Social Theory and Practice,* 7 (Spring 1981): pp. 99–119.

25. This is one of the arguments considered by James Sterba, ibid., at pp. 107 and 114 ff.

26. See James W. Nickel, "Are Human Rights Utopian?" in *Philosophy and Public Affairs* II, no. 3 (Summer 1982): 246–264.

27. B. M. Barry, "Justice between Generations," in P. M. S. Hacker and J. Raz, eds., *Law, Morality, and Society: Essays in Honour of H. L. A. Hart* (Oxford: Clarendon Press, 1977), p. 270.

28. Gregory Vlastos, "Justice and Equality," first published 1962, reprinted in A. I. Melden, *Human Rights* (Belmont, Calif.: Wadsworth Publishing Co., 1970), p. 90.

29. Barry, "Justice between Generations," p. 284. He modifies this view somewhat, but without argument, in "Circumstances of Justice and Future Generations," in Sikora and Barry, *Obligations to Future Generations.*

Chapter 14   The International Context

1. A classic statement of this position was made by George Kennan some years ago: "Morality, then, as the channel to individual self-fulfillment—yes. Morality as the foundation of civic virtue, and accordingly as a condition precedent to successful democracy—yes. Morality in governmental method, as a matter of conscience and preference on the part of our people—yes. But morality as a general criterion for the determination of the behavior of states and above all as a criterion for measuring and comparing the behavior of different states—no. Here other criteria, sadder, more limited, more practical, must be allowed to prevail." *Realities of American Foreign Policy* (Princeton, N.J.: Princeton University Press, 1954), p. 49.

2. Stanley Hoffman, *Duties beyond Borders: On the Limits and Possibilities of*

Ethical International Politics (Syracuse, N.Y.: Syracuse University Press, 1981). A few passages in this chapter are based on my review of this book in the *Journal of International Law and Politics* 14, no. 4 (Summer 1982) © 1982, New York University. They are used with permission.

3. See e.g., ibid., p. 72 (discussion of the U.S. interventions in Iran in 1953, Guatemala in 1954, and at the Bay of Pigs in 1961); p. 70 (discussion of India's involvement in Bangladesh and France's involvement in removing Emperor Bokassa I of the Central African Empire); pp. 49, 59–60 (discussion of the use of force by Britain and France in 1956 in response to the nationalization of the Suez Canal); pp. 132–34 (discussion of how the United States might deal with human rights violations in South Africa).

4. Although it has serious problems, one such guideline is the "lexical ordering" employed by John Rawls. Rawls argues that his first principle of justice, requiring equal liberty, should always take priority over his second principle, requiring a fair distribution of economic and social benefits. See John Rawls, *A Theory of Justice* (Cambridge, Mass.: Harvard University Press, 1971), pp. 42–43, 60–63.

5. Hoffmann, *Duties beyond Borders,* pp. 27–34.

6. Ibid., pp. 28–29.

7. See, e.g., Hoffman, *Duties beyond Borders,* pp. 2–5, 153–57. Hoffman says of Rawls's *A Theory of Justice:* "It is very fascinating, but it has very little relevance to reality," (p. 2).

8. See, e.g., Benjamin Barber, "Justifying Justice: Problems of Psychology, Measurement, and Politics in Rawls," *American Political Science Review* 69 (1975): 663; Virginia Held, "On Rawls and Self-Interest," *Midwest Studies in Philosophy,* 1 (1976): 57. See also M. McDougal, H. Lasswell, and L. Chen, *Human Rights and World Public Order: The Basic Policies of an International Law of Human Dignity* (New Haven, Conn.: Yale University Press, 1979), pp. 91, 454 and n.9, 458, 460.

9. Hoffman, *Duties beyond Borders,* p. 19.

10. See generally Louis Henkin, *How Nations Behave: Law and Foreign Policy,* 2d ed. (New York: Columbia University Press, 1979).

11. See especially Charles Beitz, *Political Theory and International Relations* (Princeton, N.J.: Princeton University Press, 1979).

12. Hoffman, *Duties beyond Borders,* p. 21.

13. For a discussion of this issue, see Kai Nielsen, "On the Choice between Reform and Revolution," in V. Held, K. Nielsen, and C. Parsons, eds., *Philosophy and Political Action* (New York: Oxford University Press, 1972), p. 17.

14. See Thomas Hobbes, *Leviathan,* ed. C. B. Macpherson (Baltimore: Pelican, 1968), chaps. 14 and 17.

15. See Louis Henkin, *The Rights of Man Today* (Boulder, Colo.: Westview, 1978); C. B. Macpherson, *Democratic Theory: Essays in Retrieval* (New York: Oxford University Press, 1973); and Susan Moller Okin, *Women in Western Political Thought* (Princeton, N.J.: Princeton University Press, 1979).

16. See, e.g., James W. Nickel, "Cultural Diversity and Human Rights"; Louis Henkin, "Rights: American and Human"; and Hoffman, *Duties beyond Borders*, pp. 103–8. See also chapters 5, 8, and 10.

17. Hoffmann only briefly considers these issues when he suggests the contours of an acceptable human rights policy. He states that "the minimum floor ought to entail the main elements of the right to life and health, which means a right not only against such things as torture and slavery and political imprisonment, but also against famine, epidemics, and infant mortality." Ibid., p. 121.

18. See, e.g., Richard Wasserstrom, ed., *War and Morality* (Belmont, Calif.: Wadsworth Publishing Co., 1970); and Marshall Cohen, Thomas Nagel, and Thomas Scanlon, eds., *War and Moral Responsibility* (Princeton, N.J.: Princeton University Press, 1974).

19. See, e.g., Richard Falk, *Legal Order in a Violent World* (Princeton, N.J.: Princeton University Press, 1968); Jorge Domingues et al., *Enhancing Global Human Rights* (New York: McGraw-Hill, 1979); McDougal, Lasswell, and Chen, *Human Rights and World Public Order;* and Richard Falk, *Human Rights and State Sovereignty* (New York: Holmes and Meier, 1981). See also Stanley Hoffmann, *Primacy or World Order: American Foreign Policy Since the Cold War* (New York: McGraw-Hill, 1978).

20. See Louis Henkin, *The Rights of Man Today;* Henry Shue, *Basic Rights: Subsistence, Affluence, and U.S. Foreign Policy* (Princeton, N.J.: Princeton University Press, 1980); James Nickel, "Cultural Diversity and Human Rights." See also A. S. Rosenbaum, ed., *The Philosophy of Human Rights: International Perspectives* (Westport, Conn.: Greenwood Press, 1980); and Peter Brown and Douglas MacLean, eds., *Human Rights and U.S. Foreign Policy* (Lexington, Mass.: Lexington Books, 1979).

21. See, e.g., Hugo Adam Bedau, "Genocide in Vietnam?" in Virginia Held, Sidney Morgenbesser, and Thomas Nagel, eds., *Philosophy, Morality, and International Affairs* (New York: Oxford University Press, 1974); Ralph L. Stavins, Richard J. Barnet, and Marcus G. Raskin, *Washington Plans an Aggressive War* (New York: Vintage Books, 1971); and Alexander Kendrick, *The Wound Within: America in the Vietnam Years 1945–1974* (Boston: Little, Brown, 1974).

22. See Henkin, *The Rights of Man Today*, p. 118.

23. Beitz, *Political Theory and International Relations*, p. 155.

24. See, e.g., Telford Taylor, *Nuremberg and Vietnam: An American Tragedy* (New York: Bantam, 1970).

25. Falk, *Human Rights and State Sovereignty*, p. 11.

26. See ibid., chap. 2.

27. This is a frequent claim. It is reflected in Dworkin, *Taking Rights Seriously*, especially pp. 91 and 194.

28. The claim that a nation is "nothing but" its individual members is another frequent but misleading claim. In persuasively undermining the tenets of "methodological individualism," which maintains that "facts about society and social phenomena are to be explained solely in terms of facts about individuals," Steven Lukes asks, "Why should we be compelled to talk about the tribesman but not the tribe, the bank teller but not the bank?" See Lukes, "Methodological Individualism Reconsidered," in Dorothy Emmet and Alasdair McIntyre, eds., *Sociological Theory and Philosophical Analysis* (New York: Macmillan, 1970), pp. 77 and 84.

29. See, e.g., Virginia Held, "Can a Random Collection of Individuals Be Morally Responsible?" *Journal of Philosophy* 68 (July 23, 1970): 471–82; Peter A. French, ed., *Individual and Collective Responsibility: Massacre at My Lai* (Cambridge, Mass.: Schenkman, 1972); and especially Peter A. French, "The Corporation as a Moral Person," *American Philosophical Quarterly* 16 (1979).

30. In "The Corporation as a Moral Person," Peter French argues that corporations can have privileges, rights, and duties and can be morally responsible. The internal decision structure of a corporation "accomplishes a subordination and synthesis of the intentions and acts of various biological persons into a corporate decision" (p. 212). Thus a corporation can act for a reason, as when a company joins a cartel, and can be deemed responsible. A similar argument applies to nations.

31. See chapter 6. See also Hugo Bedau, ed., *Civil Disobedience: Theory and Practice* (New York: Pegasus, 1969); Jeffrie Murphy, ed., *Civil Disobedience and Violence* (Belmont, Calif.: Wadsworth, 1971); and Edward Kent, ed., *Revolution and the Rule of Law* (Englewood Cliffs, N.J.: Prentice-Hall, 1971).

32. See, e.g., R. Falk, "Ecocide, Genocide, and the Nuremburg Tradition of Individual Responsibility," in V. Held, S. Morgenbesser, and T. Nagels, eds., *Philosophy, Morality, and International Affairs* and R. Wasserstrom, "The Responsibility of the Individual for War Crimes," ibid., p. 47.

33. Beitz, *Political Theory and International Relations*, pp. 81–82.

34. Ibid., pp. 91–92.

35. Ibid., p. 92. But see also Noam Chomsky and E. S. Herman, *The Political Economy of Human Rights. From Vol. 1: The Washington Connection and Third World Fascism* (Boston: South End Press, 1979).

36. John Stuart Mill, "A Few Words on Non-Intervention," in J. S. Mill, *Dissertations and Discussions* (New York, 1873), III, 238–63.

37. Michael Walzer, *Just and Unjust Wars* (New York: Basic Books, 1977), p. 87.

38. Ibid., p. 101.

39. Hoffmann, *Duties beyond Borders*, p. 68.

40. Ibid., p. 69.

41. Ibid., pp. 71–73.

42. Susan Brownmiller writes, "A female definition of rape can be contained in a single sentence. If a woman chooses not to have intercourse with a specific man and the man chooses to proceed against her will, that is a criminal act of rape. Through no fault of woman, this is not and never has been the legal definition. . . . Rape could not be envisioned as a matter of female consent or refusal; nor could a definition acceptable to males be based on a male-female understanding of a female's right to her bodily integrity. Rape entered the law through the back door, as it were, as a property crime of man against man. . . ." Brownmiller, *Against Our Will: Men, Women and Rape* (New York: Simon and Schuster, 1975). And Michael Walzer writes, ". . . humanitarian intervention comes much closer than any other kind of intervention to what we commonly regard, in domestic society, as law enforcement and police work. At the same time, however, it requires the crossing of an international frontier, and such crossings are ruled out by the legalist paradigm—unless they are authorized, I suppose, by the society of nations. . . . Many lawyers prefer to stick to the paradigm. That doesn't require them, on their view, to deny the (occasional) need for intervention. They merely deny legal recognition to that need. Humanitarian intervention 'belongs in the realm not of law but of moral choice, which nations, like individuals must sometimes make. . . .' But that is only a plausible formulation if one doesn't stop with it, as lawyers are likely to do. For moral choices are not simply *made*; they are also judged, and so there must be criteria for judgment." *Just and Unjust Wars*, p. 106. Walzer's view of the limitations of a legalistic interpretation of intervention is perceptive. But against his relatively easy theoretical justification of humanitarian intervention, it might be more strongly argued that even though nations may have grave internal faults, they may not wish to be rescued by outside intervention. If they, or groups within them, request outside assistance, the issues may be quite different, but first we need to understand "intervention."

43. Beitz, *Political Theory and International Relations*, pp. 103–4.

44. See, e.g., Stephen Schlesinger and Stephen Kinzer, *Bitter Fruit: The Untold Story of the American Coup in Guatemala* (New York: Doubleday, 1983).

45. Hoffman, *Duties beyond Borders*, pp. 227–29.

46. For two interesting volumes on Mexican migrants and related issues, see Peter G. Brown and Henry Shue, eds., *The Border That Joins: Mexican Mi-*

grants and U.S. Responsibility (Totowa, N.J.: Rowman and Littlefield, 1982); and Brown and Shue, eds., *Boundaries: National Autonomy and Its Limits,* Maryland Studies in Philosophy (Rowman, 1981).

47. One institution that publishes articles and studies with important methodological implications is the Center for Philosophy and Public Policy at the University of Maryland. Hoffmann cites its 1979 book *Human Rights and U.S. Foreign Policy: Principles and Applications* (P.G. Brown and D. MacLean, eds.), but does not seem to have considered the methodological implications of the center's efforts.

Chapter 15   The Practice of Moral Inquiry

1. See, e.g., Gilbert Harman, *The Nature of Morality* (New York: Oxford University Press, 1977), especially pp. 6–7.

2. For further argument, see Virginia Held, "The Political 'Testing' of Moral Theories," *Midwest Studies in Philosophy* 7 (1982): 343–63. The present chapter draws on this paper. Selected passages are reprinted with permission.

3. Karl R. Popper, *The Logic of Scientific Discovery* (New York: Science Editions, 1961), pp. 60–103.

4. See, e.g., Mary Hesse, *The Structure of Scientific Inference* (Berkeley: University of California Press, 1974).

5. For a discussion of this analogy, see, e.g., Peter Caws, *Science and the Theory of Value* (New York: Random House, 1967).

6. For discussion, see Peter Achinstein, *Concepts of Science* (Baltimore: Johns Hopkins Press, 1968); Richard E. Grandy, ed., *Theories and Observation in Science* (Englewood Cliffs, N.J.: Prentice-Hall, 1973); and Clark Glymour, *Theory and Evidence* (Princeton University Press, 1980).

7. Even those who reject the distinction between theory and observation still make sense of the notion of testing scientific theories. W. V. O. Quine, for instance, writes that "there is scope for error and dispute only insofar as the connections with experience whereby sentences are appraised are multifarious and indirect, mediated through time by theory in conflicting ways; there is none insofar as verdicts to a sentence are directly keyed to present stimulation" (*Word and Object* [Cambridge, Mass.: M.I.T. Press, 1960], p. 44). And Mary Hesse writes, "At any given time some observation statements result from correctly applying observation terms to empirical situations according to learned precedents and independently of theories, although the relation of observation and theory is a self-correcting process in which it is not possible to know at the time which of the set of observation statements are to be retained as correct in this sense . . ." (*The Structure of Scientific Inference,* p. 43).

8. Immanuel Kant, *Critique of Practical Reason,* trans. Lewis White Beck

(New York: Bobbs-Merrill, Liberal Arts, 1956). For a discussion of universalizability, see chapter 4. On the "testing" of Kantian moral theory, see Onora Nell (O'Neill), *Acting on Principle* (New York: Columbia University Press, 1975).

9. See, e.g., Thomas Kuhn, *The Structure of Scientific Revolutions* (Chicago: University of Chicago Press, 1962), and also Larry Laudan, *Progress and Its Problems* (Berkeley: University of California Press, 1977).

10. Alan Gewirth, *Reason and Morality* (Chicago: University of Chicago Press, 1978), p. 49.

11. Ibid.

12. See W. D. Ross, *The Right and the Good* (London: Oxford University Press, 1930).

13. Ibid., p. 31.

14. Amartya Sen and Bernard Williams, eds., *Utilitarianism and Beyond* (Cambridge: At the University Press, 1982), p. 16.

15. A somewhat different view of the analogy between ethics and science is offered by Morton White in *What Is and What Ought to Be Done* (New York: Oxford University Press, 1981).

16. Robert Ackerman, "Inductive Simplicity," in P.H. Nidditch, ed., *The Philosophy of Science* (London: Oxford University Press, 1968), p. 125.

17. For further discussion, see Virginia Held, "The Independence of Intellectuals," *The Journal of Philosophy* 80, no. 10 (October 1983):572–82.

Index

314